PENGUIN
BOOKS

How
Not
to Be a
Professional
Racing
Driver

Jason Plato is one of the biggest characters in UK motor racing, and one of the most controversial. Since bursting on to the karting scene at the end of the 1970s, he has gone on to either upstage or upset dozens of drivers, team owners and team managers – not to mention the odd policeman and nightclub owner. Despite that he is the British Touring Car Championship's most successful driver ever, having won an astonishing 96 races and two championships. Since 2004, Jason has also co-presented the popular motoring television magazine series *Fifth Gear*. Jason is Board Director of the British Racing Drivers' Club, which owns and operates Silverstone.

How
Not
to Be a
Professional
Racing
Driver

JASON
PLATO

PENGUIN
BOOKS

PENGUIN BOOKS

UK | USA | Canada | Ireland | Australia
India | New Zealand | South Africa

Penguin Books is part of the Penguin Random House group of companies
whose addresses can be found at global.penguinrandomhouse.com

First published by Michael Joseph 2019
Published in Penguin Books 2020
001

All images credited to Jason Plato, excluding: Peter Fox: 10, 14; Jakob Ebrey: 16, 17, 19,
50, 51, 54; Colin McMaster: 20; Lyndon McNeil: 26; Mark Bothwell: 28, 29, 31,
32, 33; raceofchampions.com: 46; Mike Hewitt/Getty Images: 47; PSP Images: 52.

Set in 11.88/14.44 pt Garamond MT Std
Typeset by Jouve (UK), Milton Keynes

Printed and bound in Great Britain by Clays Ltd, Elcograf S.p.A.

A CIP catalogue record for this book is available from the British Library

ISBN: 978-0-241-40416-4

www.greenpenguin.co.uk

MIX
Paper from
responsible sources
FSC® C018179

Penguin Random House is committed to a
sustainable future for our business, our readers
and our planet. This book is made from Forest
Stewardship Council® certified paper.

For Team Plato:
Soaf, Alena, Zia, Mum and Dad

Contents

Introduction

Once you've finished reading this book, you'll no doubt be asking yourself questions such as *How on earth did he get through school?*, *Why isn't he in prison?* and, ultimately, *How the bloody hell is he still alive?*

The answer to all of the above from the horse's mouth is: I really have no idea. None of it was premeditated, save for me trying to make it as a racing driver, and the rest of it just sort of happened. Some has been an upshot of circumstance, no doubt, but the majority is down to the fact that I have always had an issue in distinguishing between how I should behave on a racetrack and how I should behave off it. It tends to be all or nothing all of the time with me.

In spite of everything you are about to read, I have quite a good memory (which is surprising!), so I have many stories at my disposal and I've had to be quite be selective. For instance, if I were to try and cover my racing career in full, which so far comprises over 550 starts with eleven different teams, we'd be looking at about a thousand pages. Instead, I've decided to take a few ups, a few downs, and then mix them in with a bit of high jinks and a few shenanigans.

One of the beauties of me being a similar person both on and off the racetrack is that it has left me with two blueprints: how to become a professional racing driver, and how not to become a professional racing driver, hence the title. Given the fact there are probably dozens of examples featuring the former currently in print, I thought I'd turn it on its head. After all, as the renowned motor-racing fanatic and dramatist William Shakespeare once said, *Madmen have such seething brains!*

Enjoy.

The Son of Mod

Right then, you lot. Where do we start?

'At the beginning' will no doubt be a popular answer.

Ah, yes, but at the beginning of what? At the beginning of my life or at the beginning of the bit when I started driving very quickly, pissing people off and doing things I perhaps shouldn't have?

Well, it probably won't surprise you to learn that I was doing the last three from quite an early age, so we may as well go back to 14 October 1967, which is roughly nine months after my mother and father did something that half the paddock at any British Touring Car Championship race wished they hadn't.

I was born in Oxford, although when I was very young we moved to the northeast of England and remained there for about seventeen years.

When I say we, I mean me – obviously – and my dad, Tim, and my mum, Linda.

The phrase *a chip off the old block* usually refers to a son taking after his father, and although that's true in my case, I also take after my mother in many respects, as she too is a feisty so-and-so and doesn't take any shit from anyone.

Let's start with my old man, though.

There's quite a nice hotel in Oxford called the Malmaison, and a few years ago, not long after it opened, my future wife Sophie and I decided to take my mum and dad there for a bite to eat.

Not long after arriving, my mum piped up and said, 'Do you remember visiting your dad in here?'

'How do you mean, Mum,' I replied. 'It's only been open a few weeks.'

'No, no, no,' she said. 'When it was a prison!'

'Eh!? A prison. You're joking, aren't you?'

I then remember looking at Sophie. We hadn't been going out that long, and although she was aware that I'd had a pretty colourful past, I don't think it stretched to my old man being an old lag.

It turned out that when I was a little boy my mum had taken me to visit Dad when he was a few days into a fourteen-stretch for taking the odd car or two for a joy ride. Fortunately for all concerned, it was fourteen days as opposed to years, so it was over and done with in a flash. I'd love to have known what was going through Sophie's head when Mum mentioned it in what was now a very lovely luxury hotel. The word 'Help' most probably!

When I turned up, my old man was eighteen and my mum was just seventeen and a half, so they were obviously in a hurry to get little things like childbirth and going to prison out of the way. Who can blame them?

Incidentally, when it comes to being in clink, I've actually got one up on my old man as I've been there twice, although not in this country. Anyway, that's for a bit later.

When he was young, Dad was Oxford's chief mod, which probably accounts for some of the bad behaviour, although not all of it. He had a Willys jeep, a minder and at least one police car following him at all times! One night in those early days he came home in an Aston Martin DB5. I was only about three or four years old at the time but I remember thinking, *Where the bloody hell did that come from?* I never asked him. It's best not to.

Apart from being a cross between the Modfather and Norman Stanley Fletcher, and a pretty special guy, it has to be said, the most interesting and relevant fact I can tell you about my old man is that he holds the world record for being the first person ever to write off an Austin Allegro (also known as an Austin *All-aggro*).

After a quick butchers on the internet, it seems that the Allegro, which was a bloody appalling car, was launched in October 1975, so that's when it would have happened. We were up in the northeast by this time, and my old man was working in the car trade. The day it was launched he decided to take one home for a laugh and ended up writing it off at the end of the road. How the hell do you write off an Allegro for God's sake, unless you mean to? They only do about 40 mph!

So tickled was my old man at the prospect of being the first man to write off one of the worst road cars of the twentieth century that he actually did some research to try and find out if any others had gone on launch day and as far as he could make out, they hadn't. Well done, Dad! I think the world owes you a favour for that one, ridding us of at least one of those godforsaken vehicles.

Later on, after we'd moved down south, he worked in the City of London insurance market for a while, and one evening my mum received a telephone call from the British Transport Police asking her to come and get him.

'He's stuck in luggage rack on a train and he won't come down, Mrs Plato,' said the officer.

'Stuck my foot,' replied Mum. 'He's pissed, isn't he?'

'Well, he might be. We can't really tell from here.'

'I'll be there in half an hour . . .'

I wouldn't have liked to have been my old man that night. I bet my mum had a few choice words for him when they got home.

People often ask me if I'm related to the philosopher Plato, and my stock-in-trade answer is always: *How the flaming hell should I know?* He was born in Greece about 400 BC for heaven's sake! I very much doubt it, though. After all, Plato was often described by historians as being a modest man who was quiet and studious and that is pretty much the opposite of me. Then again, he was also supposed to have died in his bed while a beautiful young woman played the flute for him, so it could go either way really, he said cheekily.

If only they'd had cars in ancient Greece. Had he written something off early doors then it could well have been game on with regards to us being related. You don't hear of many Platos, so you never know.

Because I'm an only child with two daughters, you'd be forgiven for assuming that one day our branch of the Plato family will die out.

Think again!

We're a resourceful bunch, we Platos, and despite coming close to extinction previously we've always managed to cling on.

Many years ago, my great-great-grandmother Edna Plato had a fling with (so the rumours go) an Australian soldier and in 1914 gave birth to two boys, Raymond (my grandfather) and Ernest (who sadly died in his infancy). My great-grandfather was never to be seen again, presumably killed in action in WW1. No father was registered on the birth certificates, which meant the maternal name was passed down: Plato. So in tribute to my great-great-grandmother's efforts, the deal is that I will only pay for my daughter's weddings if they retain the Plato name – which is a cracking surname, let's face it. They obviously don't know that yet, but the contract's there ready for them to sign. And I don't want any of that double-barrelled nonsense either!

Until recently my old man thought we were descended from Italians as opposed Greeks. An old relative once told him that back in the day Italian families used to change their surnames in order to give themselves a leg up the social ladder and according to this relative that was why, and where, our branch of the Plato family had originated.

I don't really subscribe to that, but it's a pretty cool tale.

Then, a few years ago, a journalist friend of mine, Marcus Simmons (who actually started his journalist career at exactly the same time I started my car racing career!) did a bit of a family tree for me to accompany an article he was writing about me and he found out some absolute gems. For a start, he told me that my great-great-grandfather on my dad's side had died in the First World War and that his name is included on the war memorial in Abingdon in Oxfordshire. I have driven past that war memorial so many times over the years and I had no idea.

Perhaps more interestingly, though, I always thought that my gifts – i.e. a certain amount of madness and some creativity – must have come from my dad's side of the family, but apparently not. The madness certainly does, or at least most of it, but when it comes to the other aptitudes it appears my mum's side might well be more to blame. Her maiden name is Scott, and she's related to the singer Marc Almond from the 1980s pop group Soft Cell and the comedian Jimmy James, who was massive in the 1940s and 50s. It turns out she was also related to one of the major controllers at the BBC, so I wish I'd known about that earlier. I could have touched him up for a job!

What can I tell you about my mum – that won't get me into trouble?

Well, when I said before that she was a feisty soul, I meant it. As an only child I was always her pride and joy (I still am, bless her), and although she had no problem with me competing in sports like rugby it was on the proviso that nobody laid a finger on me under any circumstances. The first time I became aware of this was the first time she came to watch me play. It was at school, and a ruck was occurring. I was somewhere underneath when all of a sudden I heard a rather familiar, but at the same time rather unexpected, voice.

'Get off him. Get off my boy now!' screamed Mum.

The thing is, she wasn't just chastising the other players, she was physically pulling them off me and then pushing them away.

The next voice I heard was more familiar in the current location but less so overall. It was the games master.

'Mrs Plato,' he bellowed. 'Will you please put those pupils down NOW and kindly leave the playing field!'

Unfortunately for all concerned Mum wasn't having any of it, and while I was lying face down on the rugby field shouting, 'Oh Jesus Christ, make her go away!' while silently praying for Jesus' father to make the ground swallow me up, Mum continued manhandling, not just my opponents, but anyone who dared to be in the vicinity of her little munchkin.

'Get off him. Get away from him. LEAVE HIM ALONE!'

Come to think of it, she should have taken my place on the field. There'd only have been one winner.

Many people assume that because my dad's such a big

personality he's the driving force behind the family and the one who wears the trousers, but if anything it's the inverse of that. Mum's definitely the quieter of the two but she's very, very strong. She was a hairstylist in her younger days, so very creative and offered the opportunity to chat lots, and after that she became a nurse. The two professions suit her down to the ground really, as she's sociable and very caring. She's just a good egg.

There you go, then. On my mum's side you have creativity, talent and a modicum of violence, on my dad's side, out-and-out naughtiness. I am, without any doubt whatsoever, a chip off both blocks.

OK, now I've set the scene family-wise and provided you with some explanations about my future behaviour, let's get behind a wheel or two and kick up a bit of dust.

It all started for me motorsport-wise forty years ago in 1979, so I'd have been twelve years old at the time. Quite late, really. My old man was running a BMW dealership in the northeast called Priory Cars and one day he accepted a racing kart as payment for a bad debt. The debt was nothing – a couple of hundred quid at most – so it was a really good deal.

Dad used to have a mate called Brian Chivers who was into karting, so when he found out about it he was cock-a-hoop. 'Oh, mate,' he said. 'You'll love this. Karting's great!' He and Dad used to tinker around with cars all the time, and although Dad had never raced before (legally), he loved a bit of speed and was obviously into his cars. In that respect the kart was meant for him really, not for me.

The kart had a BM chassis, a Bultaco engine (there's a blast from the past) and was verging on being an antique. That said, it was fast, and the first time I remember driving it was in and out of the petrol pumps at the garage on a Sunday afternoon. Bearing in mind my lack of experience in driving anything with four wheels at speed, and the fact that I was just metres away from tens of thousands of gallons of highly flammable liquid, this would possibly be frowned upon slightly by today's health and safety executive, but back in the 70s we didn't give a damn! It was just fun.

Not far from the garage there was a company called Tyne Car Auctions, and their car park must have measured at least three acres. Being in the trade, my dad knew the owner quite well (he knew everybody quite well!), and so, after having a few words, we were given permission to drive the kart there in the evening when everyone had gone home.

This is where it started to come to life for me, as I was no longer restricted by space. The police were always having a moan, as we made a bit of noise, but it never became serious enough for us to stop. We just said sorry, waited half an hour and then started again. Dad would have the majority of the time in the kart, and I'd get ten minutes at the end. It was lush.

A few months after we got the kart the whole thing almost came to an end. My two cousins, Nicola and Amanda, came up for the weekend, and Nicola, who was about my age, asked her dad to persuade my dad to let her have a go in the kart. She'd watched me darting around for a while and obviously thought it looked fun.

We were up at the dealership at the time and, after easing her in and telling her what to do, me and my old man gave her a bump start. Unfortunately, instead of trundling along at 5 miles an hour for a few yards, like she'd been told to, Nicola completely freaked out, but instead of taking her foot off the throttle she put the pedal to the metal, so to speak. It was scary! She ended up going straight into a brick wall, and after taking her to hospital we found out she'd broken both her ankles. It could have been a lot worse, though. Because had she completely freaked out she would have garrotted herself on the chain across the entrance to the forecourt, and had she driven a few metres to the left she'd have gone straight on to the main road. It was serious stuff. Mum went absolutely bananas when she found out, and wanted to kibosh the whole thing there and then.

'It's too dangerous Tim,' she complained to my father. 'I want you to get rid of it.'

After making a few assurances, such as never allowing frightened little girls to drive the kart ever again and especially near main roads, petrol pumps and chains, Dad managed to hold on to the kart, and, after lying low for a while, we managed to find a karting track in a place called Felton, which is north of Morpeth in Northumberland. Even at this point the kart was still my old man's, and I was just along for the ride.

When we arrived at Felton for the first time I timed Dad and Brian as they drove the kart, and right at the end I managed to persuade Dad to let me have a go. With no licence this was obviously illegal, but Dad must have thought, *What the hell?* It was still the 1970s!

After handing Dad the stopwatch, I asked him to time me.

'Off you go, then,' he said. 'You've got five laps.'

I don't know exactly by how much, but all five of my laps were quicker than any of Dad's or Brian's, and that's really where it all started. Dad and Brian were amazed at the times I'd posted, but I was just having a laugh.

From then on, the kart was mine, and I was the one who

drove it. In true Plato style, the next time we went up to Felton we seized up the engine after getting the oil and petrol mixture wrong! What that meant, though, together with me spanking Dad's and Brian's lap times, was that perhaps it was time to get a new kart, and in a very short space of time Dad had done a deal with a contact of Brian's, and we had in our possession a new one.

We used to keep the kart on a stand in our dining room, and as time went on the dining room gradually morphed from being a nice place to have a meal into a perfect place to tinker around with a kart. It became a workshop, basically, and after not very many weeks the entire house stank of oil and petrol. None of us cared, though, least of all my mum, as she was just as keen on karting as me and my Dad; it was an activity that we all loved as a family, and my mum liked the fact that it was a way for us all to spend time together. There was actually an archway leading from the dining room to the kitchen, so again, with all the flammable liquids knocking around and the odd flame here and there, it's a wonder we didn't go up!

We used to have this massive sideboard in the dining room that these days might have done well on *Antiques Roadshow*. We didn't care, though. From the moment the kart arrived it was covered in tools, parts and a selection of fine lubricants.

The next investment Dad made was in a black van, which he got through a contact. That was to be our home, our workshop and our transport to and from the races for the next year or so. Once he'd bought it, Dad and I set about converting it, and within a few weeks we were all set to go. We had a new kart, a mini-motorhome/workshop/garage, a mechanic, engineer, financer and mentor (Dad), a team catering manager and team nurse (Mum), a team mascot (our dog, Castrol) and a driver, moi. Team Plato was born!

Within a matter of weeks, karting had completely taken over our lives. It was our joint hobby, if you like. We didn't do things like go on summer holidays or go skiing either. We didn't need to. I also used to give school trips the bum's rush; I can't remember going on a single one. I'd bring a letter home from school with some information about a trip, and after looking at the price Dad would say, 'That's the equivalent to five sets of tyres. Do you want to go, Jason?'

'No Dad.'

'OK, then, bin it.'

Had I not been an only child, the karting thing would never have happened, as Mum and Dad invested everything they had – time and money – into it. Had there been another child to consider, there wouldn't have been enough of either to go around.

The first time I competed was in the 1980 club championship and I can remember going into the little signing-on hut at the start of the season in order to register. The club secretary was sitting there, and the first question he asked me was what number I wanted. After looking down the list, I said to him as bold as brass, 'I'll have number 1 thanks. That hasn't got a name against it.' 'You will not, young man,' he said, laughing. 'That's reserved for the champion.' That's how little we knew at the time, me and my dad. We'd only been doing this a matter of months and had only been on a karting track a couple of times. We were totally naive.

'Can I have that one then,' I said, pointing to number 6.

'You can indeed.'

In the club championship we cleaned the board in 1980 and in between all that we started competing nationally. The circuits most local to us were Wombwell, which is near Barnsley; Rowrah, near Cockermouth, which is the other side of Carlisle; and of course Felton. That was our little triangle, if you like, and they became our second homes. There were other tracks in the area but unless they were part of the national championship we didn't bother.

It's difficult to put into words how excited I got on race weekends. I used to run home from school on a Friday, and as long as Dad had arrived home we'd set off bang on 4 p.m. Sometimes we wouldn't get home until 10 p.m. on a Sunday, so if you take into account the time we spent tinkering in the dining room or practising during the week, it really was all-encompassing. And I'm obviously not the only one to have lived this life. Heck no! Hundreds of families the length and breadth of the country used to do exactly the same thing, so there was a real family atmosphere about karting. We were all competitive, sure we were, but it was the social aspect that made it really enjoyable, as that meant everybody was included. There was a real camaraderie at the time, and it kept us all interested. In fact, Mum and Dad still keep in touch with some of the families we met during the karting years. They were great times.

To get the distances we used to cover into perspective, I remember one year racing down at Dunkeswell, which is near Exeter. This was on a Sunday, and straight after that we had to drive to Cockermouth for a Bank Holiday meeting that was taking place the following day. It was about 360 miles from our place to Dunkeswell and roughly the same again from there up to Cockermouth. We loved it, though! The van we had was an LT28 Volkswagen, and in the back there was a partition that me and Dad had built separating the workshop, which included the tyre racks and the tools, from the living quarters. The bed, which slept all of us, was probably just over half the width of a double bed and was actually nothing more than a piece of foam that we'd had cut and covered. We all slept like logs, though, as most of the time we were knackered. Our garage was nothing more than a little awning that used to strap on to the side of the van. As mad as it all sounds, it actually worked. Seriously, it was perfect.

The only reason we didn't win the British Championship in 1981 was because of a first-corner incident in the last race that knocked me off and dislodged my exhaust pipe. My old man ran straight on to the track (fathers were allowed to help restart the juniors) when it happened, and after making sure I was OK the first thing he did was try and pick up the exhaust, which was obviously red-hot. Ouch! He ended up burning himself really badly and still has the scars to prove it. You see what I mean about naive? It was a baptism of fire – literally – for all of us.

Within just a year of us starting, we had a deal in place with a team, so things had moved on very quickly. New parts would arrive at the house all the time, and I remember me and my old man pulling rear-axle bearings apart and getting all the bits out of the middle just so they'd spin a bit quicker. The bearing hangers are clamped on to the back of the chassis and if they're not perfectly straight they'll clamp the bearings. We used to spend hour after hour just sitting there trying to get these things to move as freely as possible. And I mean hours! It was wonderful though. Quality time.

One of the other great joys of karting – and I think you'll find this is common, especially with my generation – was the pre-race preparation. When I first started, I'd turn up at the circuit the day before a meeting and I'd start painting the kerbs or hanging up bunting. Whatever needed doing, basically. Everybody wanted to be involved and everybody wanted to make the place look as professional and as presentable as possible. In what other situation would you get children willingly picking up brooms and things? I just wanted to help them put a great event on and I honestly would have walked the 30 miles to the circuit if I'd had to. I used to get a bus, and it was a good two- or three-hour round trip. Having a hobby like that keeps body and mind active and is what an eleven-year-old lad should be doing. In my opinion.

I think a lot of people assume, quite wrongly, that all race circuits look like Silverstone, or mini versions of it, but nothing could be further from the truth. In fact, I'd say the vast majority would be dumps if it wasn't for the volunteers who keep them going.

That was a very big part of the attraction for me early on (it waned a bit once I got serious as I didn't have as much time) and it was almost as exciting as the racing in that it added to the anticipation and made you feel totally involved. You often hear drivers talking about feeling at one with their cars or their team – me included – but being at one with your sport is just as important, but that takes effort.

It was an important lesson for me, in that you have to give back to whatever sport you practise, and if I didn't have those memories of being involved in the preparation for a race meeting my career in motorsport wouldn't be quite as sweet or fulfilling as it is. It's all very well just turning up, taking what you can and then pissing off again, but in order to get a 360-degree experience you have to get involved at grassroots level – and properly involved. It's the only way.

The first deal we had was with a team called Mistral Racing, which was run by a lovely fruitcake of a man called Neil

Hann. The team was based in a sleepy little village just out-side Yeovil called Montacute. It's a great name, isn't it?

One of the reasons my old man had gone with Neil was that he was dead straight and didn't give him any flannel. *This is what's involved, this is what you'll get, and this is what you'll need to do. OK? Bish, bash, bosh.* There was no messing around, and that was exactly how Dad liked to do business. It was music to his ears.

Prior to me, Mistral had had one or two decent drivers on their books, most notably a lad a few years older than me called Martin Smart. Martin had represented Great Britain from 1974 until 1980 and, as well as winning the British Junior Championship once or twice, which is what I'd almost done in my first year, he'd won the European Team Championship and had finished third in the World Championship. His were obviously big shoes to fill, but that kind of challenge was exactly what I needed at the time. I was young and relatively inexperienced, but I had a smidgen of talent and bags of confidence. Although we never became friends (he was a bit older than me, and our paths never really crossed much), a few years ago I decided to touch base with Martin, as his success and reputation had been a big motivation for me and I was interested to see how he was doing. It turns out he's now an architect based in Warwickshire and is doing really well. No surprise there.

When I started driving for Neil in 1981, he had his own chassis called the Mistral MM3, and our engines were made by the gearbox manufacturer Hewland. They'd recently produced their first karting engine, and it was an absolute work of art. Neil was one of the main agents for the Hewland Arrow, which is how it came about, but he used to tune them all himself. At the bottom of his garden he had a shed which was like a huge Aladdin's cave, and that's where he did the tuning. I used to spend most of my summer holidays down there helping him out, so it was like an extension – and a progression, really – of what I'd been doing with my dad in our dining room. It was invaluable.

Neil had another company at the time called Sportac. They used to produce leather race suits but not just for karters. The Isle of Man TT legend Joey Dunlop was one of his clients, I remember, and he also used to sell suits to a lot of the speedway lads. I used to work there too when we weren't in the shed and would spend hours stitching up suits. Who'd have thought it. Jason Plato. Seamstress to the stars!

I won my first British Junior Championship with Neil in 1982; looking back, he was undoubtedly the link between me competing at a fairly high standard as a privateer and winning multiple championships. My old man and I had all the endeavour in the world, but without the necessary experience and resources we could only go so far. When Neil became involved, that immediately started to shift, and as well as us becoming part of his team, as in Mistral, he became part of ours too. We also started competing in Europe under Neil's tutelage and again we had more success.

In 1983, I started driving for Zip Kart in the European Series and the World Championship, but still under Neil's management. The man behind Zip, the late and much-missed Martin Hines, was synonymous with the sport and was known as 'Mr Karting'. He was the next link in my career chain, I suppose, and in addition to passing on some of his vast and invaluable experience to me and Dad, Martin also sorted out a tyre contract for me with Bridgestone. Having someone like that backing you makes a massive difference to your knowledge and your confidence, which in turn makes any talent you might have a lot more accessible. In many respects Martin Hines was like an early Frank Williams for me, and it's hard to overestimate the effect he had.

I'll tell you what, let's have a tale from Europe, where, if memory serves me correctly, I probably raced about six times.

My biggest achievement there was winning the Junior Federation Cup in 1983. It took place at a circuit in Kerpen in Germany, which Michael Schumacher ended up buying many years later. He was actually tipped to win the Junior Federation Cup that year and was already being tipped for great things.

What I remember most about that event, apart from winning the cup, is the fact that it marked the crescendo of a huge tyre war. Sometime in 1983, the CIK, which is the FIA of karting, had introduced a tyre regulation that said that from now on the tyres used had to be a certain shore. Shore is the hardness of a tyre and is measured by a durometer. This had obviously caused pandemonium within the industry, and it was deemed that the first team or tyre company to come to terms with the rule and get their heads around it would come out on top.

There was a tyre company at the time called Vega, who were an offshoot of Pirelli, and it became clear in the events leading up to the Federation Cup, which was a one-off competition, that they had won the battle, although perhaps not the war. Not by producing a brand-new tyre, by the way, but by circumnavigating the rule. How they got away with it I don't know, but in layman's terms Vega invented a manufacturing process that allowed them to put a very thin layer of hard rubber across the tread of the tyre that would satisfy the durometer, making the CIK believe that the rest of the tyre was the same, and then erode after about four laps.

Underneath that you had all the sexy stuff, so the moment the hard layer had gone, you were off!

Unlike Vega, Bridgestone had played it by the book and consequently they'd been annihilated at every race. Unbeknownst to Vega, however, and the teams using them, Bridgestone had been working their arses off to rectify the problem and by the time the Federation Cup came about they were just about ready.

Although a single event, the Federation Cup was the climax to a long weekend of racing, and we arrived at the track on the previous Monday. On the Wednesday evening the Bridgestone track man, who was called Mr Kakuchi, came around in his van and gave each of his drivers ten new sets of tyres. Each set looked identical except for a tiny bit of paint on the bead. I forget the colours they used, but one was for their standard tyre, another colour for a softer tyre, and two more colours that represented the harder tyres.

Anyway, these things were off the scale, which immediately put 180 of the 200 competitors out of the running. That's the way it was, though. Vega had gone for a quick fix and had painted over the cracks while Bridgestone had played the long game. Well done Bridgestone!

My abiding memory of the Thursday, which is when the shit hit the fan, is watching my dad, Delboy Plato, selling a set of these tyres for £5,000! That's at least ten grand in today's money. The thing is, unless you had a set of these tyres you might as well go home, so if you had the dosh it was definitely worth the investment – said my old man!

The driver he sold them to was called Rohan Dewhurst. He was attached to the British team and was the heir to the Dewhurst butcher empire. He wasn't much of a driver, bless him, but he must have had a few quid, and luckily for him the first person he approached about acquiring some of these fab new tyres was Timothy Plato, Esq. Dad must have seen him coming and within about two minutes he'd pocketed the wedge and was whistling away with his hands in his pockets, pretending that nothing had gone on. In fairness to Dad, nothing had gone on really. Or at least nothing untoward. As long as he sold a used set as opposed to a new set and to a British competitor, everything was OK, and that's exactly what he did. The only thing that surprised me about this was that Dad didn't make more of it. In fact, had he gone around all the other Bridgestone drivers buying up all their used tyres before erecting a stall somewhere within the track, I'd have been far less surprised. I think he was just shocked at having bagged five big ones for a set of ours and thought he'd quit while he was ahead!

We had an absolutely brilliant weekend (financially and professionally!) in Germany and went on to win the inaugural Junior European Federation Cup. The tyres, though, were so grippy it was ridiculous. Even these days the grip you get with a sticky hot tyre in a hot climate in karting is insane. It can break your ribs.

Actually, as well as the aforementioned Michael Schumacher, who is the subject of a great story later on, there were one or two other talented lads racing that weekend, although none of them were daft enough to ask my old man for any tyres. There were David Coulthard, Johnny Herbert, Vincenzo Sospiri, Alex Zanardi, Allan McNish, Mika Häkkinen and a delightful future touring car driver from France called Yvan Muller, who I ended up having a proper ding-dong with. That too is for a bit later on.

In addition to the individual race, in which I triumphed (just in case you'd forgotten), there was also a team race during the weekend, and the manager of the British team, of which I was part, was a man called Tony Temple, or so the parents used to call him. He was a very funny-looking small gentleman and he was seriously officious. A perfect team manager really.

Anyway, to cut a long story short, the parents of the team members, including my own mum and dad, decided to play a trick on him one evening, and it ended up working beautifully. To be fair to Tony, he was very pro team UK, and when the Dutch team started mouthing off one day about something insignificant, the parents decided to send Tony into battle.

I forget what the Dutch had been whinging about, but instead of telling Tony the truth, as in it was nothing really and it would be best to ignore them, the parents ended up telling him all kinds of stories, and by the time they'd finished with him he was apoplectic! But instead of just sending him into the Dutch camp with a bad temper and a load of false truths, they decided to spice things up a bit.

'Remember, Tony,' said one of the parents. 'The person you need to speak to is Hertz Van Rental. He's the one who's been complaining and he's a real troublemaker. Did you get that?'

'Yes, don't you worry. I need to speak to Hertz Van Rental. Right then!' He was completely oblivious to the fact that he was being set up.

Two minutes later Tony was storming around the Dutch camping area shouting, 'WHERE THE HELL IS HERTZ VAN RENTAL? COME ON. HE'S THE ONE I NEED TO SPEAK TO. WHERE IS HE? WHERE IS HERTZ VAN RENTAL?'

Nobody could stand it any longer, so instead of watching

Tony we all ran off and hid in our respective caravans. About an hour later – yes, an hour – Tony finally returned with his tail between his legs.

'There was no Hertz Van Rental, was there? You just made it up.'

'Really? We must have got the name wrong. Sorry Tony!'

The team event, which featured six drivers from each country, took place on the Saturday, and the individual event, which was the one we were all there for, on the Sunday. On the Saturday, shortly before the team event, the drivers had to be presented to the crowd, and I remember waiting in the holding area beforehand. We were all wearing a British Racing Green race suit with a red, white and blue stripe down the middle, and the helmets were the same design.

Bearing in mind this was the early 1980s, instead of having a mascot or something leading us into the arena they decided to give each team a dolly bird, and because we were in Germany I assumed that they would all only speak German. A reasonably fair assumption, I think you'll agree, but unfortunately not a correct one.

Because I thought she was German, and because I wanted to show off in front of my teammates, I said something along the lines of, 'Wouldn't it be fun if I went up to our dolly bird and asked her for a shag?' to which my teammates all said something very much to the affirmative. 'Yeah, that would be brilliant!'

I'm paraphrasing now, but after strolling up to her and giving her a quick wink and a cheeky grin, I asked our dolly bird, very politely, if she'd like a quick shag. I was, after all, cock of the bloody north.

The look she gave me was one of abject disgust. A proper shit-on-my-shoe type of thing.

'No thank you,' she said, just loud enough so my teammates could hear her, before rounding off the sentence beautifully about half a second later with, 'little boy.'

If a car had driven up to me at that moment, the driver would probably have stopped and waited patiently for me to change to green. I was laughed out of the track, basically. And rightly so. Game, set and match to the lovely German dolly bird who happened to speak excellent English.

Anyway, what else is there to tell you about karting?

I haven't told you about our caravan yet, have I?

As soon as I started growing a bit, the foam mattress became too small for the three of us, so we ended up getting a caravan to live in while we were touring the world (and while I was making improper suggestions to women). One of the first times we used it was when we went to do some winter testing down at Rye House, which is a karting track in Hertfordshire. Winter testing was one of the only things about karting I didn't enjoy, for the simple reason it was winter! Don't get me wrong, I quite like a bit of inclement weather from time to time, as it makes me appreciate the sun more, but not when I'm driving and certainly not when I haven't a bloody roof.

On the first day of this test the weather was absolutely Baltic, about minus 2, and shortly after arriving at Rye House we realized that we'd brought the wrong gas for the caravan. I think I've got this the right way round but I'm pretty sure we'd bought a blue gas canister instead of a red gas canister, and the reason we needed the red one was because it had a much lower freezing point. Sure enough, as soon as we tried to heat the caravan, we realized that the gas had frozen inside the pipes.

'What do we do now, Tim?' Mum asked. 'We can't stay if it's like this.'

Faced with the prospect of having to find and then pay for a hotel, my dad took drastic action.

Five minutes later, he was lying on his back underneath the caravan clutching a plumber's soldering torch and trying to unfreeze the pipes. Yes, you read that correctly, ladies and gentlemen. My old man, the modfather, was holding a soldering torch – powered by red gas, I imagine, and burning at about a thousand bloody degrees – and was holding it against some pipes that were full of gas and which led directly to a rather large and very full gas canister!

I remember thinking to myself, *What the bloody hell is he doing?* I didn't question him, though. My dad's always been a bit of a nutter, so this was just normal practice, and I trusted him implicitly. In fact, I still do. About ten minutes later, he got the gas flowing, and from then on we were as warm as toast. I remember shouting to Mum that Dad had got the gas flowing and then looking under the caravan. He had a big smile on his face and was still rubbing the red-hot soldering torch up and down the pipe. Good old Dad. It was gas engineering Plato style. Not so much Corgi registered, more Kamikaze!

This has just reminded me of something. When I was young, there always used to be a bit of a furore when the gas man came to read the meter at Plato Towers. I don't know how he did it but I'm pretty sure my old man had found out how to make the meter go backwards or something and a few days before the gas man was due to come and read it he would try and make the meter go the right way round. As far as the meter was concerned, instead of the Plato's using three months' worth of gas we'd used three days. Not that we ever made it easy for the gas man to get in. It would have been easier to make me go teetotal in my twenties.

'Go to the door, Jason,' Mum would say, 'and if it's the gas man tell him he can't come in.'

'But what if he asks why?' I'd ask.

'Tell him your parents aren't in.'

'Will do.'

On other occasions we'd turn all the lights off and pretend to be out. He probably knew we were in there, but we didn't care. It was a war, a war of attrition, and whoever blinked or moved first lost!

The thing is, it was impossible to prosecute us really as (a) the gas company couldn't prove anything, and (b) I'm sure we were far from the only ones to do it. In felony terms it was a perfect crime.

If You Need Me, I'll Be in the Vaulting Horse

I think my karting career definitely shaped my on-track character when I went professional. Karting at a very high level – we're talking national here but certainly international – is competitive beyond belief. You could go and watch a race now in Italy, and the pace would be off the scale. You'd be saying to yourself, *Fuck me, how fast is this?*

There'd be a train of about twenty karts just millimetres away from each other like a giant snake, then all of a sudden a gap would appear and – bang! Attack, attack, attack. From a driver's point of view, the problem is that if you're the one being overtaken, not just one kart will pass you. Half the snake will!

In order to succeed at that level you have to be incredibly fast and very aggressive. Those who wait or play the long game never make progress. You also need to drive defensively without slowing yourself up while still trying to attack, so anyone who says that men can't multitask should pop off and watch a karting race or two. In those conditions it doesn't matter if you're running first, second, fifth or even eighth. Every driver will have good equipment and by virtue of the fact they're up there they will know exactly what they're doing. They'll be tasty, believe you me.

One of the most famous tracks in world karting is Pista Azzurra, which is in a place called Lido di Jesolo near

Venice. The first time I raced there was in 1983 in a round of the European Championship, and it blew my head off. Seriously, it was a different world.

The Italians were so far up the road with regards to competitiveness and they also had the best equipment. The track, though, was just ridiculously fast.

What made the experience problematic for me – apart from the speed of the track, which I quickly got used to – was the weather. In those days karters from the UK weren't taken seriously by the southern Europeans, and the reason for that was we were racing in different environments and different conditions, which required a different kind of race craft. The heat alone played merry hell with my equipment and especially the tyres. I just couldn't get any grip! Things also started to bend, I remember, and we all had to think very, very quickly. I actually fared OK in the end, but it was a steep learning curve. Italians are just nutcases!

As I recall my karting days now, I realize how much I miss it. The levels of intensity and on-track competition are unrivalled in my opinion, and there are no hiding places. Make one mistake and within three corners you could go from first to fifteenth easily.

Even today I can be a bit punchy during a race, but that's what gets you to ninety-seven wins. Mind you, that fuck-it attitude can undo a promising championship campaign because, instead of settling for third or second in a race to protect your points total, you think, *Fuck it, I'm going for the win*, and if you don't pull it off and lose points you can ruin a whole season's worth of racing. I could have had so much of an easier life by going, *OK, let's settle for third this time. Let's play the long game and think about the championship*. Unfortunately, it's just not within me.

From a manufacturer's point of view, and especially the big boys, playing the long game might be preferable as not only would their driver stand a better chance of winning the championship, but they themselves would stand a better chance of bagging the constructors' title. Then again, drivers who go for the win tend to get the headlines so it's probably six of one and half a dozen of the other.

I do sometimes wonder how things might have turned out for me had I fixated on winning championships and all I know for sure is that my career, and therefore my life, would have been a lot less eventful and so a lot less exciting. At the end of the day I'm a thrill-seeker. I always have been. I'm also somebody who lives in, and for, the moment so in order to focus on winning championships I'd have had to completely change my personality.

Paradoxically, I can actually be quite methodical at times and when it comes to things like business I'll wait as long as I have to in order to get the right deal. Once the deal's done, I'll go out and celebrate as if my life depended on it, but not until then.

The only thing that's changed my mindset slightly is parenthood, I'm not quite such a risk-taker now (though I still take the odd one, I wouldn't be me if I didn't!), but when it comes to my determination to win races I'm exactly the same now as I was when I was fifteen and if I see a gap I'll usually go for it. Is it instinctive? Partly. It's a reaction-based sport, and you don't have time to sit back and make qualified decisions. By the time you've thought about it and you have analysed the risk, it's too late. If going for a gap is what you've always done and is what comes naturally to you, the chances are you're going to act on it should the situation arise, so on reflection it is very instinctive. It doesn't always come off, of course, but if you're good at what you do (it doesn't tend to work if you're not), you'll get better at it as time goes on and hopefully end up on top.

When I turn up at a track I'm there to win races. I'm not there to play a percentages game. Some drivers are obviously happy doing that and good luck to them. Fortunately for me, and the people who follow the BTCC, there are still quite a few drivers out there who are gung-ho enough to go for the win no matter what. Take Matt Neal, for instance, who I'll come on to later. He and I have had some huge ding-dongs over the years and if you take it down to brass tacks the reason we've had these ding-dongs is because we both like to go for the win. That's the top and bottom of it.

One of my fiercest competitors during my karting days was a lad called Lee Cramner, who drove for Sisley Racing, who were down near Tilbury. When I first started in karting Lee was the top junior and he looked mint. He was always well turned out, and the entire outfit was just slick and pro. I don't really go in for heroes as such but Lee was probably the closest thing I had to a role model when I first started. Also, his sister, who is called Julie, was absolutely gorgeous.

The only thing that used to cloud the glamour slightly was that his parents were called Terry and June, but we can forgive him that. They were both lovely, so as far as any young onlookers were concerned Lee Cramner had the lot and was the benchmark.

The reason I'm mentioning Lee, apart from the fact that he was my hero and nemesis all rolled into one, is because he exemplifies just how competitive motorsport is when you get to a decent level. He had the lot when he started – the full package – yet he never got beyond karting. That can obviously happen for a number of reasons, but the transition from the feeder sport to the formulas that sit above is one of the most difficult things you can negotiate in motorsport. Mark my words.

The last time I drove a kart – this was semi-competitively – was actually only a couple of years ago, when I raced Tiff on a piece we filmed for *Fifth Gear*, the TV show I went on to present, and still do. He'd never raced karts before and classed them merely as toys. I, on the other hand, knew differently, so with our differences of opinion well and truly aired it was time to teach him a lesson.

It all took place at PF International, which is one of the UK's premier circuits, and we drove KF1s, which are the best machines karting has to offer. These things only have 40 bhp but are so light that they deliver – wait for it – a staggering 250 bhp per ton, which is roughly the same as a BMW M3. Not bad, eh? The 125 cc motor also revs up to about 16,000 rpm, so you can understand why I was keen to get the old boy into one of these things. He was in for a shock.

The first thing we did was a pitstop race where, with the help of a mechanic each, we had to change our tyres and oil the chain. Even with the intervening years this was like meat and potatoes for me, and I whooped him. The next part was a straightforward dogfight: three laps around the track! With Tiff being indifferent to karting, I was expecting an easy ride here but during the first lap – well, at least a bit of it – the old boy was all over me. Then the G-forces started taking their toll on him – you get to about three at the first corner, which is the equivalent of a very fast roller coaster – and from then on he struggled. One of the biggest misconceptions about cornering in a kart is that you need to enter the corner quickly.

Wrong! You need to enter the corner at the correct speed for that particular bend and in the current conditions. If you enter a corner flat out, the kart won't be able to maintain grip, which will prevent you from accelerating through the corner and will result in you either spinning out, running wide or being caught on the exit by other drivers. In order to maximize your exit speed, you have to get the entry speed just right, otherwise you're stuffed. You see it all the time in touring cars and Formula 1. One driver will outbreak another going into a turn, yet because they've entered it too quickly they'll get passed again on the exit.

If truth be known, Tiff wasn't the only one who struggled that day, and despite all my experience I'd forgotten how physically demanding it is. In touring cars you can just about get away with not being super fit but in karting it's a prerequisite and there are no hiding places and no room for negotiation.

One thing's for sure, Tiff's opinion of karting had most definitely changed by the end of the day and he appreciated fully both its importance as a training ground for tomorrow's drivers and the fact that karts are not toys. Anything but!

What you wouldn't have seen in that episode if you'd watched it was Tiff writing off a disgustingly expensive television camera that probably cost more than the karts. We were doing some tracking shots, and Tiff was just behind me. I came out of a corner and narrowly missed the camera, whereas Tiff just nicked it, and the thing just went boom! It cost tens of thousands of pounds, this thing. Less importantly he also cracked a rib that day, but that was just because he wasn't used to the grip.

*

One thing we haven't touched on yet – and you'll realize why in a moment – is my time at school. Given what I've told you about my family's dedication to karting, you probably think that I just walked in and walked out again without giving two hoots, but it's not quite as simple as that. For a start, I was privately educated, but not at the school where my parents wanted to send me. They wanted me to go to the Royal Grammar School in Newcastle, but unfortunately I flunked the entrance exam. The next school on their list was King's School in Tynemouth, which Stan Laurel went to. Perhaps more appropriately, in terms of whose book you're reading, so did the Donald brothers, who created *Viz!* It was a good school, though. Quite sporty.

I think the school sussed me out from the word go, and had they not been as hard on me I would probably have gone off the rails. My old man was pretty hot in the discipline department but he was only there some of the time, and I fully admit that in my younger days I needed a firm hand *all* of the time. I was a bit of a tearaway.

Do you know what? All in all, I probably gave the school and my parents just enough confidence to keep me in there, in that I passed exams and handed in homework on time, although I did mess around an awful lot and got into all kinds of trouble. Detentions were commonplace, but they were always for stupid things like making eye contact with a teacher while they were giving me a bollocking. They used to hate that for some reason and obviously expected me to hang my head in shame while they were telling me off. Not me, I'm afraid. I'm quite happy to take a bollocking if I deserve it, and if staring at the teacher while it's happening winds them up, all the better!

About six months before I took my O-levels I got pulled

into the headmaster's office, and he said that if I didn't work my arse off I'd be lucky to get one. As daft as it might sound, I hadn't even thought about O-levels until then, as I honestly didn't think I needed any. After all, I was going to be a racing driver, not a bloody architect. Because of that, I'd never really felt any pressure before and was actually good at all the main subjects. Maths and science were my two favourites and after responding to the headmaster's instruction to pull my finger out I did as I was told and ended up getting nine O-levels. I was a bright boy really.

To be fair to the school they were very supportive of my karting career and although they didn't capitulate when it came to academia they allowed me to take time off for races and made sure I did the required amount. They couldn't have done any more really. I think what also made up for things was the fact that I always involved in the sports – rugby obviously being one, eh, Mother?

My favourite teacher, and I can't not mention him, was Mr Gibson, who took me for woodwork, design and technology. You know when you hit it off with a teacher? Well, from day one Mr Gibson and I were just great mates and because we got on well together he took an interest in the karting. Sometimes we'd have to make something in either woodwork or design and technology and whenever possible Mr Gibson would suggest I make something to do with motorsport. He used to amalgamate my hobby with my education, and I found that inspiring. If you happen to read this, thank you, Mr Gibson! You were mint.

There was another teacher, called Bruce Coburn, who was my form teacher in year three. He was as hard as nails, and because of his reputation everybody was petrified of him. Not me, though. For some reason he and I got on like a house on fire, and I never once had a cross word with him. My mates used to get a hammering from him time after time, but never me. Perhaps it was because I was an only child and could relate to adults a bit more easily. I don't know. I certainly never took the piss with him, though, and if he ever said jump, I would say, how high? The more I think about Mr Coburn the more things come back to me. He used to pull his wedding ring up to his knuckle and then whack you over the head with it. It felt painful even just to watch it happen. He also did a good line in judo kicks, if memory serves. It was proper public-school stuff.

Right, let's get on to the inevitable.

I said earlier that I got into all kinds of trouble at school and if I didn't give you a few examples you'd be left thinking that I'd enjoyed a pretty standard school career. There's nothing standard about me, I'm afraid, and when you've finished reading this bit you'll probably feel compelled to take a break and write a letter of condolence to the school.

Where do I start? Well, I once set fire to the school bus using magnesium ribbon. That was a goodie. We'd nicked the magnesium ribbon during a science class, and the idea was that after setting it alight on the back of the bus we'd get off and then watch it burn as the bus drove away. We were looking forward to watching the inside of the bus turn white and because it was just magnesium ribbon we thought it would burn itself out in a couple of seconds.

Alas, it did not.

As I said to the police officers as they quizzed us at the station afterwards, it wasn't so much an arson attack as a simple trick that went wrong. I can't remember the punishment I got for that – which perhaps gives you a hint as to how many times I got into trouble, as I can't recall the punishment for all my many misdemeanours – but it might well have been a suspension.

One of the best things about my school was that it was all boys until the sixth form, so there were fewer distractions. After that, it was mixed, so our introduction on school premises with regards to females – if you discount all the teachers and dinner ladies, that is, which I certainly am doing – seventeen- and eighteen-year-old girls was where it started.

Although the school became mixed in the sixth form, the girls always seemed to be in different parts of the school to me (I think it was just an unlucky timetable), and in an attempt to try and redress this travesty – and it was a travesty, ladies and gentlemen, make no mistake about it – me and my mate Simon decided to take matters into our own hands.

One of the only times the girls congregated together without the sixth-form boys being present was when they did gymnastics, so Simon and I decided to set up shop, so to speak, in the school gymnasium. The question was, where?

'What do they do in gymnastics?' asked Simon as we stood in the gym one lunchtime.

'I don't know,' I replied. 'The same as us, I suppose. They jump over things.'

At that moment we both spotted the vaulting horse that had already been put in place for the following day's lesson.

'I'll tell you what. Let's hide in there!' I said, probably quite excitedly.

'Brilliant!' replied Simon.

Simon and I used to have to get the train to school in those days and if we didn't time it correctly we could get into all kinds of trouble. You see, there was a comprehensive school just up the road from us called Benfield – there was a big rivalry between us and them because they all thought we were posh – and if we took the train that got us to Tyne-mouth shortly before school began we had to walk past hundreds of lads from Benfield. You can probably guess the rest. We were obviously seen as being the enemy by this lot and whenever they saw us we'd get kicked to bloody bits. As a result, Simon and I would always get an earlier train to school and, would you believe it, one that happened to deliver us to Tynemouth about fifteen minutes before the sixth-form girls arrived for their morning gymnastics session.

Before we turned into practising perverts we used to play around in the gym anyway, as we were always early, so in reality we weren't really doing anything different. Instead of playing basketball, like we usually did, we played hide and seek instead.

I think we were both about fourteen years old at the time and because neither of us was especially tall we managed to fit inside the vaulting box quite easily.

I don't know if any of you remember these vaulting boxes but they have thin holes running diagonally all the way round which happen to be perfect for perving. Sure enough, at roughly 8.30 a.m., the girls and the teacher assembled in the gym and, after locking it down – this was essential so as to prevent any prying eyes, or so they thought – they started running up to the little springboard in front of the vaulting box and jumping over – us! Unfortunately, the magnificence of what we were witnessing, and believe me it was truly magnificent, became hijacked by the comical aspect, and after just a few minutes we both started giggling.

Please allow me to pause for a second. Oh, the memories!

The teacher taking the session was Chris Davy, the head of sport. He was actually a mate of ours, as we were both quite sporty, and the moment he heard the giggling he brought everything to a halt.

'Hold on, hold on,' he shouted. 'What's that bloody noise?

Satisfied that he'd identified the location of the giggling, Mr Davy walked slowly towards the vaulting box, and as this happened the giggles quickly turned into *Oh fucks*.

'What have we here, then?' he said, lifting the lid off the box, and with it he took the lid off our fun. 'My word. Plato and Pattinson. What a surprise. Come on out, boys.'

Half the girls were giggling and the other half were looking on in disgust. Even so, as Mr Davy dragged us both out by our ears we gave them all a smile and a friendly thumbs up. They were very big for their age, I remember. It was epic.

As you'd expect, Mr Davy gave us both an almighty gobful as he dragged us from the gym. As he bollocked us, though, he couldn't help but smirk. He dragged us all the way down the corridor and as soon as we went through the main doors he immediately began sniggering. I wondered if he was thinking that we were boys after his own heart!

'Don't let me catch you doing anything like that again, OK?' he said.

'Yes sir,' we said obediently.

What a legend!

One of the less surprising aspects about my school career – even less surprising than leering at sixth-formers from inside vaulting boxes, believe it or not – was my aptitude as an entrepreneur. This I obviously get from my old man, and without wanting to sound big-headed I was bloody good at it.

In the junior school at King's you weren't allowed out at lunchtime. In fact, you weren't allowed out into Tynemouth until the second year of middle school when you were about eleven years old. This meant that when Simon and I were eventually let off the leash an opportunity arose involving the younger kids who were incarcerated. Basically, we started a lunch club, where, for a nominal fee, we would procure whatever their hearts' desired, basically for said young 'uns usually either fish and chips or a stotty and chips. I'm pretty sure that was my first racket, and we ended up getting caught in the end. I can't remember the punishment (there were so many!), but it wasn't too severe. After all, we were simply providing a service.

One of my most profitable rackets first came about after I started karting in Europe. I was already a committed smoker by then and after buying some cigarettes and a lighter one day in, I think, Italy, I realized that the lighter had cost me only the equivalent of a couple of pence. Within an hour or so I'd managed to procure enough lighters to burn down twenty schools and when I arrived back at mine the following Monday I set about distributing some of them – for a nominal fee, of course.

I think my favourite school story involves me, my mate Simon, some rugby posts and a large Swiss Army knife. Boy oh boy, did we get in trouble for this one! It was the closest I ever came to being expelled and funnily enough it happened off school premises.

We were due to play Benfield School at rugby the following day at Benfield and, as I'm sure you can imagine, we weren't really looking forward to it. Benfield were absolutely brilliant at football but rubbish at rugby. They were also hard as nails, and there was a rivalry between us, so the game was almost secondary in a way. It was simply a case of trying to avoid getting beaten to death.

In order to take revenge for all the batterings we'd received over the years (we did come out on top sometimes but only when the numbers were fair), Simon and I decided to have a go at their rugby posts with a Swiss Army knife and do just enough damage so that when we played them the following day they would collapse mid-game and hopefully after we'd just scored a penalty.

I remember Simon giving me a leg up one of the posts and after getting out the knife I set to work. It was surprisingly easy cutting through the post, and I remember thinking to myself that I may have gone a bit too far on this one. No matter.

After I jumped down, Simon gave me a leg up at the other post, and once again I started making like a lumberjack. I was a little bit more careful this time around and was sure that I'd got it just right.

'That's it,' I said to Simon. 'One smack of a rugby ball tomorrow and it'll be, TIMBEEEEEER!'

'Hang on a second,' he said as I jumped down. 'Aren't the posts moving?'

I quickly looked up.

'Oh, hell, they are. Quick, run for it!'

The plan had worked, just twenty-four hours too early.

It was a schoolboy error – literally – and as the posts fell on to the grass I could see my life ebbing away. Trouble? You don't know the half of it. I'd never had a bollocking like that in my entire life. As far as our school was concerned, we'd disgraced them, and in a sport they took very seriously. Also, it didn't exactly endear us to the pupils of the school whose rugby posts we'd vandalized, and for the next few months – until somebody else had done something equally heinous – we had to be super vigilant, as there were several hundred fists and shoes with our names on them.

We got two weeks' detention in the end, which had to run through the summer holidays. We ended up sanding down desks and creosoting fences most of the time. It was purgatory! I mean, all we did was break a bit of wood. People get wound up by the smallest things, don't you think?

While we're here, I may as well tell you about some of my misdemeanours outside of school, as the majority of these involve cars. That's cars, by the way, not karts. Even at thirteen or fourteen I was driving cars on a regular basis and most of the time I got away with it. I forget when I started exactly, but whenever my parents were out of the way I would get the keys and go for a spin. I didn't always go far, at least not at the beginning, but driving was already the most natural thing in the world to me and I was getting fed up with having to wait until a karting event to get behind a wheel. It was like smoking really. I started off by doing it every so often and then before I knew it I was pinching a parental car every other day. The difference in size meant nothing to me, and it felt just as natural as a kart. The performance was usually a bit disappointing, but as long as it had four wheels and some petrol in the tank I was happy.

One of the first times I didn't get away with it actually involved a van rather than a car, and if it hadn't been for Neil Hann it would have spelt the end of my racing career and I'd probably have ended up becoming a gymnastics teacher – *ahem!*

I think I'd have been thirteen at the time. Mum was working

as a nurse, and Dad was still in the car trade. Mum used to work nights a lot of the time and would return home whacked about 8 a.m. When that happened, Simon and I would wait for my old man to go to work and once we were satisfied that Mum was safely in the land of Nod we'd push her car off the driveway and down the road a bit, then start her up and go out for the day. This was only at the weekends and during school holidays, by the way. You couldn't bunk off at our school. It would have been suicide. Even I knew to draw the line somewhere.

We used to take some cushions from our living room first and then chuck them in the car. These were essential as, without them to sit on, we wouldn't have been able to see very much. Once we'd pushed Mum's car down the road a bit and started it we would set off quite slowly. Then, once we'd cleared the first corner it would be foot down and – BOOM! Away we go.

We had some absolutely epic days out over the years. We went all over the place. We always had a few quid for fuel and would take a jerry can with us so we could fill up without pulling into a garage. We had a well-rehearsed plan.

'Excuse me. My dad's run out of petrol. Do you mind if I fill this up?'

'No problem, son.'

Butter wouldn't melt.

I think my favourite excursion was driving into town, parking at the back of the snooker hall and playing snooker all day. A packet of fags, a few full-fat cokes and a few frames. Who could ask for more?

Anyway, one day during the summer holidays, Dad had gone to work and Mum had gone to sleep, having just come home from a night shift. I forget what Simon and I were up to at the time but at some point during the morning we ran out of fags. Instead of walking the 500 yards or so up to the newsagents, where I'd hand over a poorly written note saying, 'Please sell my son 20 B&H', I decided to drive there instead. Lazy bugger!

For a change I nicked Dad's LT28, which we still used from time to time and which had *Jason Plato Racing* emblazoned on the side. It also had an eight-track stereo, so from a coolness point of view it was bang on trend. I forget what music there was in there, but I didn't give a monkey's. I was in a van with my name on the side and I was driving it – illegally! It was the first time I'd ever driven anything high up before, but I don't remember feeling intimidated. In fact, I rather liked the view. What I do remember is how slow it was. It was like a tank!

The first part of the journey went according to plan as, after handing over the note and the money, I was duly handed a box containing twenty of Benson & Hedges' finest. It was only when I pulled into our drive again that things went sour as in the space on the drive where the van had been just a few moments before sat my old man's car. Oh fuck!

He'd obviously had to come home for some reason, and when he'd found out who'd taken the van he'd gone absolutely apoplectic. I'd just wound down the window to chuck out a fag when I saw him standing in the drive, and as I pulled up I heard him say, 'What the fucking hell do you think you're doing?' I don't experience fear very much, except when I'm driving with Tiff Needell. It's just not part of who I am. This was one of the few occasions where it almost overwhelmed me, and within a second of me opening the van door I was lying on the front lawn with my dad on top of me. I got a proper hiding for that and was told there and then that karting was now a thing of the past. Dad meant it too.

The following week, after hearing about what had happened, Neil Hann called Dad up and set about trying to persuade him to change his mind. I honestly thought that was it for me as for a few days Dad seemed resolute. I don't know how he did it, but after one or two conversations Neil managed to talk Dad around. Dad later told me that as a kid he'd got into big trouble for nicking cars, and the reason he'd gone so apeshit was that he could see me going the same way. We ended up missing a few races but in the end we managed to get back on track, pardon the pun. Funnily enough, that was my one big scare during my karting career and had nothing to do with money or a crash. It was completely self-inflicted.

In my defence – if you can defend such an action – I'd already been driving for over a year by then and because of that I always considered myself to be competent enough to drive on the road. That means bugger all as far as the law is concerned, but I'm looking at it from the point of view of a rather naughty teenager who'd already won a championship or two on four wheels – albeit in a slightly smaller vehicle than the one I nicked.

I can actually remember the first time I ever drove a car. I was about four or five at the time and I was with my grandad. He used to pop out in his car for a sly fag from time to time, and if I ever went with him he'd let me steer for a bit as we went over the Oxford bypass. I can still vividly remember the first time he let me take the wheel. It felt epic! Even then I got a thrill from being in control of something large and with four wheels – or at least partly in control – and what I remember most is that I didn't want it to stop. The smoking came later, although only slightly.

Given what you've just read, you'd think I'd have given up nicking my parents' vehicles after that, but I'm afraid not. Things like consequences only became real to me when I got married and had kids, and that goes for having a conscience too to a certain extent. I'm not saying I was the bloody devil or anything but I always had a very *live for the moment* attitude to life before meeting Sophie and if an idea came into my head or something interesting appeared – whatever that might be – I usually went with it. I've calmed down a lot since becoming a dad, but it's still there. I'm still Jason Plato.

Shall we have another car story? I think we should. This one's an absolute cracker.

When I was fourteen, my dad went away on a conference, and because it was term time and my mum was working nights I went to stay at Simon's house for a day or two. Rather foolishly, my mum had given me a key for our place just in case I needed to get anything, and after school me and Simon went back there, as it was a parent-free zone. Even more foolishly, my old man had left the keys to his Astra GTE in the hall, so instead of opening a bag of sweets, putting our feet up and watching a few episodes of *Grange Hill*, we decided to take the Astra out for the evening and have some fun. This car had a Turbo Technics conversion kit on it and it was the lairiest and loudest car on our street. It was just lush!

Immediately, we started tear-arsing around the streets of Tyneside in Dad's Astra looking very cool but incredibly illegal, and it's a wonder we weren't either reported or stopped, especially given the speeds we were doing.

Everything was going absolutely swimmingly until we decided to go down a long road that we'd taken a couple of weeks previously. On that particular occasion we'd been driving my dad's van (or rather I had) and at one point on the street we'd gone over a mini-roundabout at about 60 mph. Being almost flat, it hadn't made much of a difference, so as we tore down this road again in Dad's Astra I didn't give it a second thought. The only difference between this and the last occasion – that I was aware of – was that we were travelling a lot faster and, although I'm far from proud of it now, I have to admit that we were doing nearly a ton in what today would be a 50 mph zone. Naughty boy.

About 10 metres before we reached the roundabout I noticed there was something different about it. It was no longer flat – or flattish. It was now raised slightly like a large upturned dish and it had a kerb running round it. Despite managing to swerve slightly, we just caught the kerb and ended up totalling both the front wheels.

Oh Christ!

I should point out at this juncture that not only was it was about eleven o'clock at night when this happened (we'd sneaked out again after dinner and lights out) but we were also at least 5 miles from home. We were in a right pickle and no mistake.

'What the hell are we going to do?' asked Simon.

'I don't know. How about Andy?'

Simon and I used to have a dodgy mate called Andy who was a lot older than us and who could basically get hold of anything you wanted – for a price. He was a regular at a boozer that was quite close to where we'd crashed, so we hightailed it over there and prayed they were having a lock-in.

There were no mobile phones in those days, so that was our only option.

Fortunately, they were having a lock-in, so once we'd arrived we spent the next fifteen minutes trying to attract Andy's attention. We obviously couldn't go in there, so there was a lot of waving and tapping on windows. Eventually he spotted us and reluctantly came out.

'What the hell are you two doing here?' he asked.

'We've pranged my dad's Astra.'

'You what?'

'We've pranged my dad's Astra. Front wheels are both fucked.'

'Wahey lads! A normal Tuesday night for yooz two, then.'

'But what are we going to do, Andy?' I asked. 'He'll kill me.'

'Easy,' he said without so much as a pause. 'Nick some new ones.'

The man was a genius!

'Where from?'

'I don't fucking know. Find an Astra and get 'em off.'

After managing to start the engine, we drove the Astra, very slowly, back to my house. Some of the noises it made were horrific.

After having a quick think I remembered where I'd seen an Astra GTE, and fortunately the house was only about a mile away.

'What if we're spotted?' asked Simon.

'Don't worry,' I reassured him. 'I've already thought of that.

After nipping into our house, I re-emerged with two racing balaclavas.

'Here,' I said chucking him one. 'Get this on.'

After grabbing the necessary tools, we scampered off to

find this Astra, but it was only when we were taking off a front wheel that we realized that the rims were all wrong.

'Oh, for Christ's sake!' I yelled.

We had no choice but to put it back on and scarper.

Within a few minutes we were back at the pub, and fortunately they were still locked in. When Andy came out again, reluctantly, he was three sheets to the wind but could just about speak.

'What happened with the wheels,' he asked.

'We couldn't find two that matched,' I replied. 'What do we do now?'

'That's easy. You put it on bricks.'

'Eh?'

'Oh, for fuck's sake, man. Put it on bricks, ditch the wheels, and when yer mam comes back in the morning she'll think someone's nicked 'em.'

Eureka!

He really was a genius, this bloke.

We chucked the wheels down the railway embankment that was not far from our house and then made our way back to Simon's for a few hours' kip. The next morning – or rather the same morning – we went back to mine after breakfast, and after five minutes Mum charged in. She was in a right panic.

'Someone's had it away with your dad's front wheels,' she shrieked. 'Didn't you notice when you arrived.'

'No, Mum, we didn't,' I lied. 'Aw, that's awful!'

'I'll call the police.'

'No need to do that, Mum!' I shrieked. 'There'll be long gone by now. Wheels get nicked all the time.'

Mum did call the police, but by the time they arrived we were safely at school and so we managed to get away with it.

I expect you're wondering if I ever came clean about this to Mum and Dad, and, believe it or not, yes, I did. It was many years afterwards and from a safe distance, but I had to. Fortunately they just laughed, as it was obviously par for the course with me, and I can't say I really regret any of it. Not really. It was just a blast!

A Piss-up with Hunt, Followed by a Great Big Shunt

We haven't touched on girlfriends yet, have we? Actually, if it's all the same to you, I think we'll leave it, as the majority of my love interests during my karting years were sisters of fellow drivers and a lot of it was on the QT, if you see what I mean. Also, I didn't really get going in that department until I was about fourteen or fifteen. I never had any luck with the sixth-formers, by the way (although it wasn't through want of trying), and the majority of my spare time was spent karting (or joyriding), which is where all the action took place. Let's just say that, once I found my feet, a lot of fun was had by all!

The first proper girlfriend I ever had was when I went to the arts and tech college in Newcastle after the fifth form, so I would have been seventeen at the time. Lindsay McAndrew was her name. Instead of going into the sixth form and then to university, I wanted to get stuck in and I did a diploma in technology instead. The reason I wanted to do the diploma was because it was all racing related, as I figured it would give me a much broader scientific and theory-based knowledge of broad-brush technology, whether it be mechanical engineering or electrical engineering, which would in turn give me an advantage in the industry. I suppose in hindsight I might also have been feathering my nest subconsciously in case the racing thing came to naught, but had that happened I'm pretty sure I'd have done something entrepreneurial as opposed to something academic. Also, working for other people doesn't come naturally to me, and in the long term I'm sure I'd have been an awful employee.

Instead of staying the course on the tech course, so to speak, I decided to leave once I'd learned what I considered to be the required amount. I was also skint by this point and I hated that.

In order to earn a few pennies while I decided what to do next, I started selling vacuum cleaners door to door for an American company called Kirby and I made a shedload of money very quickly. Mum and Dad had moved down south by this point, and I was living in Newcastle.

These vacuum cleaners cost – wait for it £799.99 in what would have been the mid-1980s. You could have bought a bloody house for that in certain parts of the country, so you can imagine how difficult it should have been selling them door to door. For your average salesman, yes. For me, no. To be fair, we had the advantage of selling them on the never-never, on credit, which obviously made things easier, but it was still a hard slog, and the demonstrations, which were just pitches really, used to last hours.

I think my best month was thirty-eight machines, which was a record for the northeast distributor. If you sold a machine for full price you got £300 commission and if you discounted them a bit less, but that month I ended up earning about £10k commission – in 1985! Some of you will be assuming, or at least hoping, that I spent it all on cars, but in truth I just pissed it up against a wall.

If you sold two machines over a weekend the boss would take you out to buy some new clobber and after that to a swanky wine bar. It was a school for extreme capitalism to all intents and purposes, as they were forever dangling carrots in front of you. To a young man like me who enjoyed having nice clothes and a few quid in his pocket, it was tailor made, and my colleagues and I were regulars in all the best night-clubs and all the best bars and restaurants. We used to finish our last appointments by about 10.30 p.m. and nine times out of ten we'd head straight to the clubs.

'Evening, boys. Usual table?'

'Yes please!'

We were always front of the queue. Lairy lads about town you'd probably call us. Newcastle is a great city, and the nightlife has always been excellent. It's one of the few places where, regardless of what night it is or what time of year, you'll always find a few places that are buzzing. We used to go to a place called Julies, which was at the groovy end of town. That was a sexy little club, and I shudder to think how much moolah I did in there. It was money well spent, though!

Bearing in mind how strong the accent is up there, it's a surprise I never picked it up much. If I ever go back, which I do from time to time, and stay for a few days, I do start sound-ing a little bit Geordie, but it's just the odd word. There'd be a kind of sing-song in my voice. If anything, I sound like a Brummie most of the time, but I have no idea where that comes from.

In the long term, I always knew I was going to leave the northeast, because I wanted to become a racing driver, and with the best will in the world Newcastle is not the epicentre of motorsport. In fact, it's about 250 miles away as far as Britain's concerned. My nearest track up there was actually Doning-ton, as Croft was closed to circuit racing at the time and didn't reopen until 1997. I needed to be where the action was and I needed to be part of the action. It was as simple as that.

*

I stopped driving karts in 1987 after what had been a pretty successful career and once I was settled down south – I stayed with my parents in Suffolk at first – I set about trying to make the transition into single-seaters. I'd been trying for a while to find some sponsors or some openings but as I said the north-east just wasn't the place to be. Suffolk wasn't Oxford, but at least I was close to places like Snetterton and I could get over to Oxford or down to London in next to no time.

One of the first things I did when I moved down there was help my old man set up a new business selling insurance for car phones. He found a gap in the market just at the right time and made a lot of money very quickly. I helped him set up a dealer network and as well as earning a few quid I was able to identify a few potential sponsors. I wasn't driving at the time but I intended to be soon, and the more backing I had the better chance I'd have of succeeding.

Incidentally, never one to miss an opportunity, I had stipulated in my contract with Dad that my first company car should be a Peugeot 205 GTI 1.9, and I got away with it! Soon after that I negotiated a deal for a 275 bhp Lancia Delta Integrale if sales targets were hit, and, because I'd taken to this insurance game rather well, he said yes. The Lancia only lasted three weeks as, after accidentally bursting in on Mum and Dad one day when they were up to no good (quite graphic no good, as a matter of fact!), I went for a drive to try and prevent what I'd witnessed from etching its horrific self on to my consciousness for all eternity and ended up hitting a bloody tree. The impact took the front wheel off and left the engine hanging out of one side of the car, and when I realized what had happened, my ticker started going like the clappers. Boy, was I in the shit! You know what it's like, though. Mums and dads aren't meant to have things like sex lives, so if you're ever unfortunate enough to discover that they do indulge in some indoor sports occasionally it's like watching David Attenborough throwing plastic bottles at dolphins. It's just wrong!

After procrastinating for a few minutes, I finally plucked up the courage to call Dad and after I tried, and failed, to underplay the condition of the car, he agreed to drive out and rescue me. He wasn't happy. About five minutes later, I saw a police car coming towards me. Oh, bloody hell! I thought. That's all I need. My teflon coating was about to be put to the ultimate test.

'Evening sir,' said the officer. 'Had a little accident, have we?'

'You could say that,' I replied. 'I was driven off the road!'

In truth, I'd been driving like somebody who had just seen their parents having a special cuddle and had simply lost control, but I wasn't going to tell him that. Ten minutes later, I'd done a job on the policeman, and he was standing there with his hand on my shoulder saying, there, there, there sir, and telling me there was nothing to worry about. I was almost home and dry.

Just as that was happening, I heard the unmistakable sound of my Peugeot 205 GTI 1.9, which had a bad-boy exhaust and made a noise like a Harrier Jump Jet. I'd decided to keep it when I got the Lancia, and Mum had been using it to get to and from work. Dad was at the wheel now and by the sounds of things he was showing it no mercy. It was almost as if he was pissed off about something? When he eventually took the corner at which I'd had my accident he almost locked up, and for a moment I thought he was going to copy me. The policeman frowned for a second.

'Who's this, then?' he asked as Dad came screeching to a halt.

'It's my dad,' I replied nervously.

As the door of the Peugeot flew open, out popped Pater, holding a torch. The first thing he did was to shine the torch directly on to the tyre marks I'd made and given what I've just told you, that made me nervous.

'Erm, Dad,' I shouted. 'Over here!'

'I'm afraid your son's been driven off the road, Mr Plato,' said the sympathetic police officer. 'It wasn't his fault, though, and he's OK.'

'Driven off the road my arse,' said Dad. 'He's spun you a right one. He's conned you.'

Wasn't seeing him and Mum at it enough? Now he was trying to incriminate me!

'He's always joking, my dad,' I said, trying to retrieve the situation and pull the verdict from 'lock him up' to 'not guilty'. Fortunately, Dad played the game from then on, but the drive home was excruciating. I was feeling embarrassed and relieved, and Dad was feeling embarrassed and angry. Very angry.

Mum and Dad probably won't thank me for including this story, but it's bloody well going in. I'm scarred for life!

While all this was going on, it was suggested to me that I try and get into what was then called the Winfield Elf Renault Racing School in France. Winfield had been co-founded by two brothers called Mike and Richard Knight, and they also ran the school. It was regarded as the best you could go to at the time, and its alumni included the likes of Damon Hill, Andy Priaulx, Jean-Pierre Jabouille, René Arnoux, Patrick Tambay, Jean Alesi, Olivier Panis and some bloke called Alain Prost. In fact, since opening, they'd taught twenty-six Formula 1 drivers.

As a Formula Renault school, which is what I was hoping

to get into before taking Formula 3 and then Formula 1 by storm, we decided that the best course of action was for me to try and get a little bit of experience before going to the school, and at great expense to my old man he basically bought me some time in a Formula 3 car at the Pembrey circuit in Wales just so I could get a feel for what I was getting involved in. That was the first time I'd ever driven a racing car before, and it was absolutely epic! It was everything I hoped it would be.

When I got to the school I immediately enrolled in a competition they were running called the Pilote Elf Competition. Aimed at the former karting intake, or those with a tiny bit of Formula Renault experience, the winner of the competition got a fully paid-up drive in France's long-established national Formula Renault championship, so the stakes were enormous.

The school was based at Magny-Cours, and within a few days I'd caught the eye of Mike Knight, who very kindly introduced me to Renault UK. To cut a long story short, I ended up cutting a deal with Renault to drive in their inaugural Formula Renault UK championship that was starting the following year, so the Pilote Elf went out of the window. I sort of regret that in a way, as I ended up coming second in the competition and would probably have pissed it had I given it my all. If that had been the case, I would have had the support from Renault *and* Elf in an established competition and the chances are, had I continued progressing, I'd have made it into Formula 1 at their expense. It wasn't guaranteed, but I think the previous six or seven winners of the Pilote Elf had all gone into Formula 1, so there was certainly a good chance. There aren't many things I regret in my career, and that was probably the first. If anything, I think I was slightly daunted by the prospect of being based in a different country so early in my career and despite it being a new series I'd persuaded myself that all roads would eventually lead to F1.

The following year, in 1990, I made my debut in Formula Renault, but unfortunately the team I signed for didn't have very good equipment and about halfway through the season I jumped ship to a newish team based out of Yorkshire called Manor Motorsport. Manor were running the works Van Diemen (works means manufacturer supported, and Van Diemen were a race car manufacturer). When they put another car out for me, I repaid them by winning my first race. I think it was at Donington Park.

I first met the owner of Manor Motorsport, a remarkable man called John Booth, at the press launch of the new competition, which had taken place in the old Williams factory underneath Didcot power station. It was all very embryonic at the time, as John had never run a race team before and I'd never driven for one outside of karting. Although we got on, for some reason we'd gone our separate ways after that. When we finally hooked up halfway through the season, it seemed right. Boothy's number two was a man called Pete Slivinski, and basically they were a cracking couple of blokes. Good fun, very competitive and they did everything right. They were proper Yorkshire lads too and spent their money wisely as opposed to wasting it. They also had the backing of Van Diemen, who were arguably the most successful space-frame race car manufacturer in the world. Their factory was based at Snetterton, so with me being just half an hour away, everything fitted.

In my first half-season with Manor, which took in roughly half the races, I ended up beating Paulo Carcasci, who was their works driver. I remember having a brilliant race against

Paulo up at Knockhill, which was my first time racing there. I was leading the race, and he was up my arse. I managed to hold him off until eventually he ran me off the track in full view of everybody. Boothy went absolutely apeshit, as did Ralph Firman from Van Diemen, so he actually did me a favour, as it catapulted me into the works drive for next season.

Being part of Manor Motorsport so early on in its history is one of the great joys of my early racing career, and the first full year we had together, which also sadly turned out to be our last, was just epic. We raced all over Europe. We won at the Nürburgring and we won the European Formula Renault Championship. It was just incredible. We also got embroiled in an extremely acrimonious championship battle with a driver called Bobby Verdon-Roe. Now here's a story.

There were two big teams in Formula Renault back then, in the UK at least, and they were my team, Manor Motorsport, and a team called Fortec Motorsport, who Bobby Verdon-Roe drove for. Because we both had the upper hand on the rest of the field, as in better equipment, it was usually a two-horse race, and, with neither team showing any signs of slipping, you had to look for every possible advantage.

One day, our engine manufacturer, who was also Fortec's, sent one of my works engines to them by mistake. I don't know how or why it happened, but the moment the engine arrived at Fortec's factory they immediately began pulling it apart and in doing so they found something they weren't happy with.

Back in the day, these Formula Renault engines had wet sumps on them, and when the formula was first designed they weren't pulling anywhere near the amount of G they are now. This was down to a number of things really, but a lot of engines had also been going pop, which had left everyone scratching their heads. After a lot of hard work our lot came up with a solution, which I'll try and explain without boring everyone's pants off.

The basic Formula Renault 2.0 litre engine had originally been turbo-charged and in its production form it had had sprays fitted to distribute oil underneath the pistons to cool them down. Our engineer, Alan, had decided to block the sprays up using ball bearings, which meant that we didn't have oil spraying around and that, in layman's terms, made our engines slightly more reliable.

Although it was potentially a bit of a grey area, in that we could have been accused of messing with the oil baffling system, we thought it was legal, and because it gave us an advantage we wanted to keep it quiet.

Fat bloody chance!

Once Fortec had discovered what we'd done they immediately lodged a complaint, and from that moment on it was war. There was already no love lost before that to be honest, but now it was getting legal.

What made matters worse was that I'd taken out what's called a prize indemnity insurance policy, which basically meant I'd insured myself *against* winning the British Formula Renault Championship. The reason I did that was because Formula 3 was so ridiculously expensive – about £250,000 a year – so if I did happen to win the Formula Renault Championship I'd have the funds to carry on and keep the momentum going. I forget what the premium was exactly, but it was well over 10,000 quid. It was a legalized bet basically (although you can't do it any more), and funnily enough Bobby had taken out exactly the same policy. The stakes were high! Not only would we win the championship but we'd not have to worry about money in one of the most expensive Formulas out there. Formula 1, here I come!

Because of what was at stake, the fight between both the teams and drivers became quite nasty, and while the legal stuff was going on in the background re the engine, Bobby and I were knocking lumps out of each other on the track. I used to have some stickers in those days that had my helmet design on them, and, as a motivation to beat me, Bobby used to have one on his steering wheel. It was like a poor man's version of Hunt versus Lauda in a way. Guess which one I am.

In the end, and after much toing and froing, it was deemed by the powers that be to be an illegal modification, so despite me winning the championship I ended up getting disqualified. Goodbye, prize indemnity, goodbye, Formula Renault Championship, goodbye, Formula 3 and, probably, goodbye, Formula 1 . . .

In a bizarre twist of fate Bobby didn't get his prize indemnity either, as his insurance company ended up going bankrupt! Poor bastard. That must have been a real kick in the teeth. He's a good lad, is Bobby, and although he didn't take the world by storm he did go on to win the TVR Tuscan Challenge one year and he's also raced at Le Mans.

What a bugger, though. So near, and yet so far away.

The aforementioned James Hunt makes me think of another tale I want to share.

In 1991 I went over to Jerez, as a spectator, for the Spanish round of the European Formula Renault Championship, which was the support race for the F3000 Championship. Boothy was going over there to look after a young driver for Van Diemen, and I thought, I'll go with him. He was also taking a development rear wing with him that I might end up using, so if I needed a reason to go, that was it.

On the Saturday I was walking up and down the paddock, taking it all in, when suddenly I saw the great James Hunt walking towards me. As well as working for the federation he was also there in his capacity as an ambassador for the Marlboro Racing Academy (at least he enjoyed a fag!) and, not to put too fine a point on it, he was pissed. As somebody who enjoyed a drink himself and who was a fan of Mr Hunt, I decided to say hello, and after having a chat he agreed to meet me and the rest of the team later in a restaurant for something to eat and a couple of sherbets.

Like everybody, I'd heard all kinds of stories about James Hunt, some of which would make your teeth itch, and nearly all of them involved women and copious amounts of alcohol. It was with this in mind that I turned up at the restaurant like a cat with two dicks. I was only going out with James Hunt! Anything could happen and probably would.

The next thing I remember after arriving at the restaurant is waking up the following morning in our hotel with the mother of all hangovers. I'd never, ever felt pain like it! What the hell happened? I genuinely couldn't remember a thing.

About ten minutes later there was a knock on my door. It was Boothy.

'What happened?' I asked him.

He looked at me as if to say, do you really want me to tell you? 'We had to manhandle you out of the restaurant,' he said.

'Was I being a tit?'

'A tit? You were being ten thousand tits. Seriously JP, you were absolutely shitfaced. Even James was impressed.'

That was something, I suppose.

'Anyway, come on, we've got work to do. Hands off cocks, on with socks. The car's outside.'

I didn't have time to shower or even change and after stumbling down to reception I was bundled into a car waiting outside. The temperature must have been at least forty degrees and the moment I got in – sorry, fell in – I went straight to sleep. When we arrived at Jerez, they just left me in the car, and when I woke up the windows were closed and it was stifling. I remember trying to take a massive breath of air when I woke up but there wasn't any! Quickly, I opened the back door and, as I tried to get out, I stumbled and ended up rolling out on to the concrete like a massive sack of shit. Just as I landed, I looked up, and who was walking towards me? James Hunt. He was wearing shorts and flip-flops and had a freshly lit fag on the go. The moment he saw me he gave me a huge thumbs up. He was still pissed! I'm a bungling amateur compared to him.

The following day, by which time I'd just about sobered up, we had to drive from Jerez to Madrid, which is about a six- or seven-hour drive. The driver Boothy was looking after, Antonio, was at the wheel, and his girlfriend was up front with him. Boothy, who had also been on the piss all weekend, was slumped in the back with me, and I was clutching the rear development wing.

The road we were on went through miles and miles of fields and was raised about 4 feet, so it had a drop either side of it. About an hour into the journey Boothy and I started nodding off, but no sooner had that happened than I felt the brakes go, and I woke up with a start. I looked forward, and we were about to hit the back of a farm vehicle. Boothy had also woken up, and the two of us sat up and braced ourselves for the impact. We must have been going about 40 or 50 mph, but because the farm vehicle was going so slowly the impact was immense.

Boothy, who's a big bloke, went into the back of Antonio's girlfriend's seat (this was long before rear seatbelts), and she ended up smashing her head against the dashboard. After that we went flying off the road into a field and a few seconds later we came to a halt. Boothy had done his ribs in and couldn't breathe, and Antonio's girlfriend, who was bleeding heavily from her nose, was screaming her head off. It was chaos! Antonio had fallen asleep at the wheel, and he and I were unharmed save for a couple of bruises.

A few hours later, we were all released from hospital. I was still clutching the development wing, and all four of us absolutely stank of iodine, and I mean stank. All of us had a few minor cuts, and for some reason they'd doused us in it. Boothy had broken a couple of ribs and had bruised a lung, so he was in a right state, as was Antonio's girlfriend. We were also wearing the same clothes so as we emerged from the hospital we must have looked like the cast of *The Living Dead*. We were a mess!

'We'll have to get a plane to Madrid,' said Boothy.

'We can't get a plane, John,' I said. 'Not in this state. We'll have to get a train.'

After getting a cab to the nearest station, we finally boarded a train to Madrid and as far as the Spanish travelling public were concerned we were to be avoided at all costs. The looks they gave us were hilarious, and nobody would come within about 10 feet.

'Fuck 'em,' said Boothy. 'At least we'll get a carriage to ourselves.'

After settling ourselves in, Boothy suggested we get a drink, so while I went off to find some alcohol, he went to the toilet. The doctors had given Boothy some painkillers that had to be taken rectally, and before going to the toilet he'd taken them out of his pocket and had left them on the window ledge. About half an hour and a couple of drinks later, Boothy announced that he was ready to insert one of these suppositories up his Panama Canal, so off he popped to the bog again. He was absolutely ages – about twenty minutes – and just before we sent out a search party, he appeared at the door.

'Here,' he said handing me his painkillers. 'Have a look at these, will you?'

I looked inside the tub, and instead of suppositories there was just a load of yellow gunk. The suppositories had obviously melted.

'How the hell do I get that lot up my arse lad?' enquired Boothy. 'I've been trying for ages and I can't manage it.'

'Don't look at me,' I replied.

At this point I started laughing, and so did Boothy.

'Stop fucking laughing, you twat,' he cried. 'I'm in agony!'

That was development testing, Manor style!

Although I was naturally a bit disconsolate after losing out on the Formula Renault Championship, I kept on fighting, and as 1992 approached, Formula 3, as a route to Formula 1, was still my number one priority. Consequently, I ended up having a few meetings with Paul Stewart Racing, who were the team to be with back then, but, although I agreed a deal with them, I didn't manage to find the money. That was bloody frustrating.

By the time I had to decide what to do for 1992 I had two options open to me: either go with Fortec Motorsport, who were looking to break into Formula 3 for the first time and who'd well and truly ballsed things up for me the year previously, or go with another new outfit, called P1 Racing.

Back then, Formula 3 was a multi-car and multi-engine championship, and there were certain cars and engines you wanted to race and certain ones you didn't. Van Diemen, who I'd raced for previously, had recently launched their first ever carbon fibre Formula 3 car, which was going to be run by the Junior Lotus team under the name of P1 Racing and by a man called Roly Vincini. They were obviously linked to the Lotus F1 Team, so when I weighed everything up, they came out on top. The thing is, I wasn't the only driver they were interested in, and I had a horrible feeling that the other chap, a pal called Kelvin Burt who ended up doing a few years with me in the BTCC, had a little bit more wedge than I did, so one morning, before Van Diemen and Roly had made up their minds who to go with, I decided to take a bit of a drastic action. Kelvin was also a very good driver, so I must have had a bit of a premonition.

Anyway, on this particular morning I woke up and decided that I was going to go and see Ralph Firman from Van Diemen and try and persuade him to choose me. It had been playing on my mind for days, and I just had to do something. The thing is, it was just five o'clock in the morning when I came to this decision, and by the time I'd had a shit, shower and shave and had made my way to Ralph's house it was shortly before six. Undeterred, I knocked on Ralph's door with a fair bit of gusto, and a minute or so later Ralph's wife, Angie, appeared.

'Jason,' she said, opening the door ajar. 'What the hell are you doing? It's six o'clock in the morning.'

'I know, I know. I'm sorry Angie. I've got to speak to Ralph. Can you get him for me please.'

'But it's six o'clock in the morning!'

'It's actually five past now. Oh, go on Angie. I wouldn't be here if it wasn't urgent.'

Just then, Ralph appeared with a fag on the go and he said virtually the same as Angie, just with a few added expletives.

'Five minutes, Ralph, that's all I ask. You'll be back in bed in next to no time, I promise.'

'OK,' he said, opening the door. 'Come on in. That's all you've got, though. Five minutes.'

I spent the next five minutes desperately trying to persuade Ralph to give me the drive.

'What about the money, Jason,' he kept saying. 'How will you find the money?'

'I'll find the money, Ralph. Just trust me, please!'

'OK, then,' he said finally. 'The drive's yours, providing you can –'

'Yes, I know,' I said. 'Providing I can find the money. Just leave it with me.'

I left Ralph's place on cloud nine, and sure enough I got the drive. It soon became a bit of a pyrrhic victory, though, as before the season had even started I realized I'd backed the wrong horse. Fortec had gone with a Reynard chassis, the Reynard 923, and a Mugen-Honda engine, both of which were epic. While we spent all our time trying to perfect our new chassis, they charged ahead, and Kelvin, who had gone there after losing the P1 drive to me, was going great guns. The irony is that, had I not got up at 5 a.m. and gone bothering Ralph Firman, Kelvin, who finished third that year, would probably have been offered the drive with Van Diemen, and I'd have ended up driving for Fortec. Hoisted by my own petard! That's life, though. It's all character-building.

After eight races, which was exactly half the season, the money ran out at my end, and so we had to call it a day. Even though we also had the Mugen-Honda engine, the chassis had caused us all kinds of issues, so in a way it was a happy release, as all we were doing was throwing good money after bad. I was pretty miserable.

By far the worst thing to happen that season was watching a driver sadly perish at Thruxton during round three of the championship. His name was Marcel Albers, and he'd been running behind his teammate, Elton Julian, on Woodham Hill before breaking into the club chicane and then hitting Julian's car. We were all fighting mid-pack at the time, and Marcel was about forty yards ahead of me. After hitting Elton, Marcel's Ralt just cartwheeled across the track and ended up ploughing into the safety barrier. He was there for over an hour in the end, as they couldn't extract him from the wreckage, and unfortunately he died on the way to the medical centre.

Everybody who'd seen the accident knew it was game over for Marcel, and just sitting there with that feeling of inevitability was crushing. The meeting was abandoned after that, and Marcel finished the race, posthumously, in seventh position and eleventh in the championship.

It was the first time I'd ever seen anything like that happen at close quarters before, and I don't mind admitting that it spooked me big time. Not enough to make me think twice about driving. After all, we all know the risks, and as much as we want our sport to be safe, an element of danger is obviously part of the attraction.

So that was the end of my Formula 3 career. Finding the money for just half a season had been like climbing Everest backwards with no climbing boots on, and although I'm quite adept at finding sponsors and actually enjoy the corporate environment, I wanted to spend my time racing, not chasing money.

Just eight or nine months previously, I'd been on the verge of banking enough dosh to see me through at least one full season in Formula 3 and with a team of my choice, which would have been Paul Stewart Racing, who would definitely have given me the best chance of winning. It was basically just a question of what colour I wanted my Rolls-Royce.

Now, everything had turned on a sixpence, and the arse had fallen out of it. That's motor racing, though. Things are often as tight off the track as they are on it, and it can drive you absolutely crazy.

Even the second option after the windfall not materializing may well have resulted in me going to Paul Stewart Racing, as that's where Kelvin ended up going after finishing third for Fortec. It's all academic now. All pie in the sky. Kelvin ended up getting a test with Jordan in the end, but once again his career was halted by the fact that he couldn't raise enough of the necessary. Like me, he ended up in touring cars, and we raced against each other for about seven or eight years. He's a good lad.

This might be a good point to put some meat on the bones with regards to how much it costs to compete in a junior formula. In case there's any ambiguity, it's almost always up to the driver to produce the majority of the funds – usually via sponsorship or a rich relative – and what they bring in goes towards running the team. Most people probably have an idea what it costs to race in these formulas, but the true figures might surprise you. Or terrify you!

These days, a year in a kart will set your parents or sponsors back between £80,000 and £100,000, and that's without any serious mishaps. Next up, you've got Formula 3. In 1992, a season in Formula 3 would have cost you in the region of £250,000. Today, that would be about £750,000. A couple of seasons in GP2, which is the formula directly below Formula 1 and is what you'd need to commit to in order to progress, will cost you about £2 million a season.

If you add it all up, just to knock on the door of Formula 1 you're probably looking at circa £7 million. That is some serious wedge! It doesn't stop there, though, as, if you're lucky

enough to get into Formula 1, you're going to need some seriously big backers. Even a seat with a low-to-mid-table team
will set you back about £10 million a season, and your chances
of finishing on the podium or even in the top six would be
bugger all.

In touring cars it's not much different, and if I want to
race, which I do, I have to bring some sponsors with me.
Luckily, I've managed to build up a decent portfolio over
the years and I always try and make sure they get value for
money. Like it or not, sponsorship is an essential cog in the
motorsport wheel, and had I been as adept then in attaining
sponsorship I'd probably have been OK. Actually, who am I
kidding? I'd have been able to race for ever!

The period directly after F3 is what I used to refer to as my
'wilderness years'. Looking back, that's a little bit dramatic, as
I did manage to do some racing and, in addition to instructing
at Silverstone and Brands Hatch, to name but a few, several
times a week and doing plenty of other stuff, I got pissed every
night, smoked my lungs black and made friends with a lot of
female people. I'll come on to that in a minute.

My next drive after F3 came about after I was contacted by
Martin Donnelly. He was offering me a fully sponsored drive
in the following year's Vauxhall Lotus Championship, which
was, in real terms, a step down from Formula 3.

After a bit of umming and ahing on my part, Martin called
me up and told me to either shit or get off the pot, and with
nothing else on the horizon I decided to take a shit. Although
crude, this is symbolic of how I viewed the Vauxhall Lotus
Championship. It's where we were, though. There was nothing
else going.

A situation like this will affect a driver in one of two ways.
They'll either become depressed and down at the fact that

their career isn't going in the direction they wished it was or they'll attempt to hide their disappointment, knuckle down and make the best of it. What compounds the disappointment, however, is the frustration of knowing that you're punching below your weight, and that's what I found most difficult to cope with. I suppose it's subjective to a certain extent, as I'm sure that every driver on the planet who moves to a lesser formula will believe they should be higher up.

Martin had actually offered me this drive in the Vauxhall Lotus Championship a year previously. This was while I was trying to persuade Ralph to give me the drive with P1, and after I'd chatted to Martin a few times, it came to light that he was very close to Eddie Jordan. Keen to make his acquaintance, I decided to call Eddie and ask if I could go and see him.

'What about?' he asked quite guardedly.

'I need your advice on something.'

'OK,' he said. 'Come and see me.'

After I went to see Eddie and asked him what I should do, he said, quite predictably, as he was a good friend of Martin's, 'Sign with Martin for the Vauxhall Lotus Championship. It's a much better prospect.'

My arse it was. It had been interesting to meet Eddie, though, and after thanking him for his time, I buggered off, carried on bothering Ralph and forgot all about him and Martin.

Anyway, once I'd sorted out the Formula 3 drive I decided to go back and see Eddie at Silverstone and thank him for his advice. It was just networking really, and I wanted to keep him on side.

I remember calling his PA, and, after putting me on hold, she came back on and asked me if I could come over right away. I didn't know what to make of this really but in the spirit of cooperation I said yes. Literally a few seconds after I'd walked into the open-plan reception area at Eddie's HQ, the man himself appeared at the top of a staircase and as he made his way down he started shouting the odds:

'You chose to ignore my advice, you piece of fucking shit.'

I couldn't believe it!

'What are you talking about? I've just come over here to thank you for your advice, you fucking prick!' I wasn't going to let him speak to me like that. No fucking way. I gave as good as I got.

Five minutes later, I left Jordan HQ having gone toe to toe against F1's foremost Irish wigster. How about that?

It turned out that Martin had got wind of me going to see Eddie, and when I chose Formula 3 instead of him, he assumed that's what Eddie had advised me to do. As a result they'd ended up having a massive barney, which is why Eddie had been so pissed off with me. If only he'd said something?

After a few weeks, I think we all realized what had happened, and we managed to sort it out. What a ding-dong, though! It was one of the most intense five minutes I think I've ever had, on or off the track. Subsequently, when it came to me having to make a decision for 1993, I remembered all this, and with Martin and Eddie still being close, and with Eddie having recently broken into F1, that sort of sealed it. I haven't got a drive, Martin knows Eddie Jordan, Eddie's a big player who's recently moved into F1, where do I sign? Connections count for a lot in most industries, and although you also need talent and money in motor racing, a bulging contacts book can make a big difference.

Just as I always feared, my Vauxhall Lotus experience turned out to be nothing more than a badly organized, under-funded shit stain, and unfortunately it sounded the death knell on my career in single-seaters. What I was obviously hoping was that I'd succeed in Vauxhall Lotus, which would catapult me back to Formula 3. I wasn't sure how I was going to fund it once I got there, but one step at a time. Alas, moving to Vauxhall Lotus from Formula 3 was like moving from Barcelona to Northampton Town, and it lacked everything: money, crowds, exposure, press. It was just rubbish, and nobody even knew we were there. Nope. As far as single-seaters were concerned – and the ultimate dream of breaking into Formula 1, of course – I was down the tubes, mate. It was a sad end to what had been a promising career, but I was one of thousands.

The bugger is, with single-seaters, although you might *think* you have enough money for a season, all it takes is a prang or two and you're done for. It's so, so precarious, which is why it's seen as being a rich man's game. In order to get on you need to have enough money to cope with every eventuality and if you don't have that the entire thing can disappear in a split second. It's obviously not healthy having to look over your shoulder all the time, but that's the nature of the beast. It's a business endeavour when all's said and done, and every business owner in the world will tell you that the first few months or years are make or break.

Here's a quirky irony for you. I think I was the only one of the budding single-seater drivers who smoked back then (or at least openly), yet I never managed to become part of the famed Marlboro Academy, which was one of the big stepping stones to F1. I'd probably kept those bastards in business over the years, and not so much as a sniff.

The reason I didn't get into the Marlboro Academy, which

was basically a well-funded programme designed to put certain young drivers through junior motorsport with a view to them reaching Formula 1, was because I never raced for any of the teams they were affiliated to. It was a closed shop, basically, and unless you got in right at the very bottom, you didn't stand a chance. So bloody ungrateful!

LESSON FOUR

You're All Sacked! Now F**k Off to Bed

I was definitely at a bit of a loss after coming out of single-seaters and came as close to being depressed as somebody like me can be. What I mean by that is that my glass is normally at least half full so on a mental healthometer I would probably have registered as being 'quite fed up'. My main source of income was teaching at racing schools, which paid OK but put me in the vicinity of a lot of former racing drivers who hadn't made it. They weren't all like that, but a lot were, and for somebody who was down but not out, in that I was only in my mid-twenties and hoped something else might come along one day, it was not a good environment in which to be. Very few of the drivers were doing the schools out of choice. They were there because they'd given up, and I wasn't at that point yet.

The reason I kept on doing the racing schools, apart from the money, was (a) because they all took place at Silverstone and Brands Hatch, which was fun, and (b) because they put me in front of a lot of potential sponsors. The main rule for instructors at Silverstone, by the way, was never under any circumstances to engage with corporate clients for your own benefit. After completely disregarding that rule, I managed to build up a nice list of contacts! Well, what the eye don't see . . .

After I'd been doing that for a while, I was asked if I'd like to do a few days' work at a rally school called RallyDrive, owned by a pal, Howard Patterson, in north

Lincolnshire. This was for fun, more than anything, and after going up there on a Thursday all bright-eyed and bushy-tailed, I'd come back on a Sunday half dead. This wasn't down to teaching. It was down to debauchery! My fellow instructors included Richard Burns, who became one of my best mates and who I still miss terribly, Martin Rowe, who became a British Rally Champion, and Jimmy Thompson, who I'll come on to later, but who became a very bad influence on me. In the same 'bad influence' list would be 'Rapid' Rich Stoodley, Kevin 'Fatty' Furber, Ian 'Knighty' Knight and a future flatmate, Simon 'Hamster' Harrison, Penny Mallory (more of her later) and a whole host of many great pals along the way.

In fact it would be wrong of me not to mention some of the great pals and characters I've spent many a crazy time with at the racing schools in the early 90s: Simon Hill (now racing his son Jake in the BTCC!), Marco Vignali, Jonny 'Swoop' Robinson, Karl 'you know you wan' it' Jones, Johnny Mowlem, Gary 'The Slice' Ayles, Steve Deeks, Tim Pearson, Rob Murphy and many more – too many to name them all. Boy, did we have some fun.

Basically, after finishing the school we'd race back to Grimsby, where we were staying, get our glad rags on and get absolutely leathered, hence me saying that I did it for fun. I used to come back with a few pennies in my pocket having been paid quite a few quid but it was a much-needed contrast to the doom and gloom at Silverstone. Well, at least that's my excuse!

It took me a little while, but I eventually managed to get over not making it to the top in single-seaters. Some things just aren't meant to be. I'd be lying if I said I didn't wonder from time to time what might have happened, but in the same way that I wonder what would happen if I became a billionaire or the Prime Minister of the United Kingdom – heaven forbid! None of it's real.

Instead of becoming a full-time misery guts – or a racing instructor, as they were known at Silverstone – I gave myself a kick up the arse and started having a proper look at what was out there.

Fortunately, after not very long at all, I managed to get a testing job for the Nissan touring car team, who had been competing in the BTCC since 1991. A cousin of mine called Kieth O'dor was driving for them at the time and he very kindly got me the gig.

I should really have mentioned Kieth by now, as he's the only other member of my family who's ever done anything even remotely spectacular on four wheels, unless you include my old man fleeing from the police in his Willys jeep! Kieth was the son of my dad's sister and her husband, János Ódor. Back in the 1960s, János had founded a performance tuning company specializing in exhaust systems called Janspeed and after building the Nissan Skyline GTR for endurance racing that won the 24 Hours of Spa and 24 Hours of Nürburgring races, Janspeed was awarded the works contract to build the Nissan Primera for the British Touring Car Championship.

The testing I did for them took place at the Pembrey circuit in Carmarthenshire. It was just mileage testing really, stuff that Kieth and his Dutch teammate, Eric van de Poele, didn't need to be doing, and it was great. It was the closest I came to racing throughout 1994, and then, at the start of 1995, it looked like it might come to something. Eric was leaving for pastures new, and there was a seat up for grabs. It was a potential dream scenario. Kieth and I got on really well, the team had been improving year on year, and Nissan were bigger than big. Finally, a drive! I was daring to dream again.

God knows why, but Nissan ended up pulling out of the BTCC before it could go anywhere, so it was back to the drawing board for me. Unfortunately, Kieth, who had started his career in rallying and who'd finished an impressive sixth in the 1993 British Touring Car Championship, was killed in 1995 after switching to the German ADAC Super Touren-wagen Cup. It happened during a race on the Avus in Berlin, and he was just thirty-three years old at the time. He obviously knew the risks, just as we all do, but at least Kieth died doing something he loved. He's much missed.

By the middle of 1995 I was living in a flat in Northamptonshire, close to Silverstone, with my fellow RallyDrive instructor pal Simon Harrison (who went on to drive for Peugeot in the BTCC in 1995) and to relieve the boredom of doing racing schools I took pretty much every job I was offered. I was a jobbing driver, when all's said and done, and fortunately I got some absolute corkers along the way.

One of the best jobs I can remember was for a company called Drive and Survive, which was run by two ex-coppers. They started off doing training courses but then branched out into arranging promotional events for manufacturers. You know the kind of thing – punters come along and get driven around by rally drivers and racing drivers, who show them how good the cars are. Standard stuff.

This particular event was for Ford, and it took place at a track close to Edinburgh Airport called Ingliston. We drivers were entrusted to 'look after the corporate product' – that was our official job description – and Ford had taken over the track for a few days to basically stage a ginormous ride-and-drive event.

On one of the evenings, we had a party for the drivers and promo girls, and after a couple of drinks an idea came to me. Earlier in the day we'd held a competition as part of the event where you had to drive a Reliant Robin blindfolded, and it had gone down an absolute storm with the punters and drivers alike. Although I didn't know where it was parked exactly I had a good idea, so once I'd suggested my idea, a posse was dispatched to find the Reliant Robin and bring it into the room where we were partying, which was part of a conference centre.

After managing to pilfer the three-wheeler from the track, we got it back to the conference centre.

'Now what?' said one of my partners in crime.

'Easy. We drive the Robin through the front doors and into the room.'

'You'll never get it through the front doors,' he said. 'They're not wide enough.'

I was having none of this.

'Yes they are,' I reassured him. 'There's a few inches either side. You just watch this.'

There was a ramp leading up to the front doors for wheelchairs and so, after reversing the three-wheeler and then lining it up, I put it in gear, gave it some throttle and prepared to unleash the gargantuan 750 cc engine, which was now reverberating – nay, roaring – underneath the bonnet. As I set off, I did think to myself, I'm not sure if I'm going to make this, but I was already committed, so it was do or die.

Unfortunately, my partner in crime was correct in his assumption that there wasn't enough room, and because I approached the door so quickly the Robin ended up getting jammed. And I mean properly jammed! They had to smash the windscreen to get me out, not to mention the glass doors, which were concertinaed either side of the Robin. It was chaos!

The boss came out and went absolutely mental.

'You're all sacked!' he shouted. 'Now fuck off to bed.'

Because we were only halfway through the event we were almost indispensable, so after the failure to find any last-minute replacements, we all got our jobs back in the morning, on the strict understanding that no alcohol would be consumed and that I would only drive in daylight hours. I think it was a fair deal, all things considered.

As time went on, I could actually feel myself being influenced by the way others felt and became downhearted. Then again, what do you expect if you keep on accepting similar but lesser alternatives to what you originally set out to do? It's a hiding to nothing.

Eventually, after a particularly heavy weekend during which I'd done nothing really except drink and mope about, I decided to get up and have one last push in single-seaters. Back in the summer, I'd managed to find a potential sponsor at Silverstone called Swan National Leasing, and with them still interested in backing me I decided to contact Boothy at Manor Motorsport to see if he'd allow me to do some Formula Renault, just so I could get my eye back in. Manor had actually won the previous year's Formula Renault Championship, so with them flying high and me bringing some money to the table, I was hopeful he'd say yes.

After a three-way negotiation between me, Boothy and my contacts at Renault, we managed to come up with a deal that satisfied everybody, so when all was apparently lost I managed to find a reprieve. Did I have a plan beyond doing a few races in Formula Renault for Boothy? Not really. It had taken enough just getting this organized. All I could do was have some fun and see what happened.

My favourite story from this short but rather sweet interlude took place shortly after an international Formula Renault race at Monza. It was the Sunday evening, and, after piling into Milan en masse, me, Boothy and the rest of the Manor crowd went to find something to eat.

After mooching around for twenty minutes or so, we managed to find a trattoria that happened to have a table spare for about twenty people and the first thing we did after sitting down was order a round of drinks – obviously. I have no idea why, but right next to this table – and I mean right next to it – was a very large and very loud fruit machine, and about halfway through the meal an Italian chap strolled up and started playing it. After literally a few seconds this became incredibly annoying, and, despite us all looking at the Italian as if to say, *Just piss off will you, you rude bastard*, he carried on throwing money into it. Anybody with even a semi-sane brain would have buggered off. Then again, anyone with a semi-sane brain eating would have asked him to do so. Not us, I'm afraid. We wanted to take the fun route.

Instead of asking this bloke to do one, we took a napkin, sneaked behind him, put the napkin on the floor between his legs and then set fire to it. Our intention was to smoke him out, but instead he went up in flames! Or at least his trousers did. On realizing he was on fire, the bloke started doing a little dance but instead of throwing pennies at him we threw water instead. Once he was out, we were out, as in thrown out. It did the trick, though.

Now fed and in the mood, we decided to go looking for some more high jinks and after a few minutes we came across a Fiat 500 that was waiting at some traffic lights. I forget whether the driver was male or female, but while they were waiting for the lights to turn to green, three or four of us crept up behind the car and the moment they turned to amber we lifted up the rear. The poor driver was obviously a bit alarmed by what was happening – or should I say what was not happening – and after about three seconds we dropped the car, and after a little bit of wheel spin it went zooming off. What a laugh that was!

By now, word had got around that a group of undesirables was marauding through the streets of Milan, and within ten minutes of us waving ta-ta to the Fiat we were being pinned against a wall by the police and had guns in our faces. This was a turn-up for the books!

Fortunately, all we received was a telling-off, but we were assured by the Polizia that if they saw us again that night we'd be looked after accordingly. We didn't know exactly what they meant, but we had a feeling it didn't involve a chat, an espresso and a tiramisu.

When I got back from Monza, nothing had really changed with regards to my prospects in single-seaters, although I did have a few more irons in the fire, and rekindling my relationship with Boothy and the boys at Manor had been a hoot. Boothy had also asked me to tutor some of his younger drivers at Manor, so although my venture hadn't catapulted me back into the epicentre of single-seat racing like I'd hoped, it was keeping me on the fringes.

Unbeknownst to me at the time, the most important bit of relationship rekindling I'd done by driving in Monza was with Renault, and just a few weeks after arriving home I received a telephone call from them offering me a drive in a new series they were starting with Renault Spiders, which were little roadsters. Although I was grateful for the offer, competing in a one-car championship was not the follow-up I'd been hoping for after my retirement from single-seaters and even with the phrase *beggars can't be choosers* ringing in my ears I still couldn't bring myself to say yes.

'You'd be doing us a big favour,' said my contact at Renault while trying to persuade me. 'Plus, the winner of the series will get a test with the Williams touring car team.'

'Really,' I said, ears now pricked. 'OK, let's have a chat.'

To cut a long story short, I ended up introducing Renault to Swan National Leasing, who'd had a great time in Monza and who were still keen on supporting me. They ended up becoming my title sponsor of my Spider programme, and so on the face of things the future was looking up. Or was it?

Not only had I signed to race in a series that was, even at this fairly uneventful stage of my career, well below my standard, but if, for whatever reason, I failed to win it, that would be it. I'd be banished to hell, basically!

Looking back, it was a big risk, and had I appreciated the significance of what was at stake prior to signing I don't think I would have gone ahead. I ended up saying to myself, *Oh sod it, you may as well*, and I signed for a cracking team at Silverstone called Mardi Gras Motorsport run by Martin Sharpe (God bless him) and Paul Hetherington, both of whom I'm deeply indebted to.

Funnily enough, the Spider Cup, as it was called, ended up being a support series for the BTCC (among others), and in its inaugural year I ended up winning eleven of the fourteen races and the European series, which had started the same year. I don't remember who beat me in the three races I didn't win and I don't want to either! Suffice to say it had all been a means to an end, and although we'd had a good laugh and the sponsors were all happy, which was brilliant, I was hoping it would lead to bigger things. Much bigger things.

Hi, Dad, I'm Going to Ambush Frank Williams

My preparations for the test with Williams – this was in addition to winning the Spider Cup, which was obviously essential – had begun at the very start of the competition and basically involved me getting as much exposure as I possibly could. As a support series to the BTCC in which Williams were competing this presented me with an ideal opportunity, and if I wasn't walking up and down the pit lane saying hello to mates of mine – in full view of the Williams garage, of course – or at the back of the Williams garage making a nuisance of myself, I'd be upstairs in the commentary box commentating on the Renault Clio races. Anything to get myself in front of, and around, Frank Williams and Patrick Head, basically.

I've always been quite good at self-promotion (yes, really!), and at the end of the day this was my last chance at bagging a future in motorsport. Or at least one that was worthy of my talents – he said modestly. The thing is, I knew I was good enough to make a success in touring cars, just as I knew I was good enough to make it in single-seaters. The difference being, there was bugger all I could have done to prevent my career from collapsing in single-seaters whereas this was a different matter, as it wasn't down to money. Whether it made any difference or not I didn't know, but as long as there was even a speck of a chance of me getting a drive with Frank

I would do everything in my power – whether it be schmoozing, driving or making the tea, I would be up for it. It was all about maximizing my chances so by the time the Williams test came about I was satisfied I'd done everything I possibly could off the track as well as on it.

The test itself took place at Silverstone, and, as with my preparations beforehand, I gave it absolutely everything. I was testing alongside Williams' existing touring car drivers, Alain Menu and Will Hoy, and I'd heard it on the grapevine that Will's contract was coming to an end at the end of 1996 and it wasn't going to be renewed. This had given me extra impetus, as with a genuine and immediate opportunity on the table there was much more at stake.

A relative novice to front-wheel drive, just a few laps into the test I was given an opportunity to impress, although I didn't know it at the time.

Just as I was going down into Maggotts and Becketts, which is a left-right complex, I felt something go wrong. Because I thought I knew what it was I decided not to drive the car back to the garage and after turning the engine off I immediately got on the radio.

'I think the drive shaft's gone,' I said.

'Really?' replied my engineer. He didn't sound convinced.

'I honestly think it has. I think it's best I stay exactly where I am.'

As it turned out, the drive shaft had gone, and had I driven the car back to the garage I'd have screwed it up, and that would have been the end of my test. As importantly, though – well, almost – the garage were really impressed, so although I'd lost a little bit of time it had been worth it.

Gaining the respect of the team galvanized me, so once they'd fixed the drive shaft I went out, let rip, and I drove my arse off. The BTCC season had just finished, so providing I put in a good performance now I was confident that I'd at least be in the running for 1997.

Although I didn't beat Will's or Alain's times I matched them pretty closely, so as far as the opportunity itself was concerned I'd ticked every single box. I certainly couldn't have done any more.

Something else that came into play here was my relationship with Renault, who had been Williams' engine manufacturer since 1989. After me winning the Spider Cup and giving the series a decent start (it ended up lasting five years, which surprised me), they were keen to repay the favour, and while Williams were deciding on a replacement for Will Hoy, Renault were in constant dialogue with them on my behalf. It was all about reputation now, and with Renault singing my praises I was confident it would pay dividends. It was looking good.

A few days after the test I got called down for an interview with Frank Williams and Patrick Head, which was all part of the process. I'd obviously been introduced to them before (I made sure of it) but I'd never really spoken to either of them at length, so it was a big deal – and, hopefully, another opportunity to impress.

They didn't give much away at the interview, which was hardly surprising, but the lap times and the drive-shaft incident were both mentioned, so all in all I felt it had gone well.

The following day I spoke to my contact at Renault UK, a wonderful man called Tim Jackson who had helped me so much since 1990, who asked how it had gone.

'Very well,' I told him.

'Great,' he said. 'I'll call Frank this afternoon, then. One last push.'

It was hard not to get carried away while all this was going on, although I did try not to. I obviously knew how precarious motorsport was, but after everything that had happened I honestly couldn't see why Williams wouldn't go with me. I was young(ish), charming, devilishly handsome (in my own lunch-time!) and was at least on a par with their outgoing driver. And I was Renault through and through. Surely it was in the bag?

I can't remember when it was exactly, but about a week after the interview – the longest week of my life, I might add – I finally received a letter from Frank. I'm paraphrasing now, but basically he said that I hadn't got the drive but that I couldn't have done any more. In romantic terms it was a classic 'It's me, not you' scenario. He went on to say that they'd decided to go with a former F1 driver, as profile was important, and unfortunately I couldn't offer them that.

Given the effort I'd put into getting my name about, that was a real kick in the teeth, but at the end of the day they wanted somebody with a public profile, not just an industry one.

The word gutted doesn't even touch the sides on this one. I was disappointed, dismayed, angry – you name it – and, providing it represents rejection in its most extreme form, I was feeling it.

Bollocks!

The first thing I did was call Tim at Renault UK to see if there was anything they could do, but unfortunately they were all spent.

'It's out of our hands now,' they said. 'Ultimately, it's Frank's decision, and unless we can give him an unarguable reason why he should take you instead of the F1 driver, then we're done.'

To be fair to Tim at Renault UK, they'd done everything they possibly could, just as I had. They also had to maintain a good working relationship with Williams and, as amiable and as talented as they might have considered me to be, it certainly wasn't worth falling out with both Frank and Patrick over it.

Frank had actually mentioned two drivers in his letter: Gianni Morbidelli, who was retiring from F1 after six years, and their own F1 test driver, Jean-Christophe Boullion. Both were really fast and both had a higher profile than I did, so although I was gutted, I could begrudgingly understand Frank's reasoning. Or at least I could temporarily. It wouldn't last.

Over the next week or so Tim and I started chucking some ideas around, although in hindsight it was probably just tokenism. The only one worth mentioning was the idea of Renault UK purchasing a 1996 car from Williams and then running it with me as a privateer. That would have been a slight misnomer, as a privateer is somebody who races without any manufacturer support, but you get my drift. At first it seemed like a goer, but after a couple of days Renault kiboshed it due to costs. That really was it, then. I was about to become a fully paid-up member of the bitter and twisted brigade. I was completely out of options and had exhausted every possibility.

Or had I?

Sometime in November, I woke up one morning absolutely full of rage. I'm not sure if I'd had a dream or something, but the moment my eyes opened all I could think about was the injustice of me not getting the Williams drive. My understanding for Frank's situation had gone completely out of the window, and I wanted blood! I remember thinking to myself, *I'm not having this. I'm going to go to Frank's door and try and persuade him that he's made a mistake.*

The only reason he hadn't gone with me, as far as I could

1. Three years old, with my first steering wheel.

2. Destined for BTCC.

3. It all started here. This was the bad debt kart.

4. First ever trophy – Felton, 1980.

5. This baby was affectionately called Love Air.

6. Second ever race – Wombwell, 1980.

7. Mistral Racing, 1981. Neil Hann on the left. I owe so much to him.

8. A usual weekend in the early 1980s.

9. 1982 British Champion, in another 20 laps.

10. Van Diemen F3 car, sexy.

11. First ever race suit, 1989.

12. Winfield Race School, 1989.

13. My precious Lancia Integrale is now dead.

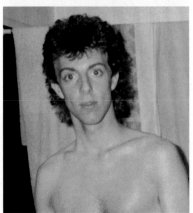

14. Come on Mum, fancy a spin in me Ferrari?

15. Check out my hairdo.

16. This season gave me the platform for BTCC. Renault Spiders, 1996.

17. Williams Renaults, 1997.

18. Manor Motorsport, 1991 – with John Booth and Pete Sliwinski.

19. Sharing a handshake with 'Short Fuse Hughes' after the debut pole position.

20. It scared me stupid.

21. With the Williams heavy hitters.

22. The Willies boys craned a car made from all the body panels I had bent into my garden.

23. This rather splendid sight is what I discovered.

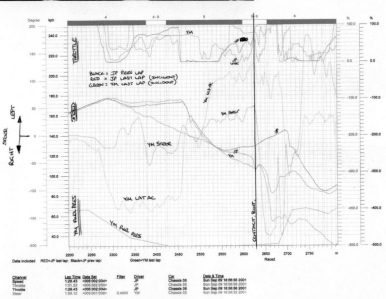

24. First Championship Win, 2001.

25. Silverstone data traces from 2001 show Yvan Muller's car had run out of fuel.

26. Yvan Muller refused to shake hands at Silverstone in 2001.

27. Trying to look cool.

28. Sea Harrier flight – before.

29. Sea Harrier flight – afterwards.

see, was because my profile wasn't high enough, and sometime during the wee small hours I'd subconsciously decided that profile wasn't a good enough excuse. Anyone can build a profile but not everyone can jump into a front-wheel-drive and hold their own against two race winners, one of whom, as in Will Hoy, had won the 1991 British Touring Car Championship. No chance. I'm not having it!

After having a quick shower, I put on a suit, polished my shoes, picked up an empty briefcase that I thought made me look important and, after buying forty fags and some mints from my local newsagent, I marched off to Williams HQ. In actual fact I drove there in my crappy old Ford Sierra and I arrived at about a quarter past nine in the morning. Early doors for me!

Because I'd only been at the Williams HQ a few weeks before, the security guards remembered me, and after laying on the old familiar charm I managed to schmooze my way in.

'You're not on the list, Jason?'

'Yeah, I only got the call from Frank an hour ago. Anyway, how're you? Is your nipper still karting?'

It was easy-peasy. Well, that bit was.

Once I'd parked up I had couple of fags, braced myself, checked my tie and then marched over to reception. Like the security guards, the receptionist also remembered me, but getting past her wasn't going to be as easy.

'Anyway,' she said after a quick schmooze. 'What can I do for you, Jason?'

'I'm here to see Frank actually.'

'Oh really? What time is he expecting you?'

This is where it was going to get difficult.

'Erm, he isn't,' I said.

All of a sudden the pleasantness turned to mild suspicion.

'It's OK, though,' I carried on. 'I only want five minutes with him.'

After making a quick call (very quietly!), the receptionist asked me to take a seat.

'Nicola will be down to see you in a few minutes,' she said.

You know the saying *behind every great man is a great woman*? Well, in my experience that should be changed to, behind every great man is a ferociously protective PA who can kill people just by staring at them and who should not be crossed by any means. Even today the name Nicola puts the fear of God into me, and it's all because of the lady who was about to meet me in reception. She was obviously Frank's gatekeeper and she was well scary: this would be my biggest test yet.

Over the next ten minutes or so I saw a lot of people I already knew – mechanics and the like – and by the time Nicola appeared I was feeling quite jolly and relaxed. It didn't last. Nicola's greeting saw to that.

'What the heck are you doing here, Jason,' she said, remaining standing. 'You can't just walk in off the streets to see Frank. Surely you know that?'

It was time to start pleading.

'Look, I know, Nicola. I just want five minutes of his time. That's all. Five minutes maximum.'

'What do you want to see him for?'

The worst thing you can do with a scary PA is refuse to tell them why you want to see their boss, but as much as I wanted to say to Nicola, *Look, Frank's chosen the wrong driver, and I'm here to take him to task about it*, the words wouldn't come out.

'I can't really say here,' I uttered, slightly pathetically. 'I just really need to see him.'

After about five minutes toing and froing, Nicola brought

the conversation to an end but by doing so she also gave me a lifeline. Whether she did it on purpose or not I don't know, but when Nicola said, 'You're wasting your time Jason. He's not even due in until twelve o'clock', I knew it was time to retreat, regroup and plan my next attack. Or, in Plato terms, go back to my car, smoke twenty fags, and then ambush him.

The latter is actually a pretty accurate description of what happened, although the ambush bit didn't occur to me until I was about ten fags in. I remember opening my car door, chucking my empty briefcase in and then lighting one up. *What the hell do I do now?* I thought to myself. I'd been given a slight reprieve, but that was it, and if I went back to reception after twelve I knew I'd get the bum's rush again. In fact, it would probably involve security guards this time.

It was about a quarter past ten when I got back to my car, and after a few more smokes I decided to move to a space under a tree that gave me a good view of who was coming in and out of the car park. I managed to do this by pretending I was leaving and then, just before I reached the barrier, taking a quick right turn towards another section of the car park, where I turned around and then parked up. After that, I wasn't sure what I was going to do. I'd decide once Frank had arrived.

Once I'd moved my car, I made a couple of telephone calls. I needed reassurance that I was doing the right thing – whatever that was going to be – and the first person I called was Mike Knight at the Winfield School over in France. He was a good pal of mine and knew all about the test and everything.

'You're doing what?' said Mike after I filled him in.

'I'm sitting in the car park at Williams HQ with an empty briefcase waiting for Frank to arrive in the hope of grabbing five minutes with him and persuading him he's made a massive mistake.'

'Well, good for you, mate,' said Mike. 'What have you got to lose?'

That was exactly what I wanted and needed to hear, although had he told me it was a bad idea I'd still have gone ahead with it.

The next person I called was my old man, and he said exactly the same as Mike. 'Just go for it, Jason,' he said.

Now galvanized, I sat there and carried on smoking, all the while wondering what I was going to say and do when, and if, Frank arrived.

At about ten to one his car finally pulled up, and as the security barrier rose so did my blood pressure – to about 160 over 100! It was showtime.

Luckily I had the packet of Trebor mints in my pocket and after throwing about ten of those into my gob I checked the old tie again, grabbed my empty briefcase and got out of the car. I assumed that Frank's car would park just in front of reception, but although I could only see the top of the car, it seemed to be going in a different direction.

'Fuck,' I thought. 'He's got a secret entrance!'

Quick as a flash I set off in hot pursuit, and as Frank's car continued going in what I thought was the wrong direction I carried on giving chase. I was running like a madman, completely flat out. The only thing I didn't do was shout, *FRAAAAAAAAAAANK!*

After I'd run about a hundred yards without a care in the world for any of Williams' nicely kept flowerbeds, the car suddenly did a one-eighty at a roundabout. Instead of chasing the car, I was now running straight towards it, and the look on Frank's driver's face said just one thing: NUTCASE! I tried desperately to go from a full-blown panicked sprint with arms flailing into a casual walk, but I didn't stand a chance, and when Frank and his driver drove past they stared at me like you'd stare at a drunk sitting on a pavement at two o'clock in the afternoon. Pity, mixed with mild revulsion, basically.

Undeterred, I carried on giving chase at a slightly more measured pace and when they pulled into Frank's spot, which was right in front of reception after all, I quickly pulled up alongside. This led to one of the most awkward five minutes of my entire life as instead of Frank simply hopping out of the back seat, his nurse, Hamish, had to lift him out and then help him into his wheelchair. It's a heck of an operation, and as Frank and Hamish set about their business, I had to stand there like a lemon. *What the hell should I do?* I thought to myself. Do I say something to Frank or do I just stand there?

Luckily, as he got out, Hamish gave me a look across the top of the car as if to say, *Don't worry, we know you're here,* and that put me at ease slightly. Even so, the moment Frank was in his wheelchair, I was in there like a rat up a drainpipe.

'Look, I'm sorry to bother you, Frank, but I need five minutes with you. It's really, really important.'

'What on earth do you think you're doing, Jason?' he said. 'I've got a full day.'

Anyway, to cut a long story short, I used the time it took to get Frank out of the car and to reception to great effect, and just as Hamish pressed the button to open the main door Frank turned to me and said, 'All right then, Jason, I'll give you five minutes.' Never underestimate the effectiveness of pester power, ladies and gentlemen.

I was in!

Frank obviously knew why I was there, and he probably

thought it was a case of going through the motions. You know what I mean. Give him a cup of tea and say, 'You did a great job, Jason. It just wasn't meant to be, I'm afraid', and then tell him to fuck off. Even so, this was my last opportunity to bag myself a decent career in motor racing, so I was going to give it everything I'd got – again!

As Hamish and Frank led on, I followed a few paces behind, and as we passed the receptionist she looked at me and mouthed, *How the hell did you do that?* It was a question I was busily asking myself!

To the right of the reception desk there was a small lift that I'd never noticed before, and as the doors of this lift opened, Hamish began reversing into it with Frank. For a moment I didn't know what to do, as the lift they were getting into was hardly big enough for two. Consequently, I hesitated for a moment, until Frank said, 'Are you coming in or not?' 'Yes,' I said, running forwards. 'Sorry, Frank. Sorry.'

In order to get into this lift I had to lean forward a bit, so my knees were touching Frank's, and, worse still, my crotch area was dangerously close to his head. Seriously, if Carlsberg made bizarrely awkward situations . . .

It was absolutely crazy!

Not only was the lift small but it was – ironically for a place where speed was their business – very, very slow, and as I was leaning over Frank, trying to keep my knob out of his face, Hamish started getting the giggles. Fortunately, the lift stopped before Hamish or I lost the plot, and as soon as the doors opened I began to reverse out. As I did so I clocked a member of staff standing about 5 feet away from me. He obviously wasn't used to seeing strange men leaving Frank's lift, and as Frank followed me out he looked at his employee and said, 'Don't ask!'

After me following on once again, we finally got to Frank's office, which had a couple sofas outside it.

'Would you mind waiting here for a minute, Jason,' said Hamish. 'We'll be with you as fast as we can.'

As the door to Frank's office closed, I literally fell on to one of the sofas. I was absolutely exhausted from all the adrenaline, and my heart was going as fast as a toilet door when the plague's in town. What a day!

Just then, Nicola came out of Frank's office and looked at me like a parent would a teenager who'd been out on the piss for the first time.

'What are you like?' she half whispered.

'I know, I know. I just needed to see him.'

'Do you want a cup of tea?' she said.

'Oh, yes please, I'd love one, Nicola. I'm gasping.'

'Jolly good,' she said. 'Kitchen's down there. You can make me one while you're at it. White, no sugar.'

I was in, but I wasn't yet part of the family.

Forty minutes he kept me waiting, during which time I basically sat there on the sofa, drinking tea and sweating like a deviant.

'OK, Jason,' said Nicola finally. 'Would you like to come in?'

It was time to pull myself together!

Once I was sat down in Frank's office, Nicola asked me if I'd like a cup of tea. I wasn't sure if she was going to have me making my own again, so I passed.

'I'd like some water if that's OK?' I said.

'Frank, what would you like?' asked Nicola.

'I'll have just some juice please,' said Frank.

I thought I'd wait until my water had arrived before I started my speech and once it had I cleared my throat and got down to it.

'Frank, the reason I wanted to see you is obviously to do with your decision not to give me the drive next year. I believe you've made a mistake and what's more . . .' I'd been rehearsing it for days, and fortunately Frank appeared to be listening.

After about a minute Nicola came back in again with Frank's juice and because of the process involved in enabling him to drink it I started losing concentration. First of all, Nicola put a book in front of Frank and then put the beaker of juice on top of it. Frank, who has feeling in his arms but not his hands, had his arms either side of the book and once Nicola had put the beaker down she then placed one of those curly straws into it. For his *pièce de résistance* Frank leaned over the beaker with his arms stretched out either side on the desk and proceeded to suck on the straw while watching me intently. It was fascinating stuff, but horrifically distracting, and it took every ounce of my concentration to hold things together.

I think I spoke for about ten minutes in all, so I ran over a bit. Frank was patient, though, and once I'd finished saying my piece he thanked me for coming and sent me on my way. I hadn't been expecting him to suddenly relent and say, *My God, you're right Jason, we made a mistake. The drive's yours!* In fact, I hadn't been expecting anything really, as even if it did spark a change of heart he'd have to speak to Patrick first. It was just a pitch, basically.

Once again, I'd turned over every possible stone and had explored every avenue, so if it didn't work out I could start again in whatever field I chose with a clean slate, a clear conscience and a bit of confidence. Win or lose, I'd given it a damn good crack, and given the circumstances and my lack of cash I'm sure the majority of people wouldn't have got this far.

One thing that gave me a little bit of hope was the way

Frank had listened to me. He was different to how he'd been at my interview during the test, a lot different, and despite the curly straw thing, which still makes me laugh and is something I'm pretty sure he does to disarm people, I thought I'd put on a good show.

Over the following few days I went about my business as normal – whatever normal is on planet Plato – and as time went on, I think I resigned myself subconsciously to having lost the war. There were no calls from Renault and nothing from Williams, so that was obviously that. At least I'd never have to wake up and go, *If only I'd tried this*, or, *If only I'd tried that*. I'd even go so far as to say that I was actually quite contented. The pubs were open, I was having a laugh, and, for now, at least, all was well with the world.

About a week after the ambush, I got a call one morning from Ian Harrison, who was one of Frank's team managers. I'd met Ian, who is from Durham, so not far from me, during the test, and we'd got on really well.

'A little bird tells me that you door-stepped Frank?' said Ian after some preliminary chitchat.

'Guilty as charged,' I replied. 'It had to be done.'

'Absolutely,' agreed Ian. 'Everybody at Williams is talking about it. You're a legend.'

'How do you mean, everyone?' I was fishing now.

'Everyone. Frank and Patrick included.'

'I made my mark, then!'

'You certainly did, mate. Look,' said Ian, 'I just wanted to say that, if you were having any regrets about it, don't. It was the right thing to do, and you left a good impression.'

I figured it was just a mate being nice and said my goodbyes. Then, exactly two days after Ian's call, at roughly the same time, the phone went again.

'Jason, it's Frank. We've decided to run another test. It'll be a shootout between you, Morbidelli and Boullion. Be at Snetterton in exactly two weeks' time. You'll all get identical equipment and the same amount of time, and the fastest man will get the job. Got all that?'

'Yes, Frank.'

'Good. See you in two weeks.'

For those of you who've never heard Frank Williams speak, regardless of what he's telling you, it's as if he's arranging the delivery of a sofa or something, and it often belies the seriousness of what he's conveying. Suffice to say that when I put the phone down I had to repeat what he'd said in my head, and once I'd done that it finally started to sink in.

I still wasn't home and dry, of course, but one more push and I'd be there. I was actually quite proud of myself.

On with the test.

From memory we had three or four sets of tyres each and four runs in the car. Also, in between two of our runs, the mechanics made some changes, and as part of the test we had to tell them what they'd done and tell them how it had changed the car's performance. After that, we did a simulated race run followed by some qualifying laps. It was hard to tell, but I thought I'd performed well overall, and after finishing the qualifying laps we all left so that Williams could start crunching numbers.

Two days later, I was summoned to see Frank, and to be honest I thought it could easily have gone either way. My friends at Renault hadn't been returning my calls, and they would definitely have known the outcome. I just didn't know.

When I arrived at Williams I was taken straight up to Frank's office and when I walked through the door I got the shock of my bloody life. Frank was standing up!

I thought he'd been healed or something, and regrettably my shock was quite visible. 'It's all right,' said Frank. 'It's just a harness. It gets the blood flowing a bit.'

I thought the Almighty had paid him a visit.

'Sorry, Frank,' I said. 'It just took me by surprise a bit.'

'There's a contract on my desk,' he said pointing his arm. 'We'd like you to drive for us next season and, if things go well, the season after and the season after that.'

No histrionics. It was time to play it cool.

'That's great,' I said, casually but gratefully.

'Are you going to sign it, then?' asked Frank.

'Can I read it first?'

'Nope. Just sign it.'

I may have been keen but I wasn't going to be railroaded into signing anything.

'I don't want to appear ungrateful, Frank, but if I can't read it, I'm afraid I can't sign it.'

'OK, then,' said Frank, relenting. 'You've got five minutes.'

'Eh?'

I stood there for a few seconds wondering what to do.

'Come on,' said Frank. 'You've only got five minutes. Four and a half now.'

I had two choices really, I either signed there and then or I stopped the meeting and insisted on taking the contract away with me. Calling Frank's bluff at this stage probably wasn't a good idea, so after having a quick shufty at the remuneration pages, I gave him my decision.

'Sorry, Frank,' I said, putting the contract back on his desk. 'I can't sign that.'

'Eh? Why not?'

'It's a one-year contract basically, with an option for you to keep me on if you want to.'

'And what's wrong with that?' asked Frank.

'Nothing, on the face of it,' I replied. 'I totally understand and accept your proposed wages for year one, as you are taking a risk on me, but if you keep me for two then clearly I would have delivered for Williams and even more so in year three, so I would like to propose a bigger salary for those two years!'

I don't think Frank had been expecting this.

'You might not be the only driver out there,' replied Frank.

'Get out of here,' I said, laughing. 'You've just turned down two very fast drivers in favour of me. Come on, Frank. The back end of the contract just needs tweaking a bit, that's all.'

I must have had balls the size of planets! Or a brain the size of a pea.

I'm not sure if it was because he was surprised or because he agreed with my argument but Frank whacked £20k and £40k on to the two optional years there and then, and two minutes later, I'd signed my first ever professional contract as a touring car driver.

And about time! OMG, what a moment that was, I can tell ya.

Damn These Horny Brakes!

After being ushered out of Frank's office, literally, once I'd signed the contract, I was told to go home and wait for some telephone calls. Sure enough, within about two hours the Williams juggernaut had well and truly kicked into gear, and the following day I had to report to the Williams touring car factory in Didcot.

Until now, the only team I'd had anything to do with touring car wise had been the Janspeed Nissan team, and although they were obviously an extremely professional outfit, it was like comparing chalk and cheese. There must have been at least sixty people working at Didcot, and they had an entire floor – about 4,000 square feet's worth – completely full of designers. It was incredible! After I was shown around the main building, we then went to the workshops, and these were even more impressive. I think they had four race car bays in all, each with its own dedicated team. There were also electronics workshops and manufacturing workshops. It completely blew my mind. Best of all, though, I was a part of this now. Young Mr Plato had finally hit the big time.

After being introduced to my engineer, Gerry Hughes, and my technical team, I was then measured up for my seat. This was a first and no mistake. Boy, did I feel special. Although I knew this kind of thing happened, I hadn't been expecting any of this, for the simple reason that I could never think beyond just getting the drive. Therefore, it was all a big surprise, and the only thing I can really compare it to is taking a kid to Hamley's and saying, 'Off you go then. Do your worst!' It was lush.

Incidentally, shortly after signing that first contract with Frank I decided to acknowledge the incredible support Mum and Dad had given me over the years and the sacrifices they'd made, which had been off the scale. Many people had played a part, of course, but theirs had been leading roles, and without them I couldn't have done it. As a thank you for all this, and to mark the occasion of me turning professional, I booked them a two-week holiday in the Seychelles. As you can imagine, I was busting to tell them about this and was expecting an enthusiastic reaction.

'When is it?' Mum said.

A bit flummoxed, I reached for the confirmation which I'd printed off.

'Erm, here it is. Right, you fly on the 3rd of August.'

The moment I said it she started shaking her head.

'We can't go then,' said Mum. 'It's Knockhill that weekend.'

'Give it a rest, Mother,' I retorted. 'It's all booked and you're going. 3rd August.'

Like most mothers, mine doesn't like being told what to do, and her response was both terse and unequivocal:

'You're not listening, are you Jason? Read my lips. It's Knockhill that weekend, and WE ARE NOT GOING! You'll just have to change it.'

'What? Have a day off, will you? It's the Seychelles, for heaven's sake.'

'And we prefer Knockhill.'

'Really?'

'Really!'

In hindsight this simply reinforces the reason I wanted to

treat them in the first place, as the only reason they didn't want to go was because they wanted to watch me race. How fantastic is that?

At the time of me joining Williams, the team were about halfway through building the cars for the 1997 season. The shells were being manufactured by a company in France called Matta, who were the best in the business, and back at the factory they were busy sorting out the ergonomics. On day two I was asked how I'd like everything set up in the cockpit and, being a bit green, I said something like, 'Oh, I'll just have it the same as Alain.' 'No, no, no,' they said. 'That's not how it works. This isn't just any car, Jason, this is *your* car, OK? Now come on. Where do you want your shit?'

For a few moments I just stood there like a lemon. This was *my* car and it was being designed and built to *my* specifications. Happy Christmas, JP!

After deciding what I wanted and where – and I wanted the world, by the way – they then started measuring my arms to make sure everything was placed in exactly the right position. I liked ergonomics. I was ergonomically friendly.

My first test with Williams, or Willies, as they're known within the industry, which is how I'll refer to them from now on, took place at the ex-Formula 1 circuit Jarama, which is just north of Madrid. We had the entire place to ourselves for the duration of the test and we went there with two development cars – one for me and one for my teammate, Alain.

I didn't start appreciating the gravity of all this until I turned up at the airport. I'd been expecting one of the mechanics to pick me up or something but instead I had my own driver wearing a suit and driving a limo to get me to the hotel where my hire car would be waiting. Get in! Unfortunately there was no champers in the back, but I didn't mind.

I'd already been told that we had the circuit to ourselves, but when I arrived there were at least eighty people running around, so I assumed we were now sharing.

I assumed wrong!

Each and every one of them was there because of me and Alain. I just couldn't get my head around it.

The first person I went to find was my engineer, Gerry Hughes, who at some point in his life had been christened, 'Short Fuse Hughes', on account of him being ever so slightly quick to temper. He's now the team principal of the NIO Formula E team, a Chinese-owned team based in Oxford, so it's obviously all gone tits up for him. What an engineer, though! Apart from my teammate, who I'll come on to, I probably learned more from Gerry than anyone else during my formative years in touring cars and because he had a heck of a lot more experience than I did I treated him like the senior partner – which he was with regards to knowledge and experience. I was like a sponge with Gerry and when he talked, I listened. Boy, was he smart, and boy, did he write in such ever so small letters, and I mean ever so small, always with a retracting pencil or uber fineliner pen!

On several occasions I had to pinch myself at Jarama, none more so than when I realized there was an articulated lorry at the circuit that was full of tyres just for me. There were about five artics in all – amazing for just two cars – and two of them were full to the roof with Michelin race tyres!

I didn't like to ask why I had so many tyres, through fear of looking like a prat, but it soon became apparent. Basically, for the full five days, the team bolted on a new set of tyres every five laps, and in that time I went through in excess of a quarter of a million quid's worth. The F1 boys will be going, *Yeah, but that's nothing.* In touring car terms, though, it was absolutely massive. The reason for us using so many tyres was so I could become at one with the car and whenever they made a change to say the diff or the damping I was able to feel it instantly. Tyre degradation would have jeopardized that, hence the need to change. It was all about attention to detail and the confidence that instilled in me, not to mention the knowledge, was invaluable. I knew what the car's ultimate limit was *and* I knew its nuances and the results of every small change we made to the set-up.

After the five days I was shattered but I was on cloud nine. The team had been so, so well prepared, but as opposed to becoming overwhelmed by it all, I rose to the challenge. It had also acted as an induction, in a way, as with everyone staying in the same hotel it had given us a chance to bond, or at least have a few drinks. As a newbie, again I found this invaluable as I needed to be at one with the team as well as the car.

To help this along I decided to position myself as the butt of all the practical jokes and made sure that I was self-deprecating enough – in a humorous way – so people could take the piss. After that I was part of the gang, and the high jinks they perpetrated, often at my expense, but not always, became legendary. I'd already been warned about this by people who'd worked at Willies before and to be honest I thought they must have exaggerated it. How wrong was I?

Some of the things they did to my hire car during the test were just brilliant. Brake fluid in the exhaust, wiring the horn up to the brake pedal and handbrake, putting talcum powder in the air vents. It was relentless.

I remember the first time they wired my brakes up to the horn. It almost gave me a nervous breakdown! Our hotel was in Madrid, and in order to get to it I had to drive all the way through the centre of the city. You can imagine how stressful that was with the horn blaring every time my foot touched the brake. Half of Madrid thought I was off my box and the other half thought I was blowing my horn at them. The day after that I thought I might get a reprieve, but that was never going to happen. When I got in my hire car – quite gingerly, it has to be said – I realized immediately that they'd painted the windscreen matt black! Drivers were usually first to leave, so they'd all come out of the garage to see my reaction.

'You utter bastards,' I said, getting back out. 'I've heard of tinted windows, but this is just ridiculous!'

Their *pièce de résistance* when it came to hire car vandalism happened on I think the last day of the test, and although it was funny it very nearly backfired.

I set off from the hotel to the track and as usual there was much giggling going on.

'Come on,' I pleaded. 'What have you done? You may as well tell me.'

'Nothing, JP,' one of them said.

'Oh aye, a likely story.'

I knew they'd done something but assumed it would be another load of talcum powder in the air vents or something. If only!

About two minutes after hitting the motorway a load of thick white smoke started coming out of my exhaust and it just kept on coming and coming. It got so bad that drivers on both sides of the motorway had to slow down because they couldn't see where they were going.

What the Willies boys had done is pump a litre of brake fluid up the exhaust pipe into the catalytic converter and once that had started burning it was just, whoosh! It took me about twenty minutes to burn it all off, and I found out later that the police had almost closed the motorway. What larks, eh! Total nutcases.

By the end of the test I was approaching my car like a zoo-keeper would an angry tiger! It was terrifying, but a lot of fun.

In terms of high jinks, hire cars were to racing teams what televisions were to rock stars before they started behaving themselves, so most of the fun that took place would involve at least one. During the test they were jumping them off the banks surrounding the circuit. Seriously! I remember being at lunch one day when suddenly a Renault Laguna literally flew past the windows in the canteen. It was just incredible, and because the circuit was on lockdown while we were there we could basically do whatever we wanted. The lunatics had taken over the asylum!

Like us drivers, mechanics and engineers are a pretty highly strung bunch of boys, and girls, and it was their way of letting off steam. I was a young(ish) lad with a taste for some naughtiness, so it was just perfect. Not only was I a driver in the best touring car team on earth but I was surrounded by like-minded people.

One of the most dangerously entertaining lads on the Willies team was Smeggy, the team sparky. He used to build all the wiring looms and before joining Willies he'd done the same thing for the Royal Airforce by building wiring looms for fighter jets. Pardon the pun, but Smeggy was not wired like normal human beings and as well as being an absolute nutcase he was also a licensed pyrotechnician. What a combination! He was allowed to play with things he shouldn't have been allowed to go anywhere near and my word didn't he make the most of it.

This happened sometime after the test, but one day at

Snetterton a red telephone box, which was at the far side of the start/finish straight, exploded and then lifted off the floor before a load of red smoke billowed out of it. This was on a race day, incidentally, with thousands of people in attendance, and the bloody bomb squad were called out! It was all Smeggy's doing, although nobody let on.

He and his lunatic counterparts once built a cannon with the aim of firing golf balls from the paddock at Knockhill to the top of Knock Hill itself, which is miles away. Do you know, they weren't far off in the end, so God knows what they used.

We were once at a tyre test at Vallelunga in Italy. It was Gerry's birthday, and because we always took our own catering unit they'd made him a cake. It was absolutely amazing, this thing, and had Gerry's name on it and everything. For some reason they'd decided to present Gerry with his cake in the garage, and pretty soon I found out why. As the candles were lit, Gerry lent forward to blow them out and just as he did Smeggy hit the button and – BOOM! Up the cake went, sponge and icing were blown everywhere. The entire garage was covered in it. You were always looking over your shoulder with Smeggy, because if he decided to play a prank on you it would always be spectacular.

All these tales are coming back to me now!

We did another test once at a circuit in the middle of Spain – again it was exclusive – and in the middle of the paddock was a toilet block. On the second day there was a bit of activity going on outside this toilet block, and I said to Smeggy, 'What the heck's going on?'

'We've got this new mechanic,' he said. 'When he goes to the loo, and he'll have to at some point, something's going to happen. Just watch.'

Smeggy had wired up some explosives in the toilet block, and the idea was that when the new mechanic went over to do his business all the toilet doors would blow off. Unfortunately, Smeggy got the charge wrong, and as well as the doors he blew all the windows out too! The mechanic must have shat himself, so thank God he was in the toilet. He was OK, by the way. It was straight out of *The Italian Job: You were only supposed to blow the bloody toilet doors off!*

There used to be a hotel near Croft, at Durham Tees Valley Airport, and the front of this hotel was shaped like a horseshoe. I don't think it's there any more but one day during a test up there Smeggy worked out that the drainage for the toilets in the hotel all met underneath the same manhole cover and after working out which he thought was the pipe that led to a mechanic's room he put a charge in it, pushed it up as far as it would go and then sealed the pipe up. Later, when he knew that the mechanic was in his room, and hopefully in his bathroom, he detonated the charge, but instead of simply making a large bang, it blew the contents of the pipe up the toilet, and the entire thing exploded. What made this even worse was the fact that Smeggy had miscalculated the layout of the pipes and had actually blown up somebody else's toilet. Somebody who had nothing to do with the Willies touring car team. It was a proper shitfest, apparently.

The police were called, and within the hour the entire team were thrown out of the hotel, which meant we had to find another one at very short notice. I could be wrong, but I'm pretty sure that didn't get back to Frank and Patrick at HQ.

We used to get the odd private jet at Willies, me and the engineers, and one day when going through passport control the woman who was checking them stopped me suddenly.

'Excuse me, sir,' she said suspiciously. 'Is this a recent photo?'

'How do you mean?' I said, trying to look at the passport.

She held it up in front of me, and instead of seeing my ugly mug, I saw a photograph of a very white and very well-manicured poodle.

'You absolute swines,' I said, addressing the band of sniggering engineers.

Fortunately, they'd simply stuck the photo of the poodle over mine, so it was easily rectified, but on another occasion they drew an indentation of massive cock and balls over somebody's passport photo – not mine, thank God – and they had to travel with that for years. They were absolute bastards!

The only other time I remember us getting into trouble, or at least proper trouble, was when a hire car ended up being pushed into a fountain in a town square in Spain. That was absolutely mental!

It's all such a paradox, really, as the entire team were incredibly professional – like nothing I'd ever seen before – and the operation ran like clockwork. It was just a load of people letting off steam.

We will get on to some racing in a minute, I promise!

All race teams have what they call a flat patch, which, in layman's terms, is where the set-up takes place. At Willies we used to have an amazing flat patch which was basically an old machine bed but it was absolutely enormous. It was about a foot and a half off the ground and had slots in it which you could clamp the measuring apparatus to. We used to refer to it as, 'Novelty Island, where all your dreams can come true', and before the season started I was in there almost every day.

By this time I'd moved to within about ten minutes from Didcot as I just wanted to soak up as much knowledge and information as I could. It was similar to being with Neil in his tuning shed in a way. It was just heaven.

One day, this was about two weeks before my first race, this young spotty lad with a Middlesbrough accent came into the building where the flat patch was and asked if he could have a word with me.

'I'm a design engineer upstairs,' he said. 'Can I be your data engineer?'

I wasn't actually sure whether it was in my power to hire data engineers but, liking the look of him, I said, 'Yes, of course you can.'

As I said, he was a bit spotty, but he seemed like a good lad.

'What's your name,' I asked.

'My name's Rob. Rob Smedley.'

'Do you live in Oxford, Rob?'

'Yes, I do.'

'I'll tell you what, then,' I said. 'Why don't you and I go out for a bite to eat and talk about it?'

'Done.'

We ended up going to ASK in Oxford and we just hit it off. Rob went on to become one of my best mates, so much so he was the best man at my wedding. He also went on to become one of Formula 1's most prolific race engineers with a long stint as Felipe Massa's race engineer at Scuderia Ferrari!

Anyway, as I think I've now demonstrated, my first few months at Willies were absolutely epic, and things were just as pukka away from the factory. I had some disposable for the first time in ages and ended up buying a lovely barn conversion just the other side of Oxford. I'd promised myself, years before, that before I was thirty I'd buy myself a Ferrari and I think I made it with about a month to spare. It was a 355 – in red, obviously – and after buying it from a German garage, I flew over and drove it back. Talk about living the dream. I was King Dick!

OK, it's race time.

The first race of the 1997 BTCC season – my debut, in other words – took place at Donington Park, and after the two qualifying sessions I got pole. Bang! Unfortunately, I got a bit too much wheelspin off the line in race one (a reasonable mistake to make on your debut) and ended up finishing second to Alain, but for a first attempt it wasn't too shabby.

For the second race (there were just two races per meeting in the BTCC then as opposed to three now) I did exactly the same again. Two qualies – pole! Thank you very much indeed. Again, Alain beat me off the line, but again I was running a safe second until my engine went bang and I had to retire, but the main thing is I'd impressed the team and, importantly for me, I was well and truly out the shop window. By some margin, here is this young(ish) lad who has just scooped the best BTCC seat in the business, and not delivering would have fuelled the critics or the green-eyed. The internal pressure was off, my selection was deserved. I was off and running. It was the most amazing feeling in my entire life up until that point by some margin.

Meeting two took place at Silverstone on 20 April, and once again I put the car on pole for the first race. I couldn't believe it. Three races in and three pole positions. This allowed me to relax a bit, as in my mind I'd already justified Frank's decision and was definitely earning my keep. It was a good feeling.

Unfortunately, the last thing I should have been doing at this point in the season was relaxing. The tenth of a second or so I had over Alain had disappeared, and all of a sudden he had the tenth of a second, and I was having to sharpen my act up. Some might find it hard to believe, but I was actually quite disciplined when it came to my social shenanigans at this point, and from the Wednesday prior to a race weekend not a drop would pass my lips. Not a drop. I'm not saying I didn't partake a little bit during the three weeks in between race weekends, but the job always came first, and if I was going to get the boot I was adamant it would be track-related.

Some of you might be wondering how long it took me to fall out with another driver in that first year, and the answer is about two months – or the first race of round four, to be exact.

It all happened at Brands Hatch and it's a prologue to a pretty epic tale.

The driver in question was me old mate Jimmy T, James Thompson, who was driving for Honda at the time and who was actually my best mate on the grid. During the first race Tommo and I were having a proper scrap. It was great. Then, just before he was about to shut a gap he'd left, I went for it and, in Jimmy eyes at least (and possibly one or two members of his team), I ended up harpooning him. Some might call it an aggressive overtaking manoeuvre; I would call it a racing incident. Anyway, after endeavouring to overtake young Tommo, and making a modicum of contact in the process, I carried on, and he went into the pits with some damage to his right rear. A lap or so later, my engine started overheating, so it was my turn to come in.

About two minutes later, my car was on its jacks in the pit lane, and I was inside, listening to the engineers chatting away. 'Turn it off, JP,' one of them said eventually. 'The inlet's broken. It's game over.' Just as I was shutting it down, I looked through the windscreen, and there, running up the pit lane, waving his finger like a madman, was Jimmy T. You didn't have to be an expert to work out that the person he was on his way to speak to was yours truly, and on reaching my out-of-action car he wasted no time getting stuck in. Not that I could hear him. I had my helmet on and my earpiece in. I could lip-read, through the windscreen, and as far as I could make out he was shouting words mainly beginning with F, C and B. The BBC were covering touring cars then and they had cameras everywhere. Needless to say, they were on him like a flash, and in an attempt to try and remonstrate with my aggressor I switched my radio on and started shouting.

'YOU CAN FUCK OFF, THOMPSON,' I began, before realizing that Tommo wasn't wired into the Willies radio and the only people who could hear me remonstrating were the team. No matter. I carried on shouting, and for the next few minutes or so we exchanged a range of different views as to what had occurred in race one and who was to blame.

In race two the same thing happened again. We didn't have to go into the pits this time, thank God, but we had a right go at each other, and like before I ended up coming off better than Tommo.

Later on, Tommo was interviewed by the BBC – possibly by Murray Walker – and after he'd been asked what his plans were for the evening Tommo had said, 'Well I certainly won't be having a drink with Plato', or words to that effect. What he and I had both forgotten was that that evening we were off to Monaco together. A few weeks prior to this, me, Tommo and a few mates of ours had hatched a plan to go out to Monaco for the Grand Prix. In fact, we'd decided to spend the entire week there, and after being picked up by helicopter at the race meeting on the Sunday night, me and Tommo would land at Gatwick, meet our mates Alex Deighton, Charles Lupton,

Keiron Bushell, Math Flanigan, Simon Wood and Olly Dodds and then head off. We'd been talking about it for ages, and it was going to be monumental.

Unfortunately, the Sunday night in question was today, as in the evening after I'd fallen out big time with Tommo.

When we got in the helicopter the first thing I did was try and smooth things over, and in the interests of us all having an epic week we decided to let bygones be bygones. Two minutes later we were clinking glasses and getting stuck in so it was full steam ahead.

Incidentally, one of the reasons I decided to offer an immediate olive branch was because we were staying in Tommo's apartment, and although I had no idea if we'd actually see it at all, what with all the partying we had in mind, I thought it best to smooth things over, just in case.

Needless to say, we were flat out the entire week and fully lit. Tommo was twenty-three at the time and I was just thirty. We were both professional racing drivers, we both had a bit of cash on the hip and we were in Monaco for the Grand Prix and one of the biggest parties on the calendar. It didn't get much better.

On the Sunday morning, the day of the Grand Prix, we got up a bit late, and the shortcut we were intending to use had been blocked. This meant we had to walk the long way around, and the distance from Tommo's apartment to Stars & Bars on the port, which is where we had our table, was about a mile and a half. It took for ever.

The reason we got up so late was because the night before we'd only got in at about 4 a.m., and even reprobates like us needed a little bit of beauty sleep, especially after being on the piss all week.

I think we were all hoping that the walk to Stars & Bars

would clear our heads a bit, but by the time we got there we were all still hanging out of our arses.

'Before we get stuck in, boys,' I announced after finding our table, 'I've just got to pop off to the pit lane.'

On delivering that bombshell, I then produced a pass that had been issued by the Willies F1 team.

'Where the hell are ours, Plato?' asked Tommo and the others.

'Sorry, chaps, but this is duty,' I lied, while sparking up a fag. 'Frank would kill me if I didn't say hello.'

With that I gave them all a wink and stumbled off to the pit lane. God, I felt rough! Six days' worth of alcoholic shenanigans were beginning to take their toll, and although I probably looked OK from a distance, close up I probably looked – and smelled – a little bit like James Hunt after, well, six days in Monaco!

By the time I reached the paddock I'd got my second wind and by the time I reached the Willies garage I'd gone from feeling decidedly shop-soiled to brand new. I had my new expensive shades on and my new shoes. I looked a million lira.

Back in those days they didn't have pit garages at Monaco, they had awnings that went right the way down the port where Stars & Bars looked on to. As I minced down the pit lane I could see the boys looking on from Stars & Bars so to make them feel part of it I gave them a wave and a thumbs up. 'All right boys! Don't worry, I'll be back in half an hour. Keep the champers on ice!'

Although I was unaware, the boys had noticed something about me that, had I known about it, might already have caused me a lot of embarrassment, but luckily for me I was in a state of blissful ignorance. For now, at least.

After finding the Willies awning I glided in, said a few

hellos and then went to find Frank. He was somewhere at the back of the tent, and as I approached my famous boss I attempted to pull myself together a bit and try to start acting like a normal human being.

'All right, Jason,' said Frank. 'Enjoying yourself?'

'Yeah, great, thanks, Frank.' I went for confidently non-chalant in the end as I thought that matched my outfit.

'Where are you watching the race, then,' asked Frank.

'Stars & Bars,' I said, 'just up the road.'

In an attempt to demonstrate to Frank the location of Stars & Bars I leaned down to point and as I did so my fags fell out of my shirt pocket before bouncing off Frank's lap and then on to the floor.

After that he gave me one of his looks, as if to say, *You're supposed to be super-fit, aren't you? Drivers aren't supposed to smoke*, I smiled meekly before bending down to pick them up and as I did so I noticed that my new Patrick Cox burgundy snakeskin loafers were on the wrong feet! Can ya catch ya breath!

Unfortunately, Frank's gaze had followed me down as I went to pick up my fags and he too had noticed my sartorial faux pas.

'Are you all right, Jason?' he asked.

'Yeah, yeah, fine, Frank, fine. Anyway, must dash. I've got some friends waiting.'

After darting out on to the paddock, I looked around to see if there was somewhere – anywhere – I could correct myself but there were people all over the bloody place. I kept on looking down and the more I looked the more I noticed how ridiculous I looked.

As well as walking about two frickin' miles in these things I must have passed thousands of people and for some reason

I hadn't noticed. I was just too hungover I suppose. There was nothing else for it. With no immediate options in the vicinity I was just going to have to suffer the ignominy of having my shoes on back to front at one of the most glamorous sporting events on the planet and walk back to Stars & Bars, where hopefully I'd find a toilet.

As I walked back along the paddock, I started to hear some familiar voices.

'Check your shoes out, Plato! You look like a right cock!'

It was, of course, The Lads.

I obviously couldn't start swearing but instead I gave them a few one- and two-fingered gestures and by the time I got back to the table my feet were almost falling off. It was time for a drink! And it was my round!

We just drank, enjoyed the company of the ladies and raised lots and lots of merry hell.

The night before, we'd been to the Stars & Bars nightclub, which was on the top floor of the marina building complex, and needless to say we were all absolutely out of control. Then again, Monaco itself is out of control on race weekends, so we fitted in perfectly.

Tommo had organized a table at the club that was shaped like a guitar and it was situated right next to, and raised above, the dance floor. It was all going on up there, if you see what I mean, and we all had a bird's-eye view. After a few bottles of everything, Alex 'the Deets' suddenly decided that he was going to try and walk the length of the guitar-shaped table, which was about three metres long, and halfway down the fretboard he went arse over tit. OMG, it was truly phenomenal how his little feet slipped and both legs shot off the side of the fretboard, which amazingly kind of flipped and inverted him up in the air. To the right and lower than our table by about a metre was another table, and the same again below that was the dance floor. Alex pole-axed the table below, knocking bottles of fizz all over the beautiful couple sat there, and then his momentum made sure he arrived on the dance floor upside down, arms flailing like a lunatic. There was hair, teeth and champagne bottles absolutely everywhere. Fortunately, one of the lads was actually quite sensible and generally always got us out of trouble, so after buying this couple a bottle of champagne, he gave them our apologies and tried to calm things down. We didn't really help matters by pissing ourselves laughing, and, after being reported to the manager – understandably, as we were acting like twats – we were thrown off the table.

After that I went to the bar and I ordered a round of double gin and tonics. Back in 1997 one gin and tonic of the single variety, let alone the double, was 36 francs, and when he told me how much the round was I nearly had a heart attack. I remember saying to the barman, 'Are you having a laugh?' He wasn't, though.

When he eventually brought these G&Ts, they'd been served in goblets, which was bizarre, and when I looked around to see where the others were, the only one I could see was Alex. He'd managed to get a chair on to the dance floor and had started spinning himself around on it.

'Hang on,' I said, racing on to the dance floor. 'I'll give you a hand.'

After handing Alex his goblet, which was about half the size of him, as Alex is quite small, I started spinning him around on the chair and pretty soon the remainder of our party joined us. The faster we pushed him the higher up in his goblet the G&T went until eventually it started spraying the entire dance floor. As you can imagine, this didn't go down well with anybody except us, and we were told there and then that one more misdemeanour and we'd be out. 'Fair enough,' we said. 'It's just a bit of high jinks.'

A bit later on, a singer took to the stage, and then after him a DJ. The singer had gone down like a pair of lead knickers, but once the DJ kicked off everyone got up and started dancing, and one of the first to do so was the Deets. The thing is, instead of making shapes on the dance floor like everyone else, he'd taken to the stage instead, and after spotting the singer's microphone he started doing one of the worst Roger Daltrey impressions known to man. Round and round the microphone went until suddenly the music came to a halt.

'Little man,' said the DJ, pointing to Alex. 'Little man, put the mic down and GET OFF the stage.'

He wasn't going to start the music until Alex had got down, but instead of just jumping down, like he should have done, Alex did a forward roll, which, I assume, was supposed to end with him standing up at the front of the stage and then jumping off. Unfortunately, this didn't come to pass: he tumbled off the stage, crashed into a punter and knocked her flying.

We then all started chanting: 'He's short, he's round, he bounces on the ground. It's Alex Deighton!'

That was it. We were out.

When we got out of the club, we were expecting the town to be deserted, but it wasn't. There were people everywhere.

'What time is it?' I asked Tommo.

'It's half past ten!'

In our minds it had been about four o'clock in the morning, so finding out the night was still young was excellent news.

'Where to now?' said Alex.

'How about La Rascasse?' I said.

'We'll never get in there,' said Tommo.

'Of course we will!'

Well, guess what . . . we did get into Rascasse, although God knows how.

About half an hour in, one of our other mates, Charles, decided that he didn't like the epaulettes that Alex had on his shirt (to be fair they looked very average) and without warning he walked up to him, grabbed hold of one and ripped it off, but in doing so he tore his shirt sleeve too. Given the amount of alcohol we'd had, this could easily have been the prelude to an almighty ding-dong, but fortunately Alex took it in good humour and instead of thumping Charles he started returning the favour by pulling at the arms of his shirt, and within a few seconds we were all at it. After catching the manager's beady eye, we stopped just in the nick of time and after another libation or two we hightailed it to Tip Top, which is on the way out of Casino Square towards Portier. This place is legendary and is where James Hunt and his crowd used to go back in the day.

By this time, we were absolutely wasted but we still had plenty of energy left. I'm not sure if this was a regular thing at Tip Top, but after we'd been there about an hour word started going around that a game would be taking place shortly that involved a load of blokes standing on chairs and poking a finger through their flies while a blindfolded woman passed along and fondled the fingers, pretended to masturbate them and then chose her favourite. It was like *Blind Date*, really, but with fingers pretending to be phalluses. I'm sure Cilla Black would have had a field day!

As a sportsman I decided to put my name down for this game, and when it started I put down my drink, leaped on to my chair, undid my flies, poked a finger out and started wiggling it, as you do. As the lucky lady passed along the line fondling the pretend penises, I suddenly thought to myself, *Wouldn't it be a good idea if I swapped my pretend penis for my real one?* and literally a second or so before she put her hand out to grab it I did the swap.

'OH MY GOD,' she said, pulling off her blindfold, 'IT'S A REAL ONE. HE'S GOT HIS COCK OUT!'

'I certainly have, madam,' I replied confidently. 'A little treat for you.'

This woman went absolutely mental, as did her friends *and* the manager.

'Right you lot,' he said. 'OUT!'

'Nobody said anything about not getting your cock out,' argued Alex. 'It was just a bit of fun!'

'I SAID OUT!'

Well, that made it three clubs that we'd been kicked out of in one night. Not bad going, really.

By now it was about three o'clock in the morning, and with a load of potential police sirens now ringing in our ears we decided to call it a day. Tommo's apartment was up the hill in Monaco-Ville, and about halfway up we realized that we'd lost Alex.

'When did you last see him?' Tommo asked me.

'In Tip Top, I think. When he was bad-mouthing the manager.'

We had no idea where he'd gone.

There was no point trying to find him, as he could have been anywhere, and after persuading ourselves that he'd be OK we continued back to the apartment for a bit of shut-eye.

Just before we hit the hay, the buzzer went. Tommo came running in.

'It's the police,' he said. 'They've got Alex.'

You know the famous Loews Hairpin at Monaco? In the middle of that there's a tiny little island with a few palm trees on it. It does actually look like a tiny desert island from a distance, and Alex, in his inebriated and infinite wisdom, had decided that would be a great place to watch the Grand Prix, so instead of coming back with us he'd decided to set up camp there. After a while the police had spotted him but instead of chucking him in the cells, which were probably full at the time, they decided to return him to his rightful owners. Apparently he'd wrapped himself up in some bunting he'd nicked and when they found him he was fast asleep. Bless him.

No OBE for Me, Then?

Back to earth, and things couldn't have been sweeter. Life at Willies just got better and better. Alain, in particular, was having a blinding season, and he and I were getting on like a house on fire. I remember being on the parade truck with him before a race early on in the season, and he turned to me and said something along the lines of, 'You've come just at the right time, Jason. The car is absolutely amazing. It's good to have you on board, mate.' He couldn't have been friendlier.

The only thing that made me distrust Alain slightly, apart from him being a professional racing driver, was something that had happened during the Renault Spider series. Basically, Alain had had his own team in the series, called Menu Motorsport, and during my initial interview with Patrick and Frank they told me that it had been suggested by Alain's team that the only reason I won so many races was because I'd been running on dodgy equipment, and apparently that suggestion had come from the top, in other words, from Alain.

After reminding Frank and Patrick that it was a one-model series, I told them in no uncertain terms that Alain had been talking out of his arse and that my one and only advantage on the other boys had been a greater talent for driving. Since then, Alain had actually apologized for that, but the gravity of the accusation had made me wary of him.

During that first year at Willies, as well as getting involved in as much as I could at the factory, I also endeavoured to go above and beyond for any sponsors or commercial partners. Again, it was all about making up for lost time really and announcing to as many people as humanly possible that I was on the scene. What made it easier for me was that I had a genuine interest in things like sponsorship and, as with all the goings-on in the factory and the workshops, I wanted to learn as much as I possibly could. In that respect I was a sponsorship manager's dream, albeit not especially well known yet, and so when I was asked if I'd mind going down to Southampton one day to stand in a shop for a few hours and sign some autographs I immediately replied, 'What time and where?'

Despite having to set off first thing on a Sunday morning for this event, I was happy to oblige, as it meant I had to lay off the sauce the night before, and so when I jumped into my Renault Laguna V6 in British Racing Green at about 7.30 a.m. I felt bright-eyed and bushy-tailed. Or sober, as it's also sometimes known.

About forty-five minutes into the drive I was cracking along the fast lane of the M3 doing about ninety when all of a sudden I looked in my mirror and saw a black Range Rover that can't have been more than about two or three metres behind me and flashing his headlamps. Putting it mildly, I wasn't best pleased. For a start, I absolutely hate tailgating (unless it's on a track), but this idiot had also begun to spoil what until now had had the makings of being a perfectly nice day.

For some reason there was quite a bit of traffic on the road that morning, which made it difficult to switch lanes, so, with obstinacy and indignation quickly getting the better of me, I decided to hold fast and just ignore him.

No more than about thirty seconds later, this buffoon was almost in the boot and was being even more aggressive than last time.

'Why don't you back off, pal,' I shouted, giving them the finger in the mirror. This, unsurprisingly, was about as effective as a tea bag without a kettle, and so instead of shouting and gesturing I brake-tested him. Have that!

With him now a safe distance behind me, I uttered something triumphant but profane before switching my gaze forwards again and trying to force a smile. Plato 1, dickhead in a Range Rover 0.

The tranquillity must have lasted a good fifteen seconds before he was back again, and because the middle lane was about to become free I decided to pull over, let him pass and pray that whoever was driving the Range Rover ended up contracting some nasty disease.

Despite me deciding to relent, there was no way I was going to do so without offering up a gesture, and as the Range Rover drove alongside me while passing I raised the middle digit on my right hand, looked to my right and shouted two words that were not happy birthday.

The driver of the Range Rover decided not to engage with me, so that just left the passenger. He was staring straight at me when I shouted and gestured, and unfortunately he was disturbingly familiar. I say disturbingly as, after clocking his face, it took me just a millisecond to realize that I'd just given two Fs – one mouthed and one gestured – to the future monarch of the United Kingdom.

'OMG,' I said still staring at him. 'It's Prince Charles!'

After evidently clocking what I'd said and done, he smiled – slightly – before turning to his driver and saying something. Probably: 'What a charming fellow. We must give him an OBE.'

With that, old Charlie boy and his Range Rover pals legged it, but instead of me going merrily on my way with a nice little story to tell the boys and girls back at Willies, the chaps who were looking after His Royal Highness decided to leave me with a little addition.

Behind the Range Rover were four outriders on motorbikes, and while two followed the Range Rover the other two gestured for me to pull over. Too many gestures!

After I did as I was told, they then got me out of my car, pushed me over my bonnet and gave me a proper dressing down. I couldn't bloody believe it! What would they have done if it had been the Queen. Shoot me? In hindsight, I could probably have complained about this, as it was arguably an abuse of power, but at the end of the day I'd just told the Queen's eldest son to eff off twice, and some people would give their eye teeth for a chance to do that. I was cock-a-hoop!

Talking of my Racing Green Renault V6 Laguna, which I was a few paragraphs ago. I was once driving it down the Brompton Road in London. This would have been about the same time as me saying hi to Charlie. Once again, it was first thing on a Sunday morning, except this time I'd been to a party, so, although I was sober, I was not bright-eyed and bushy-tailed.

If I'm being honest, I wasn't paying much attention at the time, as I was trying to find a radio station on the stereo, and, on looking up, as I had been doing periodically, I saw a man on a zebra crossing about 20 feet in front of me looking like he was about to shit himself. As well he might!

After coming to attention very quickly I immediately realized that the man standing in front of me, and the man I'd almost killed, was Bernie Ecclestone. Had I left it just half a second later I would have taken him out and in doing so would have changed the face of motorsport for ever. It was a proper sliding-door moment. Or in this case sliding car doors.

I think my best performance during 1997 – and my biggest buzz, after winning my first race – happened at Oulton Park for round five, which was the middle of the year. Shortly after the start, I got caught up in a shunt and spent the next ten laps or so trying to regain ground and get back into position. It was obviously coincidental, but the BBC had positioned a camera on the corner where I did the majority of my overtaking, and after a while Murray Walker, who was commentating for the BBC, suggested they change the name of the corner to Plato's Bend. I only found out about this afterwards, but it epitomizes my experience, as I drove a blinder, and everything just fell into place. Better still, I ended up hijacking Alain's interview after the race. It was pure Plato, even if I do say so myself. Allow me to fill you in.

After I had passed Alain on the way through the pack, the team had ordered me to let him back through, and after the race the interviewer had said to Alain, 'That was nice of Jason to let you through.' Instead of coming clean, which he obviously wasn't supposed to and probably wouldn't have done anyway, Alain started trying to bluff his way out of it, but before he could really say anything, I walked up to him and said something like, 'See Alain, great bloke, aren't I?' After that, I grabbed the mic, pushed Alain out of the way and proceeded to give a far more entertaining interview, it has to be said. Alain was furious!

I should point out that Mr Menu got a clean sweep at this meeting by bagging both poles, both wins and both fastest laps, and that was the only time it happened in 1997 or 1998.

Although I didn't win – or should I say wasn't allowed to win – it was one of those days when, from a racing point of view, everything just aligned. The car, the track, the performance – everything. Gaps I wouldn't normally have gone for suddenly seemed enormous, and every attempt to pass another driver came off. The track too was just perfect, and I was able to use some of the undulations and cambers to help me counter any handling deficiencies I had, and I swear to you the car was almost singing at one point. In fact, after thinking about it again, it was almost as if time slowed down for me slightly as, instead of having a split second to judge a manoeuvre, I seemed to have all the time in the world. I didn't, of course, but that's how it felt.

By the time we got to Snetterton, which was round nine, Alain had won ten races and was miles ahead of everyone in the championship. Whilst my good start hadn't been a false dawn, exactly, I'd certainly levelled off a bit after the first two meetings, but by Snetterton I'd managed to find my mojo again and was making it harder for Alain.

This meeting is significant for two reasons really. First, it's where I won my first ever race in the BTCC, and second, it's where Alain clinched the championship. What's also interesting is that's it's probably where my relationship with Alain went completely belly-up as, after I'd run him ragged during the first race and then won the second, he obviously realized that I was back in the chase again, and Alain was only friendly to me when I wasn't challenging him.

Despite this, we all left Snetterton happy people, and by the first race of the final meeting, which was at Silverstone, I was lying second in the championship. I was nowhere near Alain, but I was ahead of Frank Biela and providing I won both races – a big ask but doable – I'd finish runner-up in my debut season. That would be an epic historical achievement.

For race one I managed to get pole, and in the team meeting

before the race, Didier, our team manager, suggested to Alain that he might like to help me out. It wasn't an order, and he didn't say it in so many words, but he made it clear that it would be great for the team if I finished runner-up.

The thing is, unless you were straight with Alain, he'd always take the piss to his own advantage, so with an air of ambiguity permeating the meeting room after Didier's speech it was anyone's guess as to how Alain was going to react. What Didier should have said was, 'Right then, Alain, you Swiss cheese. Sit behind Jason, protect him, and behave yourself, OK?' You can't be grey with people like Alain.

With a few laps to go before the end of the first race, I thought Alain had been doing a great job of protecting me when what he'd actually been doing was leading me into a false sense of security. I had been driving at 95 per cent, safe in the knowledge Alain had my back, I had a couple of tenths left in the tank and was leaving a little margin in a couple of areas on the brakes. Sure enough, about five or six laps before the end, he dived late down the inside at one of the corners, and because I wasn't expecting it I ended up on the marbles. It took about a lap and a half to get all the rubbish off my tyres, and in the meantime Alain had all but won the race. You twat! Had I finished even second in the race I'd still have had a tiny chance of bagging runner-up, but as it was, I finished way down in third.

After the race an almighty argument took place, and as far as Alain and I were concerned the gloves were now off. He didn't have to do that, as he'd already won the championship, but with his dominance now in jeopardy he tried to make a point – he was obviously twitchy. And rightly so!

With the following race being the last race of the season Alain was hell bent on winning it, but with Alain being an enormous tool who'd just scuppered my chances of finishing runner-up in my debut season, so was I.

It was his turn to bag pole this time and with me slightly demoralized he must have thought he had it in the bag. Did he buggery! With no tyres to protect we basically went at each other like madmen, and we ended up having the mother of all battles. We were on a different planet to the opposition and perhaps because he wasn't expecting it I managed to get the better of him and piss on his parade, just as he'd pissed on mine. I was still absolutely seething, though, and realized that all that stuff about him being sorry for the Spider series was just BS. He was a tosser.

A few days later, while I was at the factory, I got a message that Patrick Head wanted to see me. Without wanting to appear conceited, I was rather hoping he wanted to congratulate me on a decent debut season, but after I stepped through his office door it was obvious I'd got it wrong.

'I take it you were out in Oxford over the weekend, Jason?' said Patrick.

'That's right,' I replied. 'Me and a few mates.'

'You were overheard being disrespectful about your team-mate. Something about fucking him up next season?'

I'd heard Patrick was supposed to be all-seeing and all-knowing, but I didn't think they meant it literally!

'Who told you that?' I asked, slightly flummoxed.

'Never you mind who told me that. You do that again in public and I'll tear you a new arsehole, do you understand?'

'Yes, Patrick. Sorry, Patrick.'

'OK, now fuck off.'

It just goes to show how wrong you can be. There was me expecting a pat on the back, and I end up getting a kick in the balls!

It was fair enough, though. I deserved it.

Patrick was definitely the scarier of the two with regards to the Willies bigwigs. Frank used to have a bit of a glint in his eye when I went in for a cup of tea, because he knew I was a bit of a lad and I probably brought back one or two memories for him. Patrick, on the other hand, was harbouring no such romantic recollections – or if he was, he was hiding them well – and he always maintained that distance between employer and employee. It wasn't good cop, bad cop, exactly, but they certainly complemented each other very well and obviously made a formidable team.

To be fair, and in an attempt to put the thing between Alain and me into perspective, the reason we couldn't stand each other and the reason we did what we did was because we were both fiercely competitive, and at the end of the day a win-at-all-costs attitude, which is what we racing drivers possess and is part of what makes us different to normal human beings, can manifest itself in a variety of different ways. Would I have done things differently to Alain at Silverstone? Yes, definitely, providing my teammate wasn't a complete wanker, but that doesn't mean I'm right.

From the point of view of being a young racing driver I was the luckiest man alive having Alain as a teammate, as at the time he was the best touring car driver in the business, and in that first season I learned an incredible amount from him, which still to this day I am grateful for. We are good pals now.

Speaking of being the luckiest man alive ... Just three weeks after the end of the 1997 season, I got to race in the Bathurst 1000. When I was a kid, I and my old man used to watch the Bathurst religiously, but even as a professional racing driver it had never occurred to me that I might one day get to compete.

The approach had been made – to me, at least – just a few days after the season had ended by Frank and had resulted in one of the most hilarious negotiations in which I've ever been involved. I remember him calling me in initially to ask me if I'd be interested, and my immediate reaction was, yes, of course I would be. Frank obviously knew that I was no pushover with regards to finances so before I could ask him how much I'd be getting he assured me that, although it wasn't in my contract, I'd be well remunerated.

'We'll come back to you with an offer,' said Frank.

The following day, I went to see Alain, who had already been approached by Frank about Bathurst, and I asked him what his arrangement was.

'There was no offer,' said Alain. 'I just told him what I wanted.'

'Which was?'

'Basically, I divided the amount I'm paid by the number of races in the season,' said Alain. 'Because of the length of the race, I doubled it, and then I doubled it again for winning the championship.'

Blimey! I didn't know exactly how much that was, but it must have been six figures. The next day I got called in to see Frank again.

'We've had a think Jason, and we'd like to make it worth your while. How does £2,000 sound?'

I found it difficult not to laugh, so I did. 'You've got to be joking, Frank,' I chuckled. 'Two grand?'

He looked at me quizzically.

'You've been speaking to Alain, haven't you?' he said finally.

'I might have.'

'OK, then. How does £40,000 sound?'

'Done!'

With the fiscal side now put to bed, we were all set for Australia, and Alain and I flew out at the end of September.

If racing in the Bathurst 1000 wasn't enough, I found out shortly before leaving that we'd be racing both cars, and with Alain and myself racing his car, that left two drivers for mine. The first chap was an Australian driver called Graham Moore, who I have to admit I'd never heard of, but the second was a compatriot of his called Alan Jones, who I certainly had heard of. Alan had won twelve Grand Prix and the 1980 Formula 1 World Championship and as well as being a bit of childhood hero of mine he was obviously a motorsport legend. I remember driving around the circuit with Jonesy in a road car a day or two before the race and thinking how surreal it all was. I was at Bathurst, which I'd watched since I was a kid and had dreamed of racing in, and I was now sitting in a car driving the circuit with my childhood hero who also happened to be my teammate. Things like this didn't happen, did they?

The Bathurst 1000 lasts 1,000 kilometres – yes, really – and takes place annually on the Mount Panorama Circuit in Bathurst, New South Wales. Because it's on a mountain, you might expect the gradient of the track to vary somewhat and you'd be right. In fact, there's a 174 metre vertical difference between the highest and lowest points of the Mount Panorama Circuit with grades as steep as 1:6.13. Technically, it's a street circuit, as it's also a public road, and the climb after the first corner is extremely steep. Although not nearly as steep the decline afterwards!

Alain and I were on P2 for the race, which we were more than happy with, and although I had no experience in driving endurance races I was confident I'd do OK. With Alain having driven qualifying, I was first in the car for the race and after a bit of a slow start I managed to stay with Paul Morris, who was on P1. After the pit straight you go around Hell Corner and on to Mountain Straight. Despite its incredibly steep incline, cars can reach speeds of up to 180 mph up here, and that, if you've never driven the circuit before, offers you a totally new driving experience, as there's another element to consider. In fact, very little can prepare you for driving something like the Bathurst, and I'd say it's probably my favourite circuit. The exit from the Mountain Straight is called The Cutting, and I promise you, it's like driving off a cliff – at about 180 mph!

Unfortunately, the car ended up giving way on us on lap 114, but do you know what, it doesn't really matter. I still had an amazing time. The average speed of that race was 150 kph, which included pitstops, and I ended up setting the record for the fastest lap. With super touring cars no longer being in existence, that record will live for evermore, so if you put that together with meeting Jonesy and just being at the Bathurst 1000, it wasn't a bad week.

This is in danger of sounding like the parable of the lucky git now, but shortly after the Bathurst I received a gift from my team which to this day is one of the most extraordinarily brilliant things I have ever been given. Basically, every piece of my car – every panel and every wing mirror etc. – that had either been taken off or had been damaged in a shunt had been saved by the team and, unbeknownst to me, in a far corner of a workshop somewhere they'd managed to build an entire shell with these bits.

Now, as opposed to just giving it to me, which wouldn't have been the Willies way, they decided to make it a surprise, and while I was away on a test in southern Spain they had it craned into my garden, which was walled, and placed on my patio.

When I finally got back from this test I was knackered, as my plane had been diverted to Birmingham, and after turning on the light in my kitchen I looked outside, looked again and then looked a third time. It was just totally lush.

The following spring, I asked the boys at Willies if they could make the bonnet open, as I'd had this brilliant idea of using it for a BBQ, but before they could do anything, I got a letter from the council saying that I had to have it removed. Some arsehole had complained, apparently, and it ended up costing me £600 to have it taken away!

In an attempt to try and salvage some good from the situation, I decided to sell the car at auction to raise some money for charity, and it ended up going for a good few grand.

Unfortunately, the 1998 car was nowhere near as good as the 1997 one, and despite everyone's best efforts we ended up getting stuffed by Rickard Rydell in the Volvo, who was racing for Tom Walkinshaw. It was a pity really as, despite Alain and I having differences of opinion and being very different people as drivers, we actually complemented each other, and the team, perfectly. Had the car been anywhere near as good as 97's we'd have ended up having the mother of all battles, and it would have been epic. As it was, Alain finished fourth and me fifth, so it ended up being a damp squib.

At the end of 1998, Alain left Willies, which made me the number one driver, but with the Laguna still being well under par the best I could do was match last season's effort with just one solitary win, and I came fifth in the championship.

About two-thirds of the way through the third and final year of my contract I was told on the quiet that Renault were pulling the plug on touring cars and that Willies would be doing the same. I don't mind admitting that I was absolutely heartbroken when I found out the news. It probably sounds slightly clichéd, but the entire team had become like a family to me, and like all life-changing experiences – and my time at Willies was exactly that, life-changing – I didn't want it to end. Had Willies had carried on in touring cars I'd quite happily have stayed with them for life, but unfortunately it wasn't to be.

My teammate for that season was Jean-Christophe Boullion, and no disrespect to him, but he wasn't a patch on Alain, and, may God forgive me, I might actually have ended up missing the miserable bastard! Although only slightly.

Instead of finishing on a high like we'd hoped to, the last ever race for the Willies touring car team turned out to be a bit of a disastrous fiasco and it's something that, even to this day, I find quite difficult discussing.

In the first of two races, my car developed an electrical fault and wouldn't start prior to the race, which meant race one was over before it started.

The last ever race for Williams in BTCC was a shocker. It was nobody's fault, which is some consolation, but mid distance Alain Menu (driving for Ford) was driven off the track, and when he tried to rejoin I was flying along in his blind spot and – BANG! Try as they might, the mechanics at Willies were unable to save the car, which meant I had to retire from the last race. I remember being interviewed after when I got back to the pits, and it's the first time I've ever welled up on television.

Barry Hinchcliffe was the man behind the camera, and

when the tears started appearing and the throat started croaking he started gesturing at me to carry on talking.

'More,' he started mouthing to me. 'More!'

Bugger off, Barry!

What a time, though. What an experience. Thank you so much Frank, Patrick and Tim Jackson.

Getting Bitten by a Dane

Shortly after finding out about Willies leaving touring cars I started talking to Triple Eight Racing about becoming a works driver (supported by a manufacturer) for their team, which was Triple Eight Vauxhall, so the Vauxhall works team basically. Financially, the deal was better than Willies, but there was a stipulation that in year one I'd be the number two driver to Yvan Muller. Given what I'd experienced with Alain, this wasn't ideal, but the way they sold it to me was that if a development component came along I wouldn't get it – which I was fine with – and if Yvan and I were both in with a shout of winning the championship at the end of the season, I'd drop back and support him. That wasn't quite as fine, but as long as it was at the end of the season and not the start, I was OK with it.

The opening round was at Brands Hatch, and after getting the fastest lap in race one, which Alain Menu ended up winning in his Ford Mondeo, I went out and won race two. Welcome to Triple Eight Vauxhall, Jason!

By round three, which was at Thruxton, I was leading the championship and after getting a blistering start in race one I built a commanding lead. Remember, the deal was that if Yvan and I were close by the end of the season I'd have to relent, so providing I could build an unassailable lead by the last quarter I'd have the championship. That was the plan, at least.

About halfway through the first race at Thruxton my radio suddenly went:

'Jason, it's Derek here.' (Derek Warwick, who was part owner of Triple Eight.) 'We need you pull aside and let Yvan come through and win.'

'You what? No chance. That's not what we agreed.'

'Come on, Jason,' said Derek. 'There's no room for negotiation here. We need you to pull aside.'

It was difficult trying to process this while driving at 150 mph, and the more I thought about it the angrier I became. I was miles in front, for heaven's sake, and it was only round three.

After a few more calls from Derek, during which I expressed my disgust at their decision, I decided to relent but it was going to be on my terms. Had it been up to the team I'd have spent the rest of the race trying to disguise the fact that I was giving up a lead that I'd had to work hard for, so it wouldn't look like team orders, but I was buggered if I was going to do that. No chance. I'll obey the instruction but with my best interests at heart.

When coming out of the last corner on the penultimate lap I put my indicator on and slowed down in full view of the crowd and television cameras. Then, once Yvan had caught up, which took a wee while, I picked up the speed again and carried on. The only way you wouldn't have known what was happening was if you'd gone to the toilet or had fallen asleep. The commentators were all going ballistic. 'This isn't motor racing', was the general refrain, and they were absolutely right, it wasn't. Had it been the last race or even the penultimate race of the season then fine, but race five? It was pathetic.

The way I gave up the win went down like a lead balloon

with the team, but where they hadn't stipulated – in writing – what the team orders would be I hadn't stipulated how I would obey them. The reason I did what I did wasn't to make the team look like twats, although that's what happened; it was to make a point and, hopefully, open a dialogue, but they didn't see it that way, and Vauxhall went absolutely mental. Not with me, though, with Triple Eight, for pulling what they deemed as being an unnecessary stunt. They really had backed the wrong driver here, and the whole thing backfired on them.

After everything calmed down a bit, I was called into a team meeting and was told that from now on all team orders would be displayed, in code, on pit boards, with the majority dealing with the problem of making it look like Yvan had caught me fairly and squarely. I was then told that if I didn't like the arrangement I could look for a drive elsewhere, or words to that effect, so I bit my tongue and decided to comply. I did say, however, that I would only drive under team orders for a year, and next year it would be an even playing field. 'Sure, JP,' they said. 'That's fine with us. It's only for this year. We promise.'

Fortunately, it didn't happen that often, as the situation rarely presented itself, and Yvan and I finished the season in fourth and fifth positions respectively. Fifth again! That was my hat-trick. Funnily enough, my ex-sparring partner Alain Menu won the championship, his first since 1997.

One of the best things to happen to me in a racing car during the first year of the new millennium was pissing my pants. Yes, you read that correctly, boys and girls. I said pissing my pants.

It happened during the Bathurst 1000. Yvan and I were asked to share a works car for the Holden Racing Team, and we agreed. Their regular drivers, Australian legends Craig Lowndes and Mark Skaife, were going to be in Holden's number one car, and we'd be in the number two car. Anyway, I remember arriving at the Phillip Island circuit near Melbourne to do a bit of testing, and after Mark Skaife had set the car up for us, Yvan jumped in to do a few laps. When he came into the pits and jumped out again, I could tell by the look on his face that he wasn't happy with his time.

'You're a bit off the pace, Yvan,' said the engineer.

'OK, 'ow much?' said Yvan, probably expecting it to be a few tenths.

'Four seconds,' said the engineer.

'What?' said Yvan in astonishment. 'But zis is not possible! 'Ow can I be four seconds off zee pace?'

'I don't know, but you are.'

Naturally, I couldn't wait to get in the car, and as I set off on my thirty laps I was fully expecting – and hoping – to put Yvan to shame.

'Come on, then,' I said to the engineer after coming in. 'How did I do?'

'Four seconds off.'

'What?!'

Yvan was standing next to the engineer, and the look of relief that swept across his face was almost palpable.

I remember having a word with myself in the toilet shortly after that. I actually stood there, looked in the mirror and shouted something along the lines of, *Come on, JP. Sort yourself out. Four seconds off? That's not good enough!* Seriously. I gave myself a proper kick up the arse.

To cut a long story short, Yvan and I managed to make ourselves reasonably competitive and after qualifying in nineteenth we were all set for the race. Because of a change in strategy, the team decided to double-stint me after the start, which meant I'd be doing eighty minutes instead of forty. This was due to the weather in the main part, but because I'd also be taking a shorter pitstop they figured I might gain some track position.

The car we were driving, a Holden VT Commodore, was a 5 litre V8 so there was an awful lot of downforce, and it was very, very physical. A real brute. Consequently, by the time I came in for my pitstop I was pretty dehydrated, and I must have drunk about a gallon of water.

A few laps into my second stint there was a shunt, and after cruising behind the safety car for a while, I realized that my bladder was about the size of a balloon. Now ingrained on my consciousness, all I could think about was having a pee, and a few minutes later I had to accept the fact that there was no way I could last another thirty minutes.

Because we were behind the safety car and not travelling very quickly, I thought, now's your chance JP, and just as we came on to the Conrod Straight, which is about 2 kilometres long, I gratefully began to empty my bladder. What a relief!

Then just as we were approaching The Chase, which is a three-turn sequence directly after the Conrod Straight, I suddenly heard the words, 'PIT, PIT, PIT' in my ear. Once that call comes through, there's a lot you have to do, such as putting the roll bars back, etc., and while I was doing all that I was still relieving myself! As I said, I must have consumed about a gallon. I was like a camel. An almost empty camel.

By the time I drove into the pit lane I was about done, but instead of the pee running through a little hole in the bottom of my bucket seat like it would have in the BTCC cars, before going into a tube and then being disposed of outside, it had collected at the bottom of the bucket seat, which, when I extracted myself, looked like a paddling pool of piss.

It was time for the driver change.

For those who aren't familiar with endurance racing, when a driver gets out for a driver change it's their job to help their replacement driver get ready for the off, and although it often looks a bit panicky, it's actually a choreographed routine, and each driver will know exactly what he or she is doing. My two final tasks before shutting the door on Yvan were to plug in his right shoulder strap before pulling the radio lead off his helmet and then into the seat. Just as I was doing this, I began to realize that Yvan had cottoned on to the fact that he was sitting in a bucket of piss. On closing the car door, he turned and looked at me. All I could see were his eyes, but they spoke a thousand words – the majority once again beginning with F, B or C. I don't know if it was out of sympathy, but, as Yvan sat there in a pool of my own piss, I began, metaphorically and literally, almost, to wet myself. What an angry French person he was.

After Yvan had finally squelched off, I made my way to the prat perch, which is where the engineers sit. From there I was due to talk to Yvan and advise him about any issues on the track or with the car. He already knew about one. When I plugged in he was already in mid-rant to the engineers and the first words I heard were, 'Ee iz a dirty English bastard! Ee 'az pisssed in ze car.' You betcha!

He still hasn't forgiven me.

At the end of 2000 there was a regulation change that basically killed off super touring cars in favour of similar cars to what we have today, which are called, simply, BTCC cars. Basically, these are much simpler and much cheaper cars, so a lot of the exotic materials we'd been using were ruled out, and the cars went from being saloons to hatchbacks. It was all designed to drive the costs down, as the budgets were getting ridiculous, and it was rumoured at the end of 2000 that the Ford Mondeo that Alain, Rickard Rydell and Anthony Reid had been driving cost upwards of £3 million. These days you can run a team with two cars and two drivers for an entire season for a lot less than that. Whether the £3 million is true or not I don't know, but even the suggestion was just jaw-dropping.

Whilst the budgets didn't compare to the bigger teams in F1 such as Ferrari, which even then were probably well over £100 million, they were starting to resemble those of some of the smaller teams like the Minardis of this world, and the sport simply wasn't big enough to sustain that kind of spending. At Willies we'd had qualifying engines that would do 50 km before being thrown in the bin and they cost upwards of about £100,000. The punter obviously can't see that, so if the budgets were brought down the punter would be none the wiser. It had to happen.

My first year with Vauxhall had been in the Vectra, and in 2001, which was the first year of BTC cars, we switched to the Astra Coupé. To be fair, Triple Eight produced a proper bit of kit for this season, and it was light years ahead of anything else. So much so that we ran at 85 per cent throttle much of the time just so it looked competitive.

By the end of round five of the 2001 season Yvan had developed a bit of an edge over me: he'd won six races to my three. The only other driver who'd had even had a look-in so far was Thommo, who was driving an Astra sponsored by Egg credit cards (but also run by Triple Eight), so you can see how dominant Vauxhall were.

In between rounds five and six I went for a test at Snetterton and, after trying out one or two things, I made some progress and fell in love with the car again. Before that, I'd been fighting it a bit, as the handling wasn't just perfect for me, and with the problem seemingly solved I arrived at Donington full of beans and confident that I could now catch Yvan and, with luck, take the title. Given how good the car was, and given the fact that all things were supposedly equal between Yvan and me, it was going to be my best opportunity yet.

Although nothing untoward had happened so far this season the rivalry between me and Yvan, and even between our own teams, was incredibly fierce, and that was obviously because it was deemed that one of us was going to win the championship. It created an atmosphere I'd never experienced before, and although it probably galvanized me to a certain extent it was also a bit off-putting. No quarter was being given either way, and the garage had become polarized. It was strange.

By the time we got to Snetterton for round eight, I was leading the championship by a couple of points, having won five of the eight races that had taken place between Silverstone and Knockhill, which was the round before. The rest had been shared between Yvan and Tommo, so it was still all Vauxhall.

By now they'd changed the format of the meetings, so instead of having two identical races we had a sprint race and then a longer race with a pitstop for a tyre change. The latter was called the feature race, and during the feature race in round eleven, at Silverstone, something happened that would basically catapult my and Yvan's teams from being at loggerheads to being completely at war with each other.

With a lap and a half to go Yvan was leading and I was lying second, when all of a sudden I started closing on him quite dramatically. *Brilliant*, I thought. *I'm reeling him in here!* On the last lap as we came out of Abbey towards Bridge Corner, I'd virtually caught up with Yvan, and something wasn't right. I had no idea what, but to be honest I didn't care, and all I could think about was the win.

As we turned into Priory, I went on the inside of Yvan, which, providing I accelerated out, would give me track position for the next left, which was the penultimate corner. On the way out of Priory our front wheels touched, at which point I accelerated out. Yvan, on the other hand, maintained a similar pace, so his problem was obviously still there. To cut a long story short, the collision broke Yvan's track rods, and I went on to win the race. He had problems, I took advantage, job's a good'n.

After literally hobbling over the line to finish the race, Yvan parked his car next to the pit wall, jumped over and with a look of hell about him ran into his garage and complained that, had we not collided, he'd have won the race. What utter bollocks! In reality what had happened was Yvan had run out of fuel, and that was the reason for me closing on him so rapidly. Had his car not been experiencing fuel starvation, he'd have been able to accelerate out of Priory, and the collision would never have taken place. End of. He knew this, his team knew this, but, unfortunately for me, none of them were willing to admit it. The original data traces are in the photo section of this book.

After that the stewards came to look at the damage on Yvan's car but I obviously had no idea what they were thinking. After that we all charged off to the stewards' office, where Yvan's team tried to get me disqualified for driving into him.

At the time nobody on my side of the garage knew about the fuel issue, so it wasn't mentioned, and with no evidence from my side at the time the stewards had to disqualify me, and Yvan was given the win.

Yvan may have had a look of hell about him when jumping over the pit wall but when I and my team emerged from the stewards' office, we were on first-name terms with Beelzebub himself, and I was determined to prove my innocence and get back the win.

Once the stewards have made a decision like this, you then have half an hour in which to appeal that decision with the clerk of the course, and normally what will happen is that the team will appeal on the driver's behalf. In this particular situation the team decided not to appeal the decision – surprise, surprise – which obviously didn't sit well with me. A few minutes after that, I started hearing whispers about the fuel so I immediately went to see the owners of the team, Roland Dane, Derek Warwick and Ian Harrison, to challenge them and see what they had to say.

'No, it's not true,' they said. 'Definitely not true.'

'It fucking well is,' said my engineer when I went back to the garage. 'I've seen the data.'

All the time the clock was obviously ticking, but without the data (the engineer couldn't let me have it, as he'd have got the sack) I was stuffed. In a fit of pique I went back to the owners to see if I could reason with them, but it was no good. Roland Dane wasn't my biggest fan and he basically told me to get back inside my box.

'It's not happening, Jason,' he said. 'We're not going to appeal it, and that's that.'

'Well I am,' I said.

'You're what?'

'I'm going to lodge an appeal. This is all wrong, Roland. I did not drive into the back of Yvan, and you know I didn't.'

The gloves were off now. I'd just accused the majority shareholder of my team of being in cahoots with his favourite driver. It had to be said, though, and I knew that if I didn't make a stand and just let them get away with it I'd regret it for the rest of my life.

Before Roland, Derek or Ian could say anything I left them and ran over to the clerk's office to start the proceedings. You have to pay for an appeal, by the way, and if you win you get your money back.

'I'm going to appeal it personally,' I said to them. 'I'll have the cheque for £500 with you as soon as I can.'

'You've got eight minutes Jason, and we need the cheque *and* the appeal.'

'But my chequebook is in my car and that's about ten minutes away. Can you not give me another couple of minutes?'

'No, Jason,' they said. 'There's a process.'

'Oh bollocks!'

I ran back to the team to tell them what had happened and ask them once more if they'd help me out, but it was to no avail.

'Tough shit,' said Roland. 'You're the one who wants to appeal, and if you can't submit the cheque and the paperwork in time that's your problem.'

I was literally about to tell Roland what I thought of him when Ian Harrison piped up.

'Do you know what, Roland,' he began. 'I think this is wrong. I'm going to give Jason a company cheque, and he can pay us back.'

'It's my business,' said Roland. 'You're not.'

Things were getting really, really nasty now. It wasn't good.

'All right then,' said Ian, raising his voice, 'I'm going to give him one of my own cheques.'

Unlike Roland, I always got on really well with Ian and Derek, and although he didn't say as much, I assume Ian must have known about the fuel thing otherwise he'd never have weighed in.

Within three minutes, and with about thirty seconds to spare, I'd lodged my appeal with the clerk of the course and was told a hearing would take place in a couple of hours. During that time Roland called a meeting with me and Ian Harrison and said that unless I pulled the appeal he'd fire me on the spot.

'What for?' I asked him.

'For bringing the team into disrepute.'

Oh, the irony!

The team didn't need me and my appeal to bring them into disrepute. In my eyes they were already there. My hands were tied, though, and as much as I wanted to tell Roland to go and fuck himself, I was mindful that if I did go ahead with the appeal and lost I'd probably leave the team with a reputation of being both a troublemaker and a bullshitter, and, barring a miracle, my career would be all but over. No, it was best to withdraw it.

Conversely, had I been successful with the appeal I'd have basically won the championship there and then, but on this occasion I decided to play it safe and see if I could finish the season on a high by winning the championship, in spite of Roland Dane. There were four races to go, and, providing I managed to avoid any provocations, I was in with a good chance.

From then on, as far as the team were concerned, there might as well have been a brick wall down the middle of the garage. The exchange of information and data (ahem) suddenly ceased, and there were lies and red herrings flying everywhere. I also had lawyers on standby and at races. It was just awful.

Throughout my time with Triple Eight Vauxhall all I ever did was try and challenge the number one driver within the parameters of what I had been told was acceptable, and the biggest mistake I made was not getting the details of this in writing. Although I can't prove it, what I suspect is that the reason for their behaviour was that Yvan had a clause in his contract that would have cost the team money had they not protected his number one status. There must have been something to make them act like they did, and the reason I'm so convinced is because the shenanigans continued after Silverstone, and the whole thing became a political quagmire. The press also got hold of it after Silverstone, and there were reports (not fed by me, incidentally) that I'd been gagged by the team and couldn't even shit on my own doorstep. To counter this, Yvan continued trying to convince people that I'd run into the back of him, and there was obviously no mention of him running out of fuel. Basically, it was a massive shitstorm.

On 7 October 2001 we arrived at Brands Hatch for the last round of the season, and, although it was now secondary to all the legal and political crap that had infested the team, and the sport, to a certain extent, I was ahead on points and on the verge of winning the championship.

In the pre-brief to qualifying, which takes place about an hour before, Derek Warwick came in and told me that the stewards wanted to see us now.

'What the hell for?' I asked.

'God only knows,' said Derek. 'We have to go, though.'

In five years as a professional racing driver I'd never known this to happen and the more I thought about it the more convinced I became that it would have something to do with the other side of the garage.

'What is it, gents?' I asked as we arrived. 'I've got qualifying in less than an hour.'

'It's come to our attention,' began the steward, 'that you have too many points on your licence, and as things stand we can't allow you to race.'

They were referring to my international race licence, by the way, on which – as with a normal licence – you can accrue points for indiscretions.

I was obviously conversant with the number of points on my licence and I was also conversant with the fact that two of them were under appeal.

'Ah, but you withdrew one of those appeals,' said the steward.

'So why are you telling me this now?' I asked. 'We've raced at Donington since then.'

'It's only just been brought to our attention,' he said.

'By who?' exclaimed Derek.

'By Roland Dane,' said the steward after a very pregnant pause.

I knew it!

'This is absolutely outrageous,' shouted Derek. 'I've never known anything like it.'

Roland Dane had obviously been looking for a reason to shaft me and, after eventually finding one – or at least a potential one – he'd launched the missile just when it would hurt the most.

After taking a minute or so to calm down, Derek and I spoke to the stewards and asked them if there was any way I could drive with these points under appeal, and they said that as long as we could get agreement from the majority of the other teams it would be OK, and within about five minutes Derek had done just that. Roland may have had the dosh, but Derek, who had spent ten years or so in Formula 1 and had also won Le Mans, had the respect of the entire paddock.

While all this was going on, I was still trying to get my head around the fact that my team owner was trying to screw me over. It was bonkers! Even with the agreement of the other teams, Roland was still trying to scupper things for me, and the atmosphere was toxic. There were lawyers from both sides at the race meeting, and while one side tried to find reasons to scupper things for me, the other attempted to bat them off. It was farcical.

In the sprint race I managed to take an early advantage by passing Yvan into Paddock Hill Bend and after a few incidents due to rain I ended up coming third behind Anthony Reid and Simon Graves with Yvan finishing fourth.

By the time the feature race was upon us, the weather had closed in, and it quickly became clear that we shouldn't have been out there. There were cars aquaplaning off everywhere, and had they abandoned the meeting, I'd have been crowned champion. As it was, I had a little bit more work to do, and after sitting myself just behind Yvan I was looking good. All I had to do was stay on the track.

Unfortunately, this was easier said than done, and just as I came around Surtees corner on about lap thirty I aquaplaned, left the circuit and nudged the fence. Fortunately, I managed to get going again but because I'd lost so many places it looked like I'd handed the title to Yvan. Providing he too could stay on the track, of course

A couple of laps later, Yvan aquaplaned off, as I had, and did the same again a couple of laps later. He managed to maintain his position, though, so the championship was still his. Then, on lap thirty-six, Yvan's and Roland's luck finally ran out. After a fire broke out in the engine bay as the oil cooler had been damaged when he had aquaplaned off the road twice where I had, Yvan had to retire, giving me the championship.

Talk about a bitter-sweet experience. I honestly didn't know whether to laugh or cry.

After the presentation ceremony I was called top see Roland Dane, and instead of congratulating me he sacked me on the spot. I tried reasoning with him, but he was having none of it. His pram was full of toys, and he was in a throwing mood.

'You'll never drive for this team again, Plato,' he said. Sorry, snarled.

I haven't seen Roland Dane since then and am pleased to say that he now resides in Australia. Derek and Ian, on the other hand, are good mates of mine, and I have a lot of time for both.

At the end of the day we're all guilty of occasionally running off to the stewards and shouting the odds about this, that or the other, and I dare say that most of us, if we were being honest, have been known to bend the truth slightly. It's all part of the process, and as competitive buggers it's what makes us who we are. What isn't part of the process, though, and what is alien to the way most of us behave, is making up a load of bullshit and sticking with it. How involved Yvan was with all that I have no idea, but he must have known it was happening. He refused to shake my hand on the podium at Silverstone, in full view of the TV cameras, when he *knew* the reason contact was made and he lost the win to me was because he had effectively run out of fuel. Not a good moment in the history of YM (see pic of YM not shaking hands).

Even though it was a bad experience, I took a lot away from that season, not least a championship, and I'm the first to admit that my own behaviour wasn't what you'd call exemplary. I was on the defensive, however, and although I fought hard I also fought fairly.

The most expensive lesson I learned was that motorsport can get very nasty at times, and on leaving Brands Hatch I was ready for a break. I was a champion, yet I felt nothing like one. That wasn't right.

I'm a JCB – Drive Me!

Despite being regretful about some of the more unfortunate aspects of my sport, such as what I'd experienced the previous season, I still felt privileged to be a part of it, and my two years at Triple Eight Vauxhall had, on the whole, actually been quite positive, in spite of the final outcome. Yes, I know it's difficult to believe after what you've just read, but it's the truth. Everyone worked really hard, and, as I pointed out to Roland about a minute before he sacked me, we'd just finished first and second in the championship and had left all the other teams standing.

Also, as with Alain, I'd had to play catch-up more than once with Yvan, and that had done me the power of good. The 2001 season in particular, or at least the early part of it, had been especially beneficial, and I'd spent a lot of time with Derek trying to put things right. He's a fantastic mentor and he played a big part in me turning things around and coming back at Yvan. It's difficult to put a price on things like that, so, as horrible as the latter half of the 2001 season undoubtedly was in terms of politics and bad feeling, it forced me to remember the positives and, at some of my lower points just after the season ended, cling on to them for dear life.

I was about to say that at some point after the season had ended I decided to look into giving NASCAR a go, but it was actually decided for me, really, as I didn't have a drive for 2002. That felt bloody weird. I was the best in my particular field and at the height of my powers, yet I was unemployed.

After putting out a few feelers I ended up doing a three-year deal with Rockingham racetrack in Corby, who were launching a new championship called ASCAR. It was basically the same as NASCAR except not quite as quick so it sounded like it could be a good way in. The races took place at either Rockingham or the EuroSpeedway in Lausitz, Germany, and the idea was that, providing the series did well, I'd help to launch it in the States, and in return they'd help to catapult me into NASCAR. On paper it sounded great, so by the start of the ASCAR season, which began in early May, so about a month after the BTCC, I was back to my old ebullient self. You can't keep a good man down!

At the press day, one of the first things I saw when I arrived at Rockingham was one of the posters they'd produced to promote the series, and they looked terrific. My name and ugly mug were emblazoned across it, and that added to my excitement.

My team was called Xcel Sport, and the man behind the team was the former BTCC driver John Bintcliffe. Once the press had arrived, it was suggested that the previous ASCAR Champion, John Mickel, take me out in one of the cars, and, of course, I said yes. At this point I'd never been around an oval before and had never driven a stock car, so although I agreed, I was a little bit apprehensive.

After a couple of laps John started picking up the pace a bit to the point where I felt uncomfortable.

'John, mate,' I said. 'Just calm it down a bit, would you?'

I'm a terrible passenger at the best of times but I really wasn't enjoying the experience. Half a lap later, John lost control of the car, and we ended up hitting the wall – BANG!

It was by far the biggest shunt I'd ever had, and I was lucky to be alive. Or at least that's how it felt.

In my first two races in ASCAR I came nowhere. I just couldn't get my car right. Whether this was indicative of the sport itself as opposed to just the car I'm not sure but in the sixteen races I entered I only felt comfortable in a stock car once and that was right at the end of a race. They feel like shit until you get the car up to its optimum speed, which is easier said than done, and then after that everything should fit into place. There's obviously a lot more to it than that, but you get my drift.

Also, about a third of the way through the season, the cheques stopped coming, and by the middle of the season we were going through litigation. They did pay in the end, but it took about a year to get it. It was another shitstorm, basically.

After the season finished in October, I took some time to breathe and wondered what the hell I was going to do next. The last two years had been a strange period and while it hadn't all been doom and gloom exactly (it had actually yielded a BTCC championship and a third position in ASCAR, which wasn't bad), I'd felt quite unsettled throughout and was in need of a little bit of stability.

In November, James Matthews, one of my mates, an ex-racing driver, suggested that I go to St Barts in the Caribbean for a few weeks over the winter with him and a few other mates. I'd heard from another friend that St Barts over New Year was something else, so I called James back and snapped his hand off. If I was going to plot my future and find myself some stability, I might as well do it in the French West Indies.

While I was over there, I began to hatch a plan based

around a whisper I'd heard about SEAT wanting to compete in the European Touring Car Championship and also wanting to start a new one-make series in the UK called the SEAT Cupra Championship. I'd actually made contact with SEAT about a week before leaving for St Barts and while I was over there we carried on talking.

Without wanting to bore you with all the details, their new one-make championship was going to be part of a new television series about bringing through new drivers, and my idea was that whoever won that series would partner me in the 2004 European Touring Car Championship. As with driving a stock car, there was obviously a bit more to it, but by the time I arrived back from St Barts in January I'd received a verbal agreement from SEAT, so we were back in business.

One of the first things I did after discovering that I'd be driving in the European Touring Car Championship the following year, and on a fairly decent whack, was to move to Monaco. I'd been back there a few times after the initial trip with Tommo and the lads and had been considering a move for some time.

In order to try and offset some of the ongoing costs of such a move – we're talking rent mainly, which, as I'm sure you can imagine, can be quite pricey in the Principality – I approached SEAT with yet another one of my brilliant ideas.

'How about this for a story,' I began. 'Not only does the winner of the SEAT Cupra Championship become my teammate in the ETCC but they also come to live with me for a year at my pad in Monaco!'

'Oh, wow, JP,' they cooed enthusiastically. 'That's a great plan.'

That was 80 per cent of my rent paid for. Bingo!

If truth be known, I was under the impression that who-ever became my teammate would soon become tired of paying six or seven quid for a cup of coffee, and the whole flatshare thing would peter out after a few weeks – but not the rent contribution, which would be written into the contract.

Yes, I know it's a bit cheeky. He who dares, though.

The television show that accompanied the SEAT Cup was called *Racing Rivals*, which aired on ITV and which I presented alongside Nell McAndrew.

Halfway through 2003, SEAT decided that they were no longer interested in competing in the ETCC and instead would be competing in the BTCC. This was all good and well, but in the meantime I'd moved to Monaco, believing I was going to be pan-European and would have to remain there for a number of years. Oh well. It was only ten week-ends a year, and at least it would give me a chance to see Mum and Dad and my mates.

The eventual winner of the SEAT Cupra Championship was Rob Huff, so not only did he become my flatmate in Monaco for a year but he also became my teammate for the 2004 BTCC. He ended up finishing seventh in the championship – a good effort for a rookie – and I finished third behind my old pal Tommo, who came first, clinching his second BTCC, and, would you believe it, Yvan Muller, who only lost out to Tommy by a point. What a shame. They were both driving a Vauxhall, which was still the car to have, but third and seventh in a debut year was encouraging for a manufacturer, and the guys at SEAT were happy chappies.

Incidentally, despite finishing third in the championship, I won seven races, more than any other driver, and in my eyes that's what really counts. What made the end of the championship especially sweet, however, was hassling Yvan in the final race at Donington and enabling Tommo to get the fastest lap and that precious final point. It was proper aggro out there, and when I got out of the car knowing that James had won the championship and Yvan had lost, I gave Yvan the finger. There was obviously still a hangover from 2001. A big hangover.

What can I tell you about living in Monaco? Well, the first year especially was an absolute hoot, and one of the highlights was when the Grand Prix came to town. My apartment was on the start/finish straight and overlooked the swimming pool and the port, so you can imagine what kind of view I had. The noise, though, was just incredible, and I can remember being woken during first practice and thinking, *What the hell's that?*

In years two, three and four I ended up renting out my apartment for Grand Prix weekend, as you could almost recoup your entire annual rent in three days. My rent, incidentally, was about £65,000 a year, so with my SEAT rent initiative only lasting a year I thought it would be a good idea. How bonkers is that, though?

Incidentally, one of the reasons I'd been so relaxed about living abroad was that I had my own plane and so, despite my location, I had absolute freedom and could get from Monaco to Oxford door to door more quickly than I could from Newcastle to London by car.

I'd learned to fly at the end of 1998 and in order to get my licence I'd had to go to a flying school in Florida for a couple of weeks. They taught both the British and the European syllabuses. The flying school was based at Orlando Melbourne International Airport, which is near Daytona Beach, so after holing myself up in an apartment nearby I revised my arse off and ended up completing the course in just eleven days. Because the weather was so good I managed to fly every day, and it was a fabulous experience.

While I was picking up some aviation magazines for the course I saw an advert for a Rockwell Commander four-seater. Although I'd never heard of it before, it looked fab, and the strapline on the advert was 'The Mercedes of the Sky'. That'll do me, I thought. I'm going to have one of them.

After asking around at the flying school, I got some excellent feedback about the Commander and managed to find one for sale over in California. After a few rounds of negotiations, I and the owner settled on a price, and I told them that once I'd returned to the UK, providing everything was in order at their end and checked out, I'd push the button on the cash.

Anyway, I ended up buying this plane, so once it had all gone through I set about finding somebody to fly it over. I ended up finding an American/German lady called Margaret, who was a professional ferry pilot, and she was asking buttons for the job – about £1,500 plus expenses. I couldn't believe it. Flying over Greenland in the dead of winter in a four-seater, single-engined plane weighing just 2,000 pounds? I'd want at least a million for that! Once it had been arranged, she called me up and asked me if I'd like to come along for the ride.

'No thank you very much indeed, Margaret,' I said, firmly but politely.

In hindsight I wish I had done, as it was perfect weather and she had a great flight. It was all a bit new, though. Small steps and all that.

Margaret ended up landing the plane at Newcastle, which is where I met her, and after I jumped in she flew us down to Oxford before I jumped out again. Margaret then flew the plane over to Guernsey, where it was swapped from the American register to the British register (it's a right old cuf-fuffle!), and once I'd taken another quick course (I won't bore you with it but I wasn't licensed to fly that particular plane and needed to pass a conversion course first) the plane was flown back to Oxford, where I was finally free to fly. Plato let loose in the skies! Just before I moved to Monaco I sold the Rockwell Commander and bought a Malibu Mirage, which is a pressurized, twin-turbo, single-engined six-seater. Perfect for commuting back and forth from the South of France.

It used to take me about three hours and fifteen minutes to get from Oxford to Cannes, and after putting the code into the electric gate I'd be in my car and then back in my apartment in another thirty minutes. Door to door, it was quicker than going commercial and obviously a hell of a lot more fun. That said, when flying a plane, I'm in work mode, as there's so much to remember, but it's still a privilege.

Apart from the sheer pleasure of being able to fly a plane, the most attractive aspect was undoubtedly the freedom it gave me, and right from the get-go I took full advantage. One weekend, this was towards the end of my tenure in Monaco, I decided to go to Florence for the weekend and just upped sticks and went. I didn't have to think about it. I just chucked a few things in a bag, jumped in my car and away I went. OK, I still had to sort out the flight path, fly the plane and find the hotel, but come on, it's hardly a chore!

Another time, I and a few mates went down to the San Marino Grand Prix to watch my mate Ralph Firman race for Jordan. The team sent a car for us, and, after landing the plane at Forlì Airport, I remember bombing down the autostrada to the Autodromo Enzo e Dino Ferrari, think-ing, *How the hell did I end up here?* It was crazy, but why not?

Sometimes I'd have eight or nine free days on the trot in Monaco when I didn't have to do anything, so what else could I do but go and have some fun? Whether that meant jumping in the plane with some mates and going for a weekend some-where or just hanging around Monaco getting pissed and raising some hell, the world was basically my oyster.

In 2002 I sold the Commander, as I've said, and bought a Piper PA-46, which, because it was pressurized, allowed me to fly above the weather in controlled airspace. I had radar and everything, so it was a proper piece of kit, and it was fast. With the Commander I couldn't go above 11,000 ft without an oxy-gen mask on, and it wasn't turbo-charged. I could sit at 25,000 ft in the PA-46 and could get up to about 260 mph in clean air and in the descent with a tail wind was regularly over 400 mph ground speed. I ended up doing another conversion course after this arrived that allowed me to fly anywhere in the world in controlled airspace. I was well into it.

Thank God I can't get into trouble for this, but you remember I said that when piloting a plane I'm in work mode? Well, that isn't strictly true. I had a few modifications made to the PA-46 and I was able to plug a DVD player into my multifunction screen, and after patching through my headphones, I'd lie back and watch a movie. The plane had full autopilot, and sometimes I'd remove the screen and go back and stretch my legs out for forty minutes while the computer took care of business. I could still hear air traffic control, so if they wanted to change my route it wasn't a problem. I just made it a bit more comfortable.

Somebody once asked me what it was like living in Monaco, and after mulling it over for a few minutes I came up with the example that it was a bit like living in a posh prison. People would spend days on end there, and basically we were all bored witless. You might make a couple of telephone calls in the morning but after that you were done for the day, and those days needed filling somehow. Talk about a First World problem.

What makes it worse – or better, depending on your age and situation – is that Monaco's very small, so you end up getting to know people pretty quickly, and when I was in residence there were an awful lot of single blokes who had a lot of money, a lot of time on their hands and an ability to imbibe.

This may sound ridiculous, but it's actually illegal to get drunk in Monaco. Technically, at least. The Grand Prix is obviously an exception, as they'd need cells the size of football pitches! Consequently, if you do step out of line while enjoying some refreshment you'll be in the slammer before you know it, and I myself have been a guest of the constabulary there on more than one occasion. Does that surprise you? No, I thought not.

The first time involved a lot of alcohol – obviously – and a JCB, and it's one of those stories that, if I ever am blessed with grandchildren, will be one of the first they come and ask me about. 'Grandad, tell us about the time you were arrested and put in prison for stealing a JCB while inebriated.' Pass me a Werther's Original. It warms your heart.

I forget when it happened exactly, but there'd been some construction going on between the start/finish straight and the swimming pool complex which had lasted months, and as a result there were JCBs and the like everywhere. Because it's Monaco nobody bothers taking the keys out of things like construction vehicles, and after coming out of a boozer one night with a few friends I spotted one of these JCBs, and it might as well have had a sticker on it saying *drive me!* The lure was just incredible.

'I'll tell you what, lads,' I announced. 'I'm taking that for a spin.'

Before anyone could advise me against this course of action, although I doubt that they would have, I ran across the road, opened the door and jumped into the cab. The closest I'd ever come to driving a JCB was playing with a Tonka toy as a child and, inebriation notwithstanding, I was thrilled to effing bits.

'Watch this, lads,' I shouted. 'I'm going to take her for a quick spin. Bob the Builder, that's me!'

After firing up the engine, I got her into gear, checked my mirrors – obviously – and then set off in the direction of absolutely anywhere. I was fulfilling a dream!

After I'd travelled about five yards, three police cars suddenly appeared out of nowhere, and within literally five seconds flat I was in the back of one and on my way to what I assumed would be the nick. Can we arrest him? Yes we can!

The rule in Monaco is that as long as you're a resident there the police will treat you well, unless you've done something serious. Unfortunately, I didn't have my residency card with me at the time, and so the initial exchanges between the rozzers and me were less than friendly. Fortunately, after doing some checks, they were satisfied that I was telling the truth and from then on they were lovely. I got my own cell, a blanket and even a croissant and coffee in the morning. Because of the seriousness of the crime – apparently moving a JCB without a licence and while under the influence *is* considered to be quite serious in Monaco (and I daresay elsewhere) – I had to stay there for the night, and before I left I received a bill for 120 euros. That was for my stay, and although I don't want to trivialize the seriousness of what I did, it represents fantastic value for money. The police station was also about 150 yards from my apartment, so I was back home within a couple of minutes. Tip top.

My second visit to the cells happened not long after that, and was a simple case of me being drunk and a bit silly. The following morning, after breakfast, you're then breathalysed and unless the reading is zero they won't release you. On this occasion I wasn't driving (either a car or a JCB) and, after offering this information to the desk sergeant, and the fact that I lived just a stone's throw away, I was told that it didn't make a blind bit of difference. 'Until it's zero, you're not going anywhere.'

One morning, after about two years of this, I woke up and said to myself, *Enough, JP*. As well as my liver taking a hammering, I was turning down work in the UK because of the restrictions in days you are allowed back in the UK, and I'd also lost touch with a lot of my mates. They'd all been over a couple of times, but the novelty had soon worn off, and in truth that's exactly what I'd become to my friends and family – a novelty. Nobody who I cared for lived the same life I did – and certainly not in Monaco – and I was starting to become lonely and even a bit down from time to time. It was a very vacuous existence.

The friends I'd made in Monaco were just social friends really – divorced blokes mainly – and to be honest I didn't have anybody there full-time who I could have a meaningful chat with. It's all banter when you're out and about, and as much as I enjoyed all that – and still do, within reason – I needed something real to balance it out.

As soon as I'd had this road to Damascus moment – or in

this particular case a *road back to Oxford* moment – I wanted to do something about it. I'm a doer, at the end of the day, and if an idea comes to me that I like, I want it done now. Unfortunately, it only took me a few minutes to realize that simply packing up, leaving my apartment and flying myself back to Blighty wasn't going to be an option. At least not immediately. For a start, I was tied into my lease for at least another twelve or eighteen months, and because I was a tax exile I couldn't just up sticks and leave. All of the financial tools you put in place to live somewhere like Monaco unravel if you come back early, and you get landed with a massive tax bill. Nope, I'd just have to sit it out.

Again, I know this is very much a First World problem, but now that I'd handed in my resignation at the 'Battering your liver half to death and stealing JCBs with a load of single rich blokes' club, I didn't want to go out, and I became a bit of a recluse. Had I nipped out even for a quick snifter I'd have seen a drinking buddy or six and would have ended up getting swept away. I guarantee it.

It was also a bit restrictive living in an apartment when you couldn't even put a satellite dish up. It was against the law. It was also quite restrictive in that I had people living above, below and to the side of me, and as somebody who enjoys playing their music at number eleven I was about as popular as a fart in a space suit. That really used to get on my tits.

The only neighbour who I got on well with down there was the legendary former F1 and Le Mans driver Roy Salvadori, who lived above me. He came down to complain about the noise one day, and after I'd charmed him, we got chatting. To be honest, I didn't recognize him at first, and he certainly didn't recognize me. It didn't take long for it all to come out, though, and after that we became mates. Well, friendly neighbours. Roy was born in 1922, so he had a few years on me. He was a real gent, and every so often I'd invite him down for supper or vice versa. In his ten-year career in F1 he'd raced for Ferrari, Connaught, Maserati, BRM, Vanwall, Cooper, Aston Martin and Lola and he'd won Le Mans. Needless to say, he had one or two tales to tell, and, as you'd expect, I was a grateful and willing audience. He was probably the first driver I'd ever met who'd driven against the likes of Fangio and Stirling Moss (apart from Stirling Moss), and that was a big thrill.

Funnily enough, Roy was the person who eventually solved my satellite dish problem. The authorities were really hot on this, and with the police station, or my home from home, as I called it, just 150 yards away and me being on first-name terms with the desk sergeant, I had to be extra careful. They'd literally turn up on your doorstep, order you to take it down and then whack you with a massive fine, and I couldn't be doing with the hassle.

One day, while having supper at Roy's, I noticed he had a satellite dish on his balcony and when I first saw it I almost choked. Despite the Italian name, Roy was born in England and he spoke, dressed and looked like a duke.

'What the hell's that, Roy?' I asked, pointing to the balcony.

'Oh, that. It's my satellite dish.'

'You mean the satellite dish you're not supposed to have?'

'That's the one. Come and have a look.'

Roy had worked out that if you purchased a load of plastic plants you could easily disguise a satellite dish without compromising the signal, and he'd had it for years. We had to be quite covert, but Roy gave me the details of somebody who could supply and install it on the QT, and I went and purchased the plants. Job's a good'n.

Stelios from EasyJet had the whole of the top floor in my block, and we also had the odd meet. I didn't have as much in common with him as I did with Roy, but he was an interesting fella and obviously very successful.

One of the most interesting people I met in Monaco was Gildo Pallanca Pastor, who, in 1984, had started a car company called Venturi. He'd inherited almost $4 billion from his old man a few years earlier so he was quite comfortably off, and as part of a feature for *Fifth Gear*, which I'll come on to in a bit, I was asked to go and interview him about a tiny new electric car they were launching.

To spice things up a bit, the producers of *Fifth Gear* decided to get a celebrity to try out the car and managed to get none other than Roger Moore. I was so excited! He'd lived in Monaco for decades, and although I'd seen him about here and there, we'd never been introduced – probably because when I was on my way out he was going to bed!

I'll never forget meeting him. We'd arranged to meet the great man at a restaurant somewhere, and the closer it got to the time we'd arranged the more nervous I became. Actually, nervous isn't the right word. I was excited. It was Roger Moore for God's sake!

Suddenly, at exactly the right time, I saw a tall chap with brown hair and glasses literally glide into view. He was wearing salmon-pink slacks, a dark-blue blazer with brass buttons, suede shoes and an open-necked shirt that was so white you could have lit a dark room with it. Man, he was cool.

After I'd managed to attract his attention, he and the woman he was with, who I assumed to be his wife, floated our way.

'Gentlemen,' he said, kicking off the proceedings. 'Allow me to present my beautiful wife, Kiki.'

Wow! He was as smooth as a cashmere codpiece. I can be

a bit of a charmer when I try, but this bloke was in a different league.

'My name's Roger Moore, by the way,' he said, holding out his hand. 'How do you do.'

I just stood there open-mouthed.

'Erm, I'm Jason Plato,' I said, finally.

'Plato! Any relation?'

'I very much doubt it, don't you?'

What a lovely, lovely guy. For the next two hours or so I drove him around Monaco, and he drove me, and all the while we chatted away about everything, but mainly Bond films. The first thing I said to Roger when he asked me about the car was, 'It goes like stink. Right up your street.' Why I thought that would be a good opening line I have absolutely no idea, but Roger just said, 'Really, Jason? How very interesting.'

Now he was on my radar I started seeing Roger all over the place, and now that we were mates – oh aye – I always ran up to him and tried not to say something embarrassing like, 'goes like stink'. What a frigging legend though. He was so Monaco!

To keep fit in Monaco I used to go for long walks. I've never been keen on all that running and jumping up and down on the spot cobblers, and in Monaco you've got a lot of hills, which is good, and one or two nice views. One day I decided to take a stroll up the hill towards Casino Square. When you get up the first bank on the way to Casino Square there's a row of shops – you know, Versace and Gucci etc. – and on this particular afternoon there was an enormous Rolls-Royce parked outside one of them. Being in the trade, I decided to take a quick look at the Roller, and just as I got to it the door to one of these shops opened and a line of gentlemen flounced out carrying boxes. The driver of the Rolls, who was obviously the chauffeur, then jumped out, opened the boot and started taking the boxes from the men and trying to squeeze them in. There must have been at least fifty in all shapes and sizes, so whoever was in there was obviously feeling quite flush. Two minutes later, Elton John walked out with a few of the little blokes following him, and as he walked up to the car I thought to myself, this place is just ridiculous! It's one weird, weird town.

The reason you get so many famous people in Monaco, apart from the weather and the obvious tax benefits, is because nobody gives a damn really, so you can go about your business without getting mobbed or bothered. Most of the Formula 1 drivers who were resident there when I was, such as DC (David Coulthard), Johnny Herbert and Jenson Button, were hardly ever there, and in the four years I lived in Monaco I hardly ever saw them.

I was only ill once in Monaco, and that was towards the end of what I was then calling my sentence. I'd been away to San Tropez swimming for the weekend, as you do, and on my way back I suddenly started getting earache like you can't imagine. I've had a perforated eardrum for donkey's years, and if I ever get water behind it it's agony, and that's exactly what had happened. Unfortunately, though, this became infected after a while, and the pain went from being a little bit horrible to downright unbearable.

Because I'd never been ill down there I had no idea what to do, so I rang up a couple of my boozy friends and asked.

'Have you got a doctor?' one enquired.

'Nope. Never needed one.'

After having a quick conflab with somebody at their end, my friend advised me to go to the Princess Grace Hospital on Avenue Pasteur. Quick as a flash, or as quick as I was able, I dashed up there, clutching my residency card, and within ten minutes I was seen by a doctor. After having a quick look, he confirmed that the ear had become infected and went off to get some pills. When he came back, he explained that they didn't have the ones I needed in stock at the hospital but if I'd like to wait a moment he'd call the pharmacist in town.

'He's been closed about an hour, but I'll ask him to go back and open up.'

'Really?'

It was rush hour by this time, and although the pharmacist could get back in about five minutes, he could only stay for another five, so basically I had ten minutes to get down there.

'I'll never do it,' I said. 'It's rush hour.'

'Hold on a moment,' said the doc, and with that he ran outside and called over one of the gendarmes who wear the white gloves.

'Look,' he said. 'This man needs to get to the pharmacy within ten minutes. If he goes along the one-way system he'll never make it. Would you be able to shut Avenue Pasteur for a few minutes and allow him to get down there?'

I almost interrupted the doctor when he was talking to say, 'You can't do that!', but once he'd finished talking the gendarme said, 'Sure, no problem.' I followed the gendarme out of the hospital, and he got on his motorbike and said, 'OK, follow me.' I was driving a BMW Z4 at the time, and sure enough he actually drove on to a three-lane road and stopped the bloody traffic just so I could get to a chemist.

How's that for bloody mental?

If you were to ask me what the most excruciatingly embarrassing moment was during my Monaco years you'd probably expect me to run off a tale about losing my trousers on La Rascasse or goosing Roger Moore. Nah, nothing so trivial.

In fact, there's only one possible contender for this particular accolade, and it actually took place just outside Bristol. This is a proper horror story.

SEAT had a corporate box at the Millennium Stadium in Cardiff and a few weeks before the 2004 FA Cup final they asked me if I'd fly over and press the flesh. They had a load of dealers going, so it made sense to get a driver along, and I was happy to oblige.

After flying into Oxford from Cannes I had to then get myself to Cardiff, so after taking a quick break I carried on flying. I don't consider myself to be a genius, nor am I a dunce, yet on that particular day I would have given the world's foremost village idiots a run for their money as at no point did I consider that the airport closest to the Millennium Stadium might just be a tad busy on Cup final day. With about half an hour to go and while flying at 3,000 ft and 220 mph I called Cardiff Airport on the radio and I said, as you always do in these situations, 'Inbound to land.'

'Nope, sorry,' came the immediate reply. 'We're full. Forbidden to land.'

'No, no, you don't understand,' I said. 'I've got to be at the Millennium Stadium, otherwise I'll get my balls chopped off.' (Dramatic, but worth a go.)

'You do realize it's Cup final day,' said the controller. 'We're absolutely full to bursting.'

'Look, mate,' I said, turning on the old Plato charm. 'I've come all the way over from Monaco for this. Are you sure there's nothing you can do? I'm only a little plane, stick me on the grass somewhere! You'd be getting me out of a massive hole.'

Why I told him I'd come all the way from Monaco I don't

know, but I don't think it endeared me to him. It was yet another momentary lapse of reason.

'I've told you, we're full,' he said. 'Forbidden to land.'

Bollocks!

I didn't want to go to Bristol International Airport, as it would have taken me for ever, so in the end I plumped for Filton Airport, which is north of Bristol. Fortunately, they weren't quite so busy, and after thanking them very much indeed I asked them if they could arrange for an urgent taxi to meet me there when I landed.

'Where are you going?' asked the controller.

'The Millennium Stadium,' I replied.

'You are joking, aren't you. Today?!'

'Look, please, mate, I really am in the shit here.'

'OK,' he said. 'I'll see what I can do.'

When I was about 10 miles away, the ATC controller at Filton got on the radio and said he'd managed to find me a cab.

'You're going to have to share, though,' he said. 'And you're coughing the bill.'

'Don't care, mate. That's wonderful. Thank you very much indeed!'

I was going to be late. Big-style late. But at least I'd sorted out some transport.

The moment I got out of the plane, I was on the phone to SEAT.

'Look,' I said. 'I'm so sorry. It's been a nightmare this end, but I'm literally just getting in a cab now and I should be there in about an hour.'

As the conversation went on between me and the boss from SEAT, I got in the cab and mouthed a quick apology to the driver and a thank you to the two people in the back, who I assumed were man and wife.

When I finally got off the phone I caught my breath for a second and then decided to say hello to my fellow passengers. It was going to be an hour at least, so I thought we might as well break bread. The woman, who was sitting behind the driver, was quite obviously pregnant, and so after saying my hellos I thought I'd use her imminent arrival as a conversation starter. That should keep us going for a while.

'When's it due,' I enquired merrily, gazing at her and then the bump.

Instead of receiving an answer to my question like, 'Any day now', it was met with a deathly silence. I immediately knew what had happened but unfortunately there was nowhere to hide.

'She's not pregnant,' snarled the husband.

I instinctively looked away from the rear of the car in horror and the first thing I saw was the taxi driver silently wetting himself laughing. As somebody who loves life, I'm seldom in a position where I'd like to exchange it for something else but at that very moment in time I longed for oblivion.

We were in the taxi for over an hour and a half, and after the husband had advised me that his amply proportioned spouse was not with child, not a single word was spoken. Sorry, I tell I lie. After crossing the Severn Bridge into Wales, I felt I just had to try and apologize, but after leaning around and beginning to speak I was immediately cut short by the husband. He'd leaned forward this time, and I honestly thought he was going to crack me one.

'Shut the fuck up,' he growled.

Once again, the taxi driver was silently pissing himself, and this did nothing to improve the atmosphere.

When we finally arrived at the Millennium Stadium, Jack and Jill, as I'd silently christened them, were let out first, and what made me aware of their departure, apart from them opening their doors, was that the taxi seemed to rise a few inches. A second or so later they slammed the doors shut, and as I breathed a gargantuan sigh of relief the taxi driver proceeded to howl like a banshee. I think I arrived just before half-time, and although I was obviously very late, it had given me a cracking story, and a good time was had by all.

Bugger Off Plato, I'm Not Interested!

One of the other reasons for me wanting to relocate back to the UK was because I'd met somebody who I was more than a bit keen on.

I forget when exactly, but at some point during my twenties I'd made a conscious decision not to get tied down, not that I ever had been. I was having far too much fun as a single bloke and generally I found it quite an easy rule to stick to. Suffice to say that if somebody started getting serious they would be dropped quickly but kindly.

One of the reasons I made this decision and stuck to it, apart from wanting to have fun, was that if one day I ever did decide to get married I'd like it to last and that would have a much better chance of happening if I'd sown all of my wild oats. Whether I actually believed that or not I couldn't tell you but I'd convinced myself that that was the case. My career had also started quite late in life, and in the early days I hadn't been in a position to have that much fun – although I did try. Having a few quid, driving cars quickly for a living and having a pad in Monaco, not to mention your own aeroplane, was what a lot of blokes dreamed of, so I was happy living that dream. Or was I?

I'd first met the woman in question at a PR event for SEAT in the UK. We were still filming *Racing Rivals* at the time, and she was on a university placement with SEAT as a press assistant. Her name was Sophie; she was about 5 feet

5 inches tall, had long dark hair, olive skin and was very, very attractive. She was also fifteen years younger than I was, but because I usually acted like somebody much younger and had quite a youthful outlook on life, it was actually perfect. When I first clapped eyes on Sophie my immediate thought was, *I want to get to know you.* Not just physically, by the way. Give me some credit! I was a new man.

Well, almost.

The venue of that first meeting was Thruxton. She was on a PR shoot, and I was filming *Racing Rivals*, and one evening, while everyone was sitting around having a few libations, Sophie just walked in. She was the last to arrive from SEAT, and from the moment she sat down I couldn't, and wouldn't, take my eyes off her.

Sophie later told me that she could feel me staring at her immediately after walking in, and every time she looked over, which was often, I gave her a great big grin. I don't remember any of that. I just remember being a bit smitten.

By the end of the night the people who were left standing were me, Sophie and Jean Kelly, the PR manager for SEAT UK. We were all telling stories while drinking gin and tonics and there was definitely a mutual attraction between me and Sophie. How could I tell? Well, I'd been chatting to her all evening, and at no point had she said to me, 'Bugger off Plato, I'm not interested,' which happens to the best of us from time to time. That was good enough for me. She was obviously smitten too – or at least I hoped she was.

The following evening there was a big party. I forget what it signified, but it could have been the wrap party for *Racing Rivals*. Anyway, Sophie had had to go and see her parents for a while, as it was their wedding anniversary, and by the time she got back we were all buzzing. Apparently, the first

thing I did when Sophie arrived at the party was to persuade her to stand on her head and inhale vodka through
her nose. Again, I'm afraid I don't remember this, but in my
defence, as well as me being three sheets to the wind, nobody
made her do it!

Something I've forgotten to mention is that, for a few
weeks before that, I'd been having a bit of fun with a young
lady, who worked for a marketing agency that was engaged
by SEAT, and she'd been down at Thruxton too. Consequently, when I started making a beeline for Sophie she
wasn't too happy, and while I was busy pursuing Sophie
and trying to make her ingest spirits from an upside-down
position, this girl was giving Sophie some pretty evil looks.
It had all the makings of something you'd see in a really
bad soap opera, and the more infatuated I became the
angrier this girl became. I think Sophie was just amused
by it all.

After asking Sophie do the vodka thing – allegedly – I
thought the next natural step was to get her telephone number, but with prying eyes everywhere, how? It was just a huge
room, so to anybody looking on it would be pretty obvious
what was happening. You have to remember I'd had a few
jars by this point, so instead of biding my time and attempting to be circumspect, which was the original plan, I decided
to throw caution to the wind and take action. Pretty drastic
action, as it goes.

About half an hour later, I saw Sophie go to the toilet and,
after leaving it a minute, I followed her in, as you do.

'Bloody hell,' she said. 'What are you doing in here?' She
was half smiling, so I could tell she liked me. Anyone else
would have screamed, kicked me in the balls and called for
the police.

'Give us your number, will you?' I said.

'Yeah, OK,' said Sophie. 'But why ask me in here?'

'It's safer,' I whispered, before giving her a wink and a knowing look.

'Really?' she said, gesturing to the row of closed cubicle doors.

At this point I almost wet myself.

'Oh bollocks,' I hissed.

'Look, I'll give it to you later,' whispered Sophie. 'I think you'd better get out before somebody flushes.'

At about 4 a.m., by which time Sophie had had a bit and I'd had rather a lot, we ended up going back to my room. We were both far too drunk to get up to anything untoward and after a quick snog and a cuddle we went to sleep – me on top of the bed with all my clothes on and Sophie half on the bed with all her clothes on and with one of her legs on the floor. I have to say she looked dead classy when I woke up and saw her lying there asleep and I was just about to lean over and wake her up by breathing alcohol fumes on her when there was a knock at the door.

'JASON. I NEED TO GET MY STUFF!'

It was the girl from the marketing agency.

OK, hands up. She had stayed over once or twice but only for a sleepover (ahem). It was time to wake up Sleeping Beauty.

'Sophie,' I whispered, giving her a nudge. 'Sophie. I've got a visitor. You'll have to hide in the wardrobe for a minute.'

'What?'

'I'll explain in a few minutes. Come on, chop chop.'

Reluctantly, Sophie got her other leg off the bed before sneaking into the wardrobe and within five minutes 'x' had stormed in, grabbed her toothbrush, called me a few names and then buggered off. She had no idea Sophie was there, otherwise!

'You can come out now,' I said, opening the wardrobe door. There before me was a stunning, and I mean stunning, young woman with a cheeky grin on her face and her clothes and hair in a right mess who had just spent five minutes skulking in a wardrobe avoiding a jealous woman. What a gal. Surely we were made to be together!

The following Monday, Sophie was called in to see her boss at SEAT. Somebody had obviously seen her coming back to my room, and after putting two and two together they'd come up with something rude. If only.

SEAT made the point that regardless of what had or hadn't happened, Sophie was a placement student and shouldn't be fraternizing with the drivers, and especially Jason Plato! According to them, I was bad news, and as well as advising Sophie to keep well away from me, from now on any press requests that she received regarding me had to be handed over to somebody else. I'm not sure if it was company policy or my reputation that made SEAT so vociferous in keeping Sophie away from me, but it worked a treat, and unfortunately I didn't see her again for about four months. I could have called, I suppose, but as well as being here, there and everywhere I knew SEAT's position and didn't want to cause any trouble. And there would have been trouble!

The next time I saw her was at the SEAT Christmas party and I only decided to go at the last minute. Although I hadn't spoken to Sophie, I obviously knew what they'd said to her – i.e., keep away, he's a cad! – so, when I saw her at the party, I wasn't sure what to do. Then I thought, *Sod it. I'm going to go over and speak to her.*

Time had obviously done nothing to negate the attraction

between us, and within a few minutes we were chatting and flirting away like a couple of good'ns. Unfortunately, and understandably, Sophie soon became paranoid, and she had every right to be, as all eyes seemed to be on us.

'Look, Jason, I can't be seen talking to you,' she said, taking a short step back.

'I'll tell you what,' I replied, defiantly. 'You see that gap in the velvet curtain?' (The perimeter of the room had been draped in several.) 'I'll meet you behind there in five minutes.'

The old ticker was going like the clappers at this point, so something was definitely up. Was I actually in love? Me, Plato the player? It then occurred to me that over the past four months I'd actually thought about Sophie almost constantly, and that wasn't like me at all. Of course, I felt compelled to call Sophie, but my head was doing cartwheels, and we still had the team orders hanging over us! It was all a bit strange to be honest.

Once safely behind the curtain I told Sophie that I'd been thinking about her and that I was very keen on her, and fortunately she felt the same. To err on the side of caution we avoided each other for a few hours after that, and then at the end of the night we arranged to meet in Sophie's room. I went up there first, to avoid suspicion. Sophie joined me about ten minutes later. By the time she got there it was about 5 a.m., and literally a minute after Sophie had closed the door there was a knock on it.

'Oh fuck,' hissed Sophie. 'What if it's Jean? Quick, get behind the curtains.'

The second time in one night!

As soon as I was out of sight Sophie shouted, 'Who is it?'

I obviously can't name him, but instead of it being Jean, as we'd feared, it was actually a member of the SEAT Racing

Team – one of my colleagues – and he was trying to get into Sophie's knickers.

I would have had no problem whatsoever telling an unwanted suitor to bugger off, but Sophie was very kind and considerate and for the next ten minutes or so she proceeded to let this randy little bugger down very, very gently. The problem was that, as the conversation went on, I started to find it funny, and had this lad not been three sheets to the wind I dare say he might have heard one or two guffaws in the vicinity, not to mention the curtains twitching around like a poltergeist had moved in.

Once this bloke had buggered off, we chatted for a couple of hours until Sophie had to go to work. The whole thing was just incredibly lush, and I'd properly fallen for her. She was still very cautious, both about the reaction from SEAT and over my reputation, so I was going to have to try and prove to her that it was the real deal and that my feelings for her were genuine.

I was going up to Newcastle over Christmas for a few days, so before I left I asked Sophie if she'd like to come with me. Fortunately, she said yes, and after swapping numbers – again – we arranged to meet at Oxford Airport on whatever date it was. Sophie seemed a little unsure why we were meeting there and not the train station or wherever and when she realized that I'd be flying us up there she went a whiter shade of pale. I was also giving Rob Smedley a lift up, as he was heading home to Middlesbrough, and he turned up wearing a cap, a puffer jacket and some very dark sunglasses.

'This is Rob,' I said to Sophie. 'And he's quite obviously suffering from a monumental hangover!'

'Pleased to meet you,' he said, holding out a shaking hand.

Even with the shades and the cap on he looked like death warmed up!

By the following March, Sophie and I were both head over heels in love, and so the next step was to try and sort things out with SEAT. I ended up going to see Jean, the head of PR, and said that in addition to Sophie and I being an item I'd like her to be there when I race. It was like asking her parents for permission to go courting!

'We can't have that,' I'm afraid, said Jean. 'Not until her placement finishes.'

It was fair enough, I suppose, but I was still pissed off.

Almost in defiance of SEAT's decision, and because we wanted to be together whenever we could, I ended up renting a house in Oxford that we could share when I was over there racing. This made everything much more real, and the moment Sophie's placement finished she started coming to the race meetings.

It had taken a while, but I think I'd finally started growing up a bit. I certainly hadn't become a paragon of virtue straight away. This was a process, not a miracle, after all! The main thing is, it felt right.

At the time of us getting together properly, Sophie was at university in Leeds, and one Sunday, after we spent a nice weekend together, I suggested that instead of her driving back we jump in the plane. I didn't get rid of it until 2005, and I was still looking for any excuse to fly it.

When taxiing out of Oxford Airport, because of the prevailing wind, you're often forced to take off towards the south and when that happens you have to pass the control tower. The chaps in the control tower are always standing there looking through their binoculars, bored witless, and whenever I used to pass I'd always have a bit of banter with them.

Sophie and I used to call our little plane *Love Air*, and, as people do in our situation, we sometimes got up to no good. For a bit of fun I suggested to Sophie that we fly up to Leeds completely starkers and, like a fool, she agreed. I knew full well that we were going to have to pass the control tower because of the wind, and because the pilot sits on the left I knew Sophie would be in full view of the control tower, but she didn't!

After taking our clothes off, I started the engine and then requested permission to taxi off.

'Yeah, no problem, Jason,' said the guy in the control tower.

He then started talking about the route we were taking, and as we approached the control tower during taxi he was still talking, and I could see him standing there at the window, looking through his binoculars. As we began to pass the control tower, I lost sight of him, but the way he suddenly stopped talking meant only one thing!

'Golf Juliet Papa . . . Are you having a laugh? Christ on a bike, are you naked as well?!'

'Affirmative,' I said. 'And what's more, it's just for you!'

Because she was obviously in on the joke, Sophie gave them a little wave, once she'd put her head gear on. You should have heard them all sniggering, though. They were like a bunch of twelve-year-olds. I think they ended up giving us a round of applause!

After we landed at Leeds Bradford Airport, the chap with the dayglo table tennis bats started guiding me to the hanger, which is on the opposite side of the runway to the airport terminal.

'Right, I'm getting dressed,' said Sophie, reaching for her clothes.

'You are not,' I ordered. 'We agreed not to put our clothes on until the engine has stopped. Come on, Sophie, a deal's a deal.'

As game as ever, Sophie remained *sans* clothes, and as we approached the man with the table tennis bats his countenance changed from one that said *God, I'm bored* to *Christ on a bike*.

When he'd given me the signal for brakes-on, the bloke started sidling gingerly up to the side of the plane to do some checks, and as soon as she saw him coming Sophie started waving him away. 'No, no, not now,' she mouthed in a panic. 'Come back later!'

Normally I'd have had the engine off after a minute or so but for some reason the checks I had to make took me a little bit longer to complete this time around. I wonder why?

It was a sweet little airline, *Love Air*. Small, perfectly formed and a headcase for a CEO. Foxy first officer, though.

In October 2004, I went out to Australia again to compete in the Bathurst 1000. My teammate was the legendary Peter Brock, who'd won the event God knows how many times, and it was to be his last ever Bathurst. For me personally the race was a disaster. On lap 28, the front tyre blew literally a second or so after I passed the pit entrance, so I had to do an entire lap on three wheels. It was right at the end of my stint, and I'd forgotten to adjust the brake balance with the amount of fuel I was burning, and the wheel had just locked up. It was a schoolboy error and completely my fault. Peter was due in after me, and the thought of denying Mr Bathurst, as he was known, a run in his last ever appearance was almost too much to bear.

As I was trying to nurse the car back to the pits, there was all kinds of chit chat going on over the radio, and because of my speed, or lack of it, the white and yellow flags were being waved. I was well off the racing line. Then, just as I was coming out of the final corner, with the chasing pack driving at a slower pace because of the flags, but a lot more quickly than me, John Cleland, who was *in* the pack, decided to make a move despite the flags and despite me being visible. There was a gap in between me and the pack but it was less than the width of a car and Cleland ended up ploughing into the driver-side rear door of my car before flipping over. It was a pretty spectacular shunt and no mistake.

I ended up getting the blame for the accident despite the flags and despite me being visible to the pack. The stewards' argument was that I should have been either off the track or at least on the edge, but I was trying to nurse the car back to the pits, so that was just bollocks. My retorts were futile, unfortunately, and on top of Peter not being able to race, which was obviously demoralizing, I ended up getting fined 10,000 Aussie dollars.

Needless to say, I couldn't wait to leave the circuit, and before managing to do so I received all kinds of abuse from the spectators. It was a really, really bad day. One of the worst.

After regrouping with Sophie back at the hotel we decided there and then to get out of Dodge and, after packing up the car, we headed in the direction of Byron Bay. On the way we decided to take a detour past Byron Bay and we spent a couple of nights at the Versace Hotel in Surfers Paradise. Despite the extra drive it was a great idea, and within a few hours of arriving I felt like a new man. Sophie and I had had a brilliant time until the Bathurst fiasco, and

I was buggered if I was going to let it spoil our time together. Absolutely no chance. We were in a gorgeous hotel in a great part of the world, and there wasn't a racing car in sight. Perfect!

The following day we decided to drive down to a village called Nimbin, which is about 50 miles west of Byron Bay. The reason I wanted to go there is because it was one of the only places in Australia where you could smoke cannabis openly and in my ongoing quest in seeking out new and interesting places to visit, it ticked a box – or two.

I'd heard about Nimbin but I'd never been there, and the friends of mine who had all said that it was like walking into a zombie film, as the entire village was stoned. Naturally, I took the majority of these tales with a ginormous pinch of salt, as I figured that the people who'd told me must have been stoned for the duration of their visit, and so the truth might just have been skewed somewhat. Wrong!

As we drove into Nimbin the first thing we noticed was that everybody was walking at a snail's pace, and I mean everybody! It was such a weird place. The difference between it and a zombie film is that, instead of looking gormless or, in a zombie's case, dead, everyone was either smiling or giggling. Everyone was so blissed out and happy it must have been impossible to have an argument there.

One of the most alarming things I noticed was that the pedestrians in Nimbin didn't seem to be aware of passing cars and so instead of looking both ways before crossing a road they just stepped off the kerb and walked on. After literally ten minutes of being in Nimbin we'd very nearly killed about six people! The first one almost got a mouthful until he gave me a massive thumbs up followed by a wave.

'What's he on, Sophie?' I asked.

'What do you think? Probably a bit of everything.'

Within moments of parking up we'd been offered gear of all descriptions and, with a view to supporting the local economy, we decided to buy a bag and then stuff it in the glove compartment. The stench of this gear was just incredible, and when we arrived in Byron Bay later that day we'd convinced ourselves that the whole of New South Wales could smell it. We were paranoid and we hadn't even had a joint yet!

Near Byron Bay, we'd booked ourselves into a lush hotel called the Raes on Wategos Bay but had arrived a day early and were hoping they'd be able to move our reservation forward. Unfortunately, that wasn't possible, as they were full, so we ended up renting a little apartment in Byron Bay for a night.

Unbeknownst to Sophie – obviously – before travelling to Australia I'd been building myself up to proposing and now we were settled in Byron Bay where we'd be spending a few days I thought, *OK, Jason. This is it!* I didn't have a ring or anything, but providing she said yes, which I was hopeful of, we'd go ring shopping together once we arrived home. We'd discussed getting married previously (although tentatively), and Sophie had mentioned that she'd rather buy a ring together, so I was merely following orders.

Before we went out on that first night in Byron Bay, we rolled a couple of spliffs and then headed off to a bar. After smoking one of these spliffs I thought to myself, *OK, the time is now*, but when I went to say, 'Sophie, will you marry me,' what actually came out was – and I'm obviously paraphrasing here – 'Ill moo arry be, Sloppy?' I was completely stoned!

To be fair, it was years since I'd smoked cannabis, back

in college days (honestly), but this stuff was off the bloody scale.

The following night, I tried again and but after another bloody spliff it came out no better.

'Ill moo arry be, Sloppy?'

'Eh?'

'Dunt matta.'

Three nights this went on for, until eventually we decided to chuck the gear in the bin and stick to alcohol. We were in the hotel by this point, so having a nice little stash with us probably wasn't a good idea. After dumping the gear, I readied myself for the big question.

I chickened out of asking her before dinner, and by the time we'd finished, and I was ready again, I'd had more than my fair share of booze. No matter, we could have married and gone on honeymoon in the time it had taken me to ask her, and although I was a bit pissed, my speech was still just about intelligible, if a little slurred.

After dinner we went on to a bar and, after finding a table and then downing a couple of stiff ones, I went to lean forward in order to pop the question but ended up falling off my stool and, as luck would have it, straight on to my knees. Bingo!

It was ungainly, sure, but I'd committed myself now and there was no turning back.

Fortunately, Sophie had taken slightly less alcohol than me, so if she did say yes, I'd be sure she meant it, and, fortunately, she did!

We didn't get married until two years later, but while we're here I may as well tell you about the wedding because, *quelle surprise*, it wasn't exactly conventional. It's also no surprise that the two intervening years between me falling on to my knees to pop the question and tying the knot were fairly eventful, so by the time we got around to it we were more than ready. Well, at least I was. I was knackered!

As is often the way, the first thing we started looking for after deciding to get spliced was a venue, and after having a bit of a hunt we eventually came across a fabulous place in the Cotswolds, so not too far from Oxford, called Cowley Manor. It's the original ancestral home to the Horlicks family (no sleepy drinks required, though) and from the moment we saw it we thought, *Yep, this is it.* There was even a little chapel just next door to the hotel, but better still they'd never done a wedding before, so we'd be the first. That would probably put one or two people off, but we loved the idea and after pencilling in a couple of dates we got in touch with the local vicar, told him of our intentions and arranged to meet him at the vicarage.

Sadly, he was of the opinion that unless you were avid churchgoers you shouldn't be allowed to get married in God's house, and it's fair to say that we weren't regulars at worship. Can you imagine me hopping out of bed at 10 a.m. on a Sunday morning, donning my favourite suit and then bombing down the road to sing 'All Things Bright and Beautiful' and be told about the error of my ways? No, of course you can't.

I think his reverence was expecting us to naff off and book a registrar once he'd given us the bum's rush, but it was going to take a lot more than a quick no to put us off.

'I'll tell you what, vicar,' I said, patting him on the back. 'We'll become churchgoers for a few weeks. How's that?'

'No, no, no,' he said. 'I'm afraid that won't do. You'll have to become regular churchgoers and at your local church. I can put you in touch with your vicar, if you like?'

I couldn't believe it. I was being blackmailed by a vicar! That was a first.

If it wasn't for heretics like us, churches would lose an absolute fortune, and vicars would have bugger all to do on a Saturday. Fortunately, the majority don't mind. Not like this one. He obviously hated working Saturdays.

Instead of verbalizing my potentially controversial thoughts and opinions to the good vicar, I thought I'd try giving him a bit of his own medicine first. It would be bribery as opposed to blackmail, but it can be just as effective. I'm told.

'I'll tell you what, vicar,' I said, turning on the charm full throttle. 'Don't you have some lead that needs replacing on your roof?'

'You mean the church roof?' he said.

'That's right. All churches need a bit of lead replacing every now and then, don't they? I could make it happen.'

'In return for . . .' he replied sceptically.

'In return for us not having to go to church every week and being allowed to use the chapel next to the hotel.'

Apparently, a vicar attempting to blackmail a racing driver and his betrothed is OK, but a racing driver trying to bribe a vicar isn't. Can you catch your breath!

'I think you'd better leave,' snapped his holiness.

'Well,' said Sophie after we'd shown ourselves out. 'You handled that very well. I'm surprised a big blue hand didn't come down and strike you dead!'

'It was worth a try,' I pleaded.

By now we'd set our hearts on getting married at Cowley Manor, and although our first choice had been to hold the service in the chapel, we had no choice other than to resort to plan B and after strolling back to the hotel we asked them to look into getting a licence.

Cowley Manor is one of these places where historic meets modern, and although that's not to everyone's taste, we loved it. For a start, instead of wearing something very corporate, like you'd expect, the staff all wore lime-green tank tops, and it was full of the quirkiest art you've ever seen.

When it came to finalizing the date of the wedding, we surprised the hotel by informing them that it wouldn't be lasting just one day. Oh no. It would be lasting three days!

'Really?' gasped the manager. 'But this will be our first ever wedding.'

'You'll be prepared to give me a very good deal, then, won't you,' I said, jumping on the manager's insecurity.

In the end, we had the entire place all to ourselves for the entire three days, so it was like the Willies at Jarama, where we had the whole track. We had a lot more booze at the wedding, but far fewer explosions!

The day before the wedding, we held a party for just our closest friends and family. Then, for the wedding itself, we had a few more people, and for the evening do every bugger turned up.

The pre-wedding party was supposed to be quite a quiet affair, really, as we were all meant to be on form the following day, but at 4 a.m., me, my best man, Rob Smedley, and a few others were still at the bar, having been on the widdle for – let me think now – ooh, about twelve hours? I was supposed to be getting married at 11 a.m.!

I think we all retired at about 4.30 a.m., and I set my alarm for 8 a.m. Given how much we'd drunk, I was surprised I could sleep at all, but when my alarm went off I actually felt OK. Might that have had something to do with me still being pissed? A tenner says it did.

The first thing I did was give Rob a ring and ask him to come to my suite.

'Right then,' I said, lying on the bed in my undies. 'Have you got the rings?'

'Yep. They're in my room.'

'And how about your speech?'

'Don't worry, I'll have it done in time.'

Eh?

'What do you mean, you'll have it done in time? Have you actually started it?'

'Not really,' said Rob, shrugging his shoulders. 'I've got a couple of ideas, though. I'm going to go back to my room in a bit and write it.'

'You're going to wing it, aren't you?' I said.

'Naaah, don't worry. It'll be fine.'

'It won't be fine, Rob!'

As this started to sink in, so did my hangover, and it's fair to say that with Rob's bombshell and my impending nuptials I was feeling a teeny weeny bit stressed.

Rob could obviously sense my anxiety and in an attempt to calm me down he said four words that, had she known what time we'd gone to bed and how much we'd had to drink the previous evening, would have put the fear of God into Sophie.

'How about a drink?' he said.

We both knew it was wrong but at the same time we both knew it was going to happen. It was as inevitable as the sun rising over the Sahara Desert. Even so, we still went through the ritual of trying to justify what we were about to do and exonerate ourselves of any potential blame.

'We could have just the one,' I said. 'Just to get us going again.'

'A livener!' agreed Rob.

'That's it. Sophie won't mind, will she?'

'No, of course she won't. She'll probably be having one herself.'

We went on for a few seconds longer but within a minute we were both tucking in to a large glass of champagne each, and I'll tell you what, it tasted fabulous. By the time we rolled down for the service we'd had at least three glasses each, and when Sophie turned up at the altar, or whatever the secular version of an altar is, she made the acute observation that I was indeed sweating alcohol and smelled like a brewery. Or in this case a brewery, a distillery *and* a winery. There'd been no bias alcohol-wise. I think she'd been expecting it. Everyone else had.

The party in the evening was absolutely legendary, and everybody there, regardless of their age, danced like their lives depended on it. We'd managed to hire a big band called the Jazz Dynamos who we'd seen play at the Dover Street Wine Bar, and they were tremendous. There was no marquee, which meant everything – marrying, drinking, dancing, sleeping, flirting and goodness knows what else – all took place under the same roof with the reception – or party, should I say – taking place in the ballroom. We did the speeches slightly differently, so, as opposed to everyone standing at their tables, the entire crowd congregated at the bottom of a beautiful staircase that was close to the ballroom, and whoever felt compelled to speak went to the top of the stairs and did so. It was just the best three days ever and the perfect end to my bachelor years.

Even Rob's speech was fabulous, and the claims of him not being prepared were merely a ruse to wind me up and, I suspect, to get me on the sauce again.

We started our honeymoon with a South African safari, which was incredible, and then made our way to Mauritius, which I'm afraid wasn't. The whole thing was a bit too formal for us, and the staff were ludicrously subservient and wouldn't leave us alone.

'Just chill out, will you?' I kept on saying to them. 'You don't have to stand on ceremony.'

Unfortunately, the more formal they were the more uncomfortable we became, and the more uncomfortable we became the harder they tried to make us happy, and usually failed. It was farcical, really – a bit of a vicious circle – but at the same time it was nobody's fault.

I forget what had happened, but after cocking something up one day pretty drastically, one of the people looking after us announced that to make amends they were going to arrange a special candlelit dinner for us on the beach. Once again, instead of just apologizing, leaving it be and buggering off, they were fussing around and over-promising and so as not to hurt their feelings we said, 'OK, thanks.'

'Tonight will be unquestionably perfect,' said the chap. 'We guarantee it. Everything you want and need will be there, and you will have the best night of your holiday.'

The best night we'd had so far was when we'd managed to get rid of them for the evening! That had been tip top. Christ, it was hard though. They were like limpets.

When we got down to the beach, everything had been set up as promised, and at first glance and from a distance you'd have thought, *Yeah, that's pretty smart*. Move a step closer, however, and you'd have realized that right in between the two chairs which had been placed next to each other around a small square table was a massive bamboo stick, which meant that if I fancied gazing at my beautiful wife at some point during the evening or wanted to go in for a quick kiss I'd be sadly out of luck. What the hell it was doing there I have no idea but after being shown to the table I purpose-fully stared at the bamboo stick and then turned to our host. He still hadn't clicked.

'I can't think of anything you could have done to improve on this,' I said, staring at the stick. 'This is perfection. Abso-lute perfection.

With that, I leaned forward to give Sophie a kiss and whacked my head on the bamboo pole.

'Oh my God, sir, I am so sorry! Please, allow me to remove the pole.'

'Why did you put it there?' I said, despairingly. 'You're not very good at this, are you?'

Rather than getting it removed, we used it as a comedy prop in the end and took photos of it. We also had the meal and, despite them lighting a citrus or two, we got bitten to smithereens. It was a painfully imperfect end to a comedic-ally imperfect evening.

After that we went to Cape Town for three weeks (it was supposed to be two, but we loved it so much we stayed on), and the highlight of the trip was a spot of cage diving, during which we got to see some great white sharks. The reason I'm including this story is because Sophie almost got eaten by one of them, and I found it quite a hoot.

The diving centre was about a three-hour drive from Cape Town, and when we arrived the first thing we saw was a large, sturdy and actually quite ornate aluminium cage out-side the premises. Whether this was meant to reassure the punters I'm not sure, but it did the trick on us, and after receiving a tutorial on all the dos and don'ts we jumped on a boat with our instructor and his crew and set sail. After about an hour at sea, we came to a halt and dropped anchor, which is when they showed us the cage.

'That's nothing like the one at the diving centre,' I said to Sophie. 'It's just welded rod!'

Any courage we'd managed to muster had now evaporated, but after being reassured by the instructor that it was up to the job, I stuck my hand up to go first and jumped in the cage. After about ten minutes or so a great white shark passed within about ten feet of the cage, and to this day it's probably the most amazing thing I've ever seen in my entire life. It was about the length of a caravan – 5 or 6 metres maybe – and despite it swimming past me calmly, I obviously knew that it was capable of causing all kinds of mayhem. The instructor had understandably told us not to try and touch the sharks, but as it swam past me I'm afraid I couldn't resist. It's difficult to describe really, but it felt incredibly solid and just a little bit evil.

Next it was Sophie's turn, and as she got into the cage, I opened an unfortunately warm beer and took over the filming duties. To attract more sharks, the crew put some tuna on the end of a rope and then lowered it into the water, but instead of it floating away from the cage it ended up getting stuck between the bars. About two minutes later a great white shark appeared, and as Sophie was bobbing about inside the cage the shark opened its mouth and actually tried to eat it! Seriously, instead of just nibbling away at the tuna it went for the whole kit and caboodle and at one point it actually had its mouth around the cage, which meant Sophie could see its bloody tonsils!

While she and the cage were being eaten by a great white shark, I was on deck looking at the video screen, but instead of leaping around and shouting, 'Help! My beautiful new wife is in the process of being consumed by Jaws', I just sat there giggling away nervously. After all, if Sophie was going to be eaten, I just had to have it on camera! The attack went on for a couple of minutes, and every time the shark bit the cage you could see it creaking, and as the cage creaked poor Sophie went into meltdown. As you probably would, if you were on the verge of being eaten by a great white shark.

And the moral of this story? If you're going cage diving make sure you take a cool box.

30. Who put that parasol pole there?

31. What do you mean you haven't written the speech?

32. What a wonderful day.

33. Platos and Smedleys party on.

34. I say.

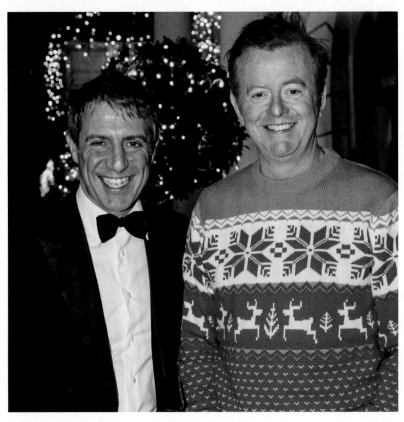

35. And I told him it was black tie.

37. Aaah, it's the *Fifth Gear* gang.

36. On the podium in 2007 after the *Fifth Gear* fire accident.

38. I love that winning kiss.

39. Soaf with Alena, in Scotland.

40. The girls.

41. My gorgeous girls, Alena and Zia.

42. A regular night at the Plato's.

43. Hangovers like this are not so bad.

44. We like to get smartly dressed on weekends.

45. Thanks, Mr Cleland.

46. Race of Champions.

47. Race of Champions winners.

48. I love racing with my buddy Craig Davies.

49. The lads on tour – Messrs Thompson, Lupton, Deighton and Plato.

50. Athlete personified – at the Goodwood Drivers Cricket Match.

51. On the absolute ragged edge.

52. WTF.

53. BTCC Awards live link1. JP unable to attend.

54. Williams Drivers.

55. Me and Soaf on the Grid at the British Grand Prix, 2017.

The Fruitcake That Is Tiff Needell

Some of you might not be aware of this, but I've been working on TV almost as long as I've been racing cars, at least professionally, so I've got a story or two, that's for sure. The first approach for me to appear on the box came completely out of the blue and happened about halfway through my first year at Willies. The enquiry was from Television South, as was, who were based in Southampton, and they were about to launch a new Friday-night magazine-style show subtly titled *Members Only*. This was in the era of magazines like *Maxim* and *FHM*, so it fitted perfectly for the time, and apparently so did I.

The show was hosted by Iain Lee, who went on to do the breakfast show RI:SE and now presents a radio show, and an ex-page 3 girl, whose name escapes me but who now works as a make-up artist in television and films. They wanted me to do car reviews every so often that would last about five minutes, and after getting permission from Willies, who were happily very keen as it would obviously be good publicity, and then agreeing terms, I said I'd do it.

I said yes partly on the basis that it would be good exposure and despite me only just joining Willies I was still mindful of Frank's reason for not signing me originally. Profile was massively important in this game, and as far as I was concerned the bigger mine was the better.

Appearing on *Members Only* turned out to be a hoot, and

the majority of my filming was done away from the studio and obviously during the day, so as well as building my profile up and earning a few extra quid I still had my Friday nights free. As with many of those magazine shows it was a bit rubbish, really, but it was something to watch after the pub.

The following year, 1998, again, out of nowhere, a friend of mine called Penny Mallory, who I knew from racing schools, got in touch and asked me if I'd be interested in appearing on a car show she'd recently joined on Channel 4 called *Driven*. The series had originally been presented by Mike Brewer, Jason Barlow and another chap I'll name in a moment, but after just one series Barlow and the other chap had left the show, with Barlow joining the BBC's *Top Gear*.

Penny had been the first to get snapped up as a replacement and, after seeing me on *Members Only* and then speaking to Mike, she thought it might be a good idea to have a word. Thank you, Miss Mallory!

Instead of being uber keen about this and biting their hands off, I decided to play it cool – even to the point of appearing uninterested. The reason I did this was to test the water and try and gauge my worth in the eyes of the producers and television companies, and the best way of doing this was to play it cool, which I'd now done, and then ask for a massive fee, which I was about to do.

After I confirmed to the producers that I was at least interested in their offer, they suggested I come down for a screen test at a place called Crowthorne, which is in Berkshire. There were one or two other hopefuls, but according to the lady I spoke to on the phone I already had it in the bag, so basically all I had to do was turn up and not make an arse of myself. In addition to this, Mike and Penny had said that they were both keen for me to come on board, so by the time

I arrived at Crowthorne I was quite excited. The only thing I'd have to sort out, should they offer it to me, was the amount of time off I'd need from Willies, but the producers were aware of this beforehand so they knew that as long as they didn't take the mick everything would be fine.

When I arrived in Crowthorne, the first person I saw was Richard Hammond, and I thought, *Oh dear!* Back in my Renault Spider days, Richard had been working for Renault and was the main point of contact between them and the team I raced for, so we knew each other quite well and had always got on like a house on fire. We'd had a PR day down at the Beaulieu National Motor Museum once, and my one abiding memory of it is that Richard and I spent the entire day laughing our socks off. The reason I wasn't that pleased to see him was that in the intervening years he'd done loads on radio and a bit on TV and he was tipped for big things. Surely he'd be chosen ahead of me?

Funnily enough, the other bloke who either me or Richard (but hopefully me) would be replacing on *Driven* was James May, who had also left to join *Top Gear*.

I don't know the full ins and outs, but luckily for me Penny and Mike bigged me up to the producers and made sure I got the gig, and so as the Hamster disappeared into obscurity, never to be seen again, I started negotiating with Sarah Brailsford, the producer.

Having been given some intelligence about what kind of money was flying around, I decided to double it just for a laugh, and she immediately said yes. My first thought was, *Why the hell didn't I triple it?*

The fee was well into six figures. Peanuts to your average *Top Gear* presenter, I imagine, but to a struggling racing driver like me with a penchant for nice things it was a very welcome emolument. Or, as my old man might say after flogging a set of tyres to a butcher, *a nice little earner.* The only thing I had to be a bit careful about, at least at first, was Mike and Penny getting wind of the disparity between their wages and mine, but because of the sheer size of the disparity it ended up driving their money up a bit, so everyone won in the end.

From 1998, when it started (I joined in 1999), until about 2001 *Driven* was the top car show in the UK. Although that was quite an admirable achievement on paper, *Top Gear* was declining at the time, and *Fifth Gear* hadn't started, so as far as competition went it was minimal. That said, *Driven* was still a good little show, and at its height we were getting audiences of about 4 million. The most popular feature was the Driven 100, in which we'd get three cars from the same class and then pitch them against each other by judging their desirability, their practicality and their cost of ownership. Sound familiar? It started off in magazines, but as far as I know *Driven* was the first car show to try it on TV, and it obviously worked.

The first time I remember getting into trouble on *Driven*, so this will probably be my first ever bollocking while working in television, happened when we were filming some cutaways one day. A cutaway is when a film cuts away to something else for a split-second and is designed to break things up a bit. For instance, if I'm filming a car review and am talking to camera while I'm driving, they'll insert a shot of the instrument panel or of me changing gear and then go straight back again. You know the kind of thing.

One day, while filming an item, I asked Penny if she'd mind doing my cutaways, which were going to consist of a couple of gear changes. She got the joke immediately, and so instead of the film cutting away to a shot of my hands or feet they cut to Penny's, wearing nail varnish and a pair of high heels. The idea was that it would all be spotted and removed during the editing process, and so Penny and I forgot about it. Unfortunately, they must have been half asleep as it went to air, and the following day I was given a right ticking-off. 'What's up,' I asked. 'Wrong shade of nail varnish?'

Not long after that, Penny and I were guiding Mike Brewer, who was driving a new Mini, out of a tight spot in France and instead of informing him that there were two giant plant pots that he obviously couldn't see, we waved him on and told him he was fine. 'Loads of room, Mike. Loads of room!' We laughed at the time. Two pots written off and a bump on the Mini.

The format we used of having three presenters in the studio and cutting to pre-recorded segments featuring one or sometimes two of us was also quite unique at the time and it became even more so when we decided to include a studio audience. That was decided during a meeting one day, when the production company suggested us moving the show to a hangar at RAF Bentwaters in Suffolk called The Hush House, which was where they used to test American jet engines.

While we at *Driven* may have started the hangar and live audience format, the boys at *Top Gear* obviously went on to perfect it, but that wasn't before a certain Mr Clarkson had asked me to switch sides. You see, before *Top Gear* was relaunched in 2002 it had been cancelled and had spent a year off air, and one of the catalysts for its demise had been the success of *Driven*. Then, before it was relaunched by Jeremy and his producer, Andy Wilman, I received a telephone call from the former asking me if I'd be interested in doing a screen test for them. Prior to this, I'd already done some filming with Jeremy, so knew him fairly well, and if it hadn't been for the fact that he was asking me to screen test for something that we'd already blown off the air, I'd have turned up there with my best smile on and with a view to winning the gig. As it was, I got halfway through the screen test before telling them that I'd decided to stay where I was. They hadn't offered me anything, by the way, so the chances are I might not have got the job. I have a feeling I might have, though, had I actually wanted it.

As crap decisions go, this was up there with the one the record company executive made when he decided not to sign the Beatles (well, to me at least), as just a few weeks after the relaunch of *Top Gear*, by which time *Fifth Gear* had also kicked into life and was doing quite well, *Driven* was cancelled! And what was *Top Gear*'s format? Three people in a hangar talking shop and taking the piss out of the audience while every so often cutting to a VT of a pre-recorded feature. Funnier still, the very first feature on the all-new *Top Gear* was a three-car test, and the presenters were the aforementioned Jezza, Richard Hammond, who I'd pipped to the post at *Driven*, and Jason Dawe. Apparently, James May had refused to be involved in the relaunch. That's until it became immensely popular. After that he was in like Flynn, and what a move that was.

Although our two concepts were the same, the boys and girls at *Top Gear* executed their version a lot better than we did, and this was down to two things really: first, the budget, which was much bigger than ours; second, Jezza. Love him or loathe him, we didn't have a Clarkson, and that was what really gave them the edge. The man's a genius in my opinion. Then, once James May had got on board, the dream team was complete, and away they went.

Ironically, had we stayed with our original format, we might have been OK, as we wouldn't have been seen as being a poor man's *Top Gear*. It was all academic, though, and in December 2002 *Driven* came off air. To be honest, this didn't worry me too much, as I was a racing driver first and foremost, and if I never presented another television programme ever again at least I could say I'd given it a go. Luckily for me, the makers of *Fifth Gear*, which was going great guns on Channel 5, obviously thought there was life in the old dog yet and in 2004 they asked me if I'd be interested in recording a couple of items for them, and I said, yes please! Fifteen years later, I'm still a presenter on *Fifth Gear*, and over the years we've had a couple of giggles.

I think my biggest USP at this point, although it's less so today, is that I was the only active racing driver who also presented television car shows (Tiff Needell, my co-host, had all but retired by this point) and although I could obviously hold my own in the role and was comfortable, it was probably what gave me the edge and allowed me to command a bigger salary. The thing is, not all racing drivers are confident in front of a camera, so without wanting to blow my own trumpet I was a unique entity at the time.

About the same time I got the *Fifth Gear* gig, a producer I knew called Hamish Barbour got in touch with me about a new show he was planning for Sky Television that, funnily enough, didn't involve cars. It was called *Mission Implausible*, and the premise was that each week a male and a female presenter, together with a team each, would compete against each other in a series of challenges. It was standard boy-versus-girl stuff, or so I thought.

Hamish had been involved in the first couple of series of *Driven* as an executive producer, which is how I knew him, and when I asked him what kind of challenges they had in mind I was half expecting him to describe some sort of

Gladiators type of thing where each week we'd have to run up a moving conveyor belt or dart up a climbing wall.

'Jumping from one speedboat to another' was Hamish's first example.

'What, moving? Across water?'

'No, stationary on concrete! Yes, of course they'll be moving across water. It wouldn't be very entertaining if they weren't.'

'How fast will they be going?'

'I don't know!' said Hamish, becoming a bit irritated. 'As fast as they need to go for it to be dangerous. About 60 mph I think.'

'What the heck!' I exclaimed. 'Are you completely off your trolley?'

'Oh, don't be such a big girl's blouse, Jason,' said Hamish. 'You drive cars at ridiculous speeds for a living. This should be child's play in comparison. There's another one I can tell you about and that's walking on a tightrope stretched across the top of a quarry with a crash mat underneath.'

Easy-peasy!

'I'm not saying no, Hamish,' I said finally, 'but I'm going to need a lot more information first.'

Joking aside, I was driving for SEAT at the time, and this was obviously a bit different to what had been demanded of me on *Members Only* or *Driven*. Sure, they'd have insurance and ambulances standing by, but at the end of the day I was a racing driver first and presenter second, and if the latter ever jeopardized the former at all there'd be trouble. Consequently, SEAT weren't happy when I finally showed them a detailed premise from Hamish, but in the interests of keeping my profile topped up I managed to persuade them to rubber-stamp it. Like Willies, they could see the advantage of having one of their drivers presenting a primetime television show, albeit on SKY1, so with a smaller audience than *Driven*.

My co-presenter on the show was Tania Zaetta, an Australian lady who had appeared in a couple of episodes of *Baywatch*. She was great fun and looked fabulous, so despite the element of danger involved I was looking forward to getting going.

We made ten one-hour episodes in all, and the only task I got injured on was, ironically, jumping from one speedboat to another! I ended up cracking my bloody ankle, and it was touch and go at one point as to whether I'd be able to carry on. It just had to be that.

What surprised me most about the entire experience on *Mission Implausible* was the launch party. SKY took over the whole of Portland Square in the West End of London, cordoned it off and put a load of screens up everywhere, as well as providing food and plenty of drink. It must have cost them tens, if not hundreds, of thousands of pounds and I remember getting properly stuck in. We were sharing the launch party with Ross Kemp's new show, *Ross Kemp on Gangs*. One of the two shows became immensely successful!

Between *Mission Implausible*, *Driven* and *Fifth Gear* – and one or two other things in between – I've done some pretty groovy things over the years, so life off the track – in daylight hours as well as after hours, which has always been a bit mad – hasn't really been that much of a contrast to life on the track. Certainly when it comes to things like danger and excitement.

Some drivers go fishing or cycling to wind down when they're not racing, but not me. I'm either listening to very loud music, jumping off moving speedboats on to other moving speedboats, rolling cars, back-flipping cars, driving cars off cliffs, covering a fast-moving conveyor belt with fairy liquid and then jumping on it to see what happens or abseiling down a skyscraper in London. That last one was part of *Mission Implausible*, and to start with they wanted me to run down it head first! I kid you not. Being terrified of heights, I had to decline their kind offer and went down backwards instead, like normal lunatics! Moving very quickly a foot and a half off the ground comes naturally to me but going very slowly 200 feet in the air doesn't. Spider Plato, I am not.

My real bread and butter with regards to TV, and the place I undoubtedly call home, is *Fifth Gear*, a television car show which has, not one, not two, but three professional or ex-professional racing drivers presenting it. What an interesting concept for a car show, don't you think? Ahem.

Anyway, let's start with the fruitcake that is Tiff Needell, shall we? I've known Tiff for, ooh, about twenty-five years? It must be getting on for that. Despite what I said about working at racing schools earlier, they provide a very useful service, as they prevent people who are good at driving fast from having to get a proper job and that, believe you me, is a blessing for all. Had I not been involved in racing schools, I might never have met Tiff, as he used to run manufacturer events like the one at which I squashed the Robin Reliant. He was the interface between the instructors and the manufacturers basically, so I'd worked with him – or should I say for him – quite a few times before landing the gig on *Fifth Gear* and as he was a fellow nutcase we'd always got on very well. Funnily enough, I also knew Vicki Butler-Henderson through racing schools, so in addition to the fact that we'd all raced professionally that was our link – and we all got on like a house on fire and still do, I'm pleased to say.

Fifth Gear's been through lots of changes over the years,

such as the locations we've used and the guest presenters we've had, but at the end of the day it has remained a factual entertainment car show with real-life reviews and real-life tests of cars from each end of the monetary and performance spectrum.

Anyway, enough of the bloody adverts. Let's have a few stories.

I suppose the biggest in terms of the effect it had on my racing career happened in 2007, when, after an accident on set, which seriously affected my performance in the final round of the BTCC at Thruxton, and after going into that round leading the championship, I ended up losing it by three points to the driver who'd been second. That doesn't happen every day.

The driver in question was Fabrizio Giovanardi, who is to winning touring car championships what I am to winning touring car races. In terms of championships, he's probably the most successful touring car driver in history, as he's won the BTCC twice and the Italian Touring Car Championship and the European Touring Car Championship three times each. In terms of races, Fabrizio still has a way to go, as he's about nineteen behind me, but if it's championships you're after, he's your bunny.

In the week leading up to that last weekend at Thruxton, I'd been asked to put a car called the Caparo T1 through its paces at Bruntingthorpe Aerodrome in Leicestershire. Designed and built by two engineers who'd worked on the MClaren F1 project, the Caparo T1 was basically a racing car for the road, and it looked very much like an open-top Le Mans car. It had a 3.5 litre V8 Indy Car engine in the back, a semi-automatic gearbox and a top speed of about 215 mph. Oh yes, and it cost about £200,000 – in 2007.

That's not all, though, as in addition to doing 0–60 mph in

just over two seconds and o–100 mph in less than five, it was capable of achieving an estimated lateral acceleration of 3 g with virtually the same for the braking deceleration. It was, so the blurb said, the fastest-accelerating production car in the world. It was like a flaming rocket ship.

I might be wrong here but I'm pretty sure I was one of the first people in the UK to review the Caparo T1, and because of its performance – and because it looked like a Le Mans car – I turned up in Leicestershire carrying my race suit.

'Ooh, we'd rather you didn't wear that,' said the manufacturer. 'After all, it is a road car.'

I looked at them and then looked at the car.

'Is it?'

'Yes, yes, it is,' they reassured me.

'OK. But I will be wearing my helmet.'

It was the first time I'd ever driven a car like that with road tyres on and as a result I could feel the front end understeering away from me. God, it was bizarre. As a track car it was like nothing I'd ever driven before, but if the track you were having to drive it to was any more than about 20 miles away you'd have been in trouble, as the vibrations were just immense. It was a road car in name only (or blurb only), and even things like a canopy and air con were going to cost new owners at least an extra two grand each. Even the tool kit was going to be over five grand. Five grand! It was obviously meant to rival the new supercars that were coming through at the time, but they had performance *and* comfort, whereas this just had the former.

During the review, I was coming down the straight when I felt a sudden loss of power. I looked in the left mirror, and there were some flames coming from the rear. I remember thinking, *Oops, that's not good!* As this was all happening, a strong burning smell filled the cockpit, and then I felt an intense heat quickly engulfing me. The car spontaneously erupted into a ball of flames. I was in the middle of a fireball!

After hitting the brakes, I brought the car to a stop as quickly as I could and jumped out. Roasted Plato, anyone? I don't think I'd never panicked as much in my entire life and although I was desperate to get out I'm surprised I could, as the heat was almost petrifying.

By the time I came to a halt, the cockpit was already in flames and my hands, neck and face bore the brunt of it. I'd been forced to take my hands off the wheel before coming to a halt as the heat was so intense and, after managing to undo my belt, I leaped out while the car was still moving. After I'd slowed to about 15 mph, the fire extinguished itself, as there was no vacuum in the cockpit, but the damage had already been done.

For some reason there were no paramedics on site (not a good idea when testing a car that does over 200 mph, but health and safety wasn't what it is now), but fortunately a mate of mine, Phil Bennett, who'd come to watch the test, whisked me off to Kettering Hospital, where I was immediately shown into a specialist cubicle. Straight away they said they wanted me to go to the burns unit at Stoke Mandeville Hospital in Buckinghamshire.

After cutting off my clothes at Kettering, the doctors had discovered there was no skin left on my right hand and very little on the left. According to the doctors at Stoke Mandeville, who I saw later, another couple of seconds more in the fire and I'd have lost the use of my right hand, as the tendons and ligaments would have been burned beyond repair.

Stupidly, I'd decided against wearing a balaclava that day (daft really, as it was October), and as a result the flames had poured down my neck, and that too was in a right mess and just as painful as the hand.

I think the problem they had with the car – or rather, I had – was to do with the oil filter. The engine was American, so it had American threads on it, and they'd put a Porsche oil filter on, which had metric threads.

About a month later Mr Clarkson reviewed the Caparo T1 for *Top Gear* and after making an understandable quip about my accident prior to starting his review – he christened me 'Baked Potato', which was rather clever – a floor panel came loose as he was driving the car at speed, and he almost crapped himself. Karma, Jezza, my old pal! Baked Potato indeed.

After that, there was a problem with the car's fuel injection system, and during his review Jezza mentioned two more incidents that had occurred beforehand: one at the press launch, when the front suspension came adrift while a journalist was driving, causing him to veer off-road, and one at the Goodwood Festival of Speed, when the throttle had stuck open. It was jinxed, basically, and as of 2012 only sixteen units had been sold in the UK.

After staying overnight at Stoke Mandeville, I made my way home, and then later that day the team came to see me. This was Tuesday, by the way, and I was supposed to be driving in just three days. As you can imagine, they were more than a bit shocked to see me covered in bandages, and their first reaction was there was no way I could race.

'It looks a lot worse than it is,' I lied. 'Seriously guys, I think I'll be fine by Friday.'

'I think we'd better organize a replacement just in case,' said the team.

Although that pissed me off a bit, I obviously couldn't argue against them organizing a replacement as, regardless of what I told them, it was obvious there was every chance I was going to need one, and the only person I was fooling by claiming otherwise was myself.

After popping back to my local hospital once or twice to get my dressings changed, I made my way down to Thruxton, which for those who don't know is in Andover in Hampshire. The first thing I did after arriving at the track was to go and see the medical director of the BTCC, Paul Trafford.

'Before I make any decisions about you racing,' said Traff, 'I've got to see the burns. We need to take the bandages off, JP.'

'I'd really rather you didn't, Traff,' I asked. 'Seriously, they feel OK at the moment.'

'I can't sign you off unless I see them,' he reiterated.

After having a look, Traff said I could race, but only after a lot of heavy persuasion from me. Even then it was probably against his better judgement, but I just had to give it a go. Because of the bandages we had to get gloves flown in especially, and I doubt they'd have even fitted Thing from the *Fantastic Four.* They were bloody huge! I was also in absolute agony, so although I had Traff's go ahead I still had an absolute mountain to climb.

When I first climbed in the car for free practice, I was obviously quite nervous, and because I was so worried about the pain my senses had become heightened to the point where I felt absolutely everything.

Because of the effect they have on you, I hadn't been allowed to take any strong painkillers, so with nothing but a couple of paracetamol swimming around inside me I set off.

Had it been a right-hand drive car, I'd have been fine, as my left hand could have done all the work, but as it was a left-hand drive my right hand had to do everything. Despite wearing bandages and gloves the size of tennis rackets, I still had no skin on my right hand, and every gear change – and I mean *every* gear change – was utter torture. I tried blocking it out, but the more I tried the worse it became.

God knows how, but I managed to finish second in the first two races, and although Fabrizio won both, I still had a one-point advantage going into the final race. This was enhanced slightly when I managed to qualify in front of him, but after battling the pain for free practice, two qualifying sessions and two races, I was really hanging out of my arse. As a result I got a less than perfect start and ended up finishing fourth to Fabrizio's second, which gave him the championship by just three points. Bugger. To be fair, Fabrizio had won ten races over the season as opposed to my six, so I couldn't begrudge him anything. He'd played a blinder.

It was the second time I'd finished runner-up in the BTCC, and it's happened four times since then, so I'm becoming quite prolific. Shit happens, though.

In hindsight, I should never have been racing at Thruxton, and had I been a less experienced driver who was less familiar to the BTCC bigwigs – and less persuasive – I would have gone straight home with my tail between my legs.

Icelandics Only Drink Milk, You Know

One thing I'm forever doing on *Fifth Gear* is punching Tiff Needell, and the reason I do this is threefold. First, he's an absolute nutcase behind a wheel; second, I'm a terrible passenger; and third, he knows I am a terrible passenger and enjoys putting the wind up me. The thing is, as he's up to all this, we're supposed to be doing a piece to camera, and the only thing that makes him slow down is a clump. Some might say it's foolhardy punching Tiff in the face when he's behind the wheel of a car and driving rather erratically, but it's the only language he understands in those circumstances. Believe me!

That's not to say I don't trust him. I do. In fact, in my opinion Tiff is the best TV driver in the world, in some respects bordering on being a genius, and he does things even I would never dream of doing. He's completely fearless, so if you put all that together you've got the makings of a supreme but ultimately unhinged pilot.

A few years ago Tiff and I went down to Dunsfold Aerodrome, which is the *Top Gear* test track, where we were due to do back-to-back tests of a Ferrari 458 Italia and a McLaren MP4-12C. In terms of notoriety, this was the test that everyone had wanted to see, and because I'd already done the original review of the Ferrari 458 Italia in Italy and had been told a few things about the MCLaren, I kind of knew what we were in for.

Normally what would happen in these circumstances is that I would drive one car and Tiff would drive the other, but because of the sheer gravity of the situation and the reputation of the marques we decided to swap around and both review each car. Tiff would take them for a general spin, as only he can, and I would do the fastest laps.

It's hard to put this into words really, but from the second Tiff got into the Ferrari 458 you could tell that he was completely in tune with it, and the lunacy that followed was just breathtaking. He'd never driven one before, yet everything aligned immediately. Everything!

When I got in I had a pretty similar experience (although I'd already driven one), and to cut a long story short we both agreed that it was one of the best cars we'd ever driven. It was just sublime.

The MClaren, on the other hand, was a completely different kettle of fish; although it looked incredible, it was hard work to drive. In terms of handling it was the antithesis to the Ferrari and within just a few minutes Tiff had ended up on the grass several times. He didn't hit anything, but there was one big moment where he went off in the direction of the old Jumbo Jet that's parked there and for the first few seconds he didn't look like he was going to stop.

When it comes to setting up the cameras for these tests it's all about trust. The cameramen will say to us, 'OK, guys, we want you coming out of that long fast corner sidewards, and in a perfect world we'd have the camera over there. Are you happy with that?' Then we'll say either yes or no, based mainly on our experience, the feel of the car and where we think our exit routes are going to be if something goes wrong. To the untrained eye you'd look at what the cameramen are doing and look at what we're doing and think, you lot are just seriously psychotic. We know what we're doing, though, which is why we always get such great shots.

Bearing in mind Tiff had been off a few times, when it came to setting up the other shots for the MClaren we erred on the side of caution to the point where on one particular shot, which was on the runway, we had to remove the cameraman altogether and do everything long distance. This had never happened before, but there was something about the MClaren that just didn't work for either of us, and at the time we couldn't put our fingers on it.

When it came to filming the shot, Tiff went off once again, and had the cameraman been in the same position he was for the Ferrari, which is the position he'd requested, he would have been wiped out. Lordy, that was scary.

As you'd expect, the MClaren ended up getting a really bad review. It had a layer of control that you couldn't turn off, so, unlike the Ferrari, which allowed the driver to be in control, it was always fiddling around in the background. Despite us believing everything had been turned off – the traction control and stability management, etc. – it hadn't at all. In layman's terms, the car wasn't programmed to cope with drivers like Tiff and me, who want to drive on, and over, the limit. It was programmed for people who would only drive up to the limit, and it would intervene at the earliest opportunity in order to prevent an accident. To make matters worse, we'd been driving both within, on, and over the limit, which confused the computer and resulted in all kinds of weird stuff. The way we put it off camera was that there was a level of *Ron-ness* in the car, as in Ron Dennis, who, so we'd heard once or twice, liked to maintain a level of control in everything he did. Speaking of whom . . .

When Ron saw our review he went absolutely orbital and was straight on the phone. We told him that as far as we were concerned there was something wrong with the car, and that our review had been fair. At the end of the day, it's up to the manufacturer to give us the ultimate example of the car they want us to review, and if the car isn't as it should be, it isn't our fault. Ron wasn't having any of it, though, and as far as he was concerned we'd unfairly screwed it up.

It turned out that there was a layer of torque reduction, and when you're hard on the throttle the last thing you want is the engine being wound back. When that happens it loses power to the wheels, and if you're on opposite lock it gets to the point where the front grips so much it snaps you off the track.

In my and Tiff's opinion, that summed up the problem in a nutshell, and MClaren ended up rectifying it with the next iteration of the car. When that came out, Tiff and Chris Goodwin, who was MClaren's chief test driver, went up to Rockingham to review it, and sure enough, the level of *Ron-ness* had been removed and it was a totally different proposition. Were we the sole reason for the change? I doubt it. I think a fairer hypothesis would be that our review perhaps catalysed the change. One claim I will make, however, is that there is no other car show on the planet that could have reviewed those cars the way that we did, because there's no other car show on the planet that has the likes of Tiff and me presenting it. Subsequently, all the driving you see on *Fifth Gear* is done by us, unlike the rest of them. Take *Top Gear*, for instance. Or *Top Gear*, as was. Do you really think that Jezza, Hammond and James did all their own driving? James probably did, as he rarely went above 30 mph, but Jezza and Hammond didn't. Or at least not all of it. Take their sliding shots, for instance. You never see the end of the slide because they've usually spun off and for all the really sexy stuff they use polarizing filters so you can't see inside the car. Jeremy Clarkson is a brilliant writer and a brilliant presenter but he is not a brilliant driver. He ain't bad, but he can't do what Tiff and I do. Likewise Richard Hammond.

Don't get me wrong. I totally get why they do what they do with regards to making it look like the Clarksons, Hammonds and Matt LeBlancs of this world are brilliant drivers, as they want viewers to believe that they're the whole package, but the truth is, they aren't. Tiff and I might not have the edge as presenters, although we're not bad, but at least we do all our own driving. That has always been, and remains, our USP on *Fifth Gear*, and it gives me great pleasure to brag about it.

I think the maddest thing I've ever been asked to do on *Fifth Gear* – so far – is to go to Reykjavik in Iceland and ride a buggy up the side of a cliff. On the face of it that doesn't sound too peculiar, I suppose, but once I've filled in the gaps, you'll realize why. For a start, the cliffs were often sheer and went up hundreds of feet, and the buggies we used to ascend them had around 800 brake horsepower. It was the people, though, who made it really scary, as they were absolutely off their nuts and made Tiff and me look like Ant & Dec.

When we arrived in Iceland, it was absolutely freezing, and the first thing we did was go to the workshop of the chap who'd be teaching me how to drive one of these things. Because it was so cold, I asked this mad Icelander, who was called Hafsteinn, if he could pop up to the kitchen and get us a round of teas or something, but apparently that wasn't going to be possible.

'We only drink milk,' he said. 'Nothing else but milk.'

'You must have a kettle or something,' I pleaded. 'It's minus ten outside, pal!'

'No, no. We only drink milk in Iceland.'

The people were lovely, but they were bloody weird.

We eventually decamped to where they drove these buggies, which was inside an old quarry, and my first words to the Icelandic milk drinker and our producer were, *You have got to be joking*. I could not get my head around how a buggy was going to make it up the side of this quarry. It was like trying to comprehend infinity. It must have been at least 300 feet from top to bottom and at least half of the climb would be up sheer cliffs. It must have been 80 degrees from top to bottom. Had I known that something like this existed, I'd have been able to research it a bit and get my head around doing it beforehand, but just turning up there was a complete bloody head screw.

'Come on, JP,' said the producer. 'He's going to take you up there now.'

'He is not! I'm sorry, but that's just stupid.'

'You'll have a neck brace, and the buggies obviously have roll cages.'

'I don't care,' I said. 'I'm an intrepid racing car driver and television presenter, not a kamikaze pilot!'

After watching some locals give it a go, I started warming to the idea, but only because it looked like fun. My opinion hadn't changed on how dangerous it looked.

The sport itself is called Formula Off-Road, and they've been doing it in Iceland for over thirty years.

Before he took me on a run, I asked Hafsteinn if he'd had

any recent injuries, and he said, nonchalantly, 'No, not injuries. I did lose my memory for two days a couple of weeks ago, but that's it.'

I was about to ascend an 80 degree cliff with a man who didn't consider two days of memory loss to be an injury. Wahey!

Because we both had helmets on and because of the incredible noise the buggy made – which, incidentally, had a higher power to weight ratio than a Ferrari 458 Italia – I couldn't hear a bloody thing Hafsteinn was saying. In fact, the only time I heard him speak in the buggy was when he said, 'Ready?', about a second before we set off.

The aim of the ride was to teach me how to drive one of these buggies and build up my confidence, but when the ascent you're about to make genuinely doesn't seem possible that confidence is very hard to come by.

In terms of fear that initial run was up there with driving with Tiff and if memory serves they had to cut out some pretty fruity language. We cleared it, though, and as we did so I might just have let out a very small, 'Woohoo!'

'OK,' said Hafsteinn. 'Now we drive down.'

Oh shit. I hadn't even considered getting down again.

'The quicker the better,' said Hafsteinn.

This bit was even scarier, because as opposed to not believing it possible to descend the cliff you just thought you were going to die. Or at least I did. I remember the front of the buggy falling over the brow of the cliff, and as it did so the *I am actually going to die* thing kicked into gear. Quickly, and under my breath, I started saying, 'Oh fuck, oh fuck, oh fuck.'

When it came to me having a go we moved to what I suppose they'd call the nursery cliffs, which, although almost vertical, were a mere 150 feet high. Simples!

Hafsteinn obviously stayed in with me, and the first thing we tried was a descent.

'OK, make sure you take it quick,' he advised me. 'There'll be less chance of an accident.'

'You mean the quicker we get down the less chance we have of dying?'

'That's correct,' said Hafsteinn.

While I wasn't exactly hyperventilating, my breathing was speeding up and my ticker going like the proverbial poorhouse door. Because the idea of bombing down there was so unnatural, my instincts took over and we ended up descending like a couple of octogenarians in a Mini Metro, but for a first attempt that was all I could muster.

'We must go faster next time,' said Hafsteinn.

'Next time?'

After faring slightly better on the ascent, in that I took Hafsteinn's advice this time, which was, and I quote, 'Just point it and pull the trigger', he then asked if I'd like to have a go on one of the larger cliffs.

Not knowing what the Icelandic was for *Look, just bugger off, will you. I want to go home*, I did the decent thing and accepted his ridiculous offer.

What really turns up the fear factor with Formula Off-Road is that you don't even do a run-up to the cliffs, as it's counterproductive, so you literally drive up to the foot of one, stop and then set off.

Once again, the old lungs and ticker were working overtime as we approached the climb, but I was up for the challenge. The producer had said beforehand, 'Do this and we can go home JP', and with that as my maxim I pointed Hafsteinn's buggy in the direction we wanted it to go, pulled the trigger and tried not to close my eyes. This time I forgot to speak, or wasn't able to, which is quite important when you're recording a piece to camera. The last 50 feet or so was completely vertical, and as we continued scrambling upwards, although at an increasingly slower pace, all I could think about was the 300 or so feet below us. It was frigging horrible!

Somehow we managed to conquer the last 50 feet, and after getting my breath back, I vowed there and then never to try Formula Off-Road again. Never! Then, like a horrible little gravity goblin, Hafsteinn said, 'OK, now we go down. Quickly!'

Oh bollocks! I'd forgotten about that.

After we managed to descend the cliff safely, Hafsteinn went up one of the really big cliffs on his own and ended up taking a proper big shunt. There was no memory loss, fortunately, but he got one or two bumps and bruises. Regardless of which, I think it was time to leave Iceland.

Formula Off-Road is a constant fight against gravity that you can lose in the blink of an eye, and although I'd enjoyed dipping into it, I longed for terra firma and tarmac. I did offer to buy Hafsteinn a kettle, though, and some tea and coffee.

'No thanks. We drink milk in Iceland.'

Laced with acid, perhaps.

Incidentally, one of the most amusing things about being in Iceland was discovering that they're all a bunch of piss-heads. Or at least a lot of the people I witnessed during my stay were. We were only there for two or three days, but one evening we went out, and the whole of downtown Reykjavik seemed to be full of people on a mission to get hammered. Even by 8 p.m. there were people bouncing off shop windows and stuff. It was just epicly weird.

The difference I found between there and other places is that, despite being three sheets to the wind, the people were still warm and friendly, and that remained the case the entire evening. Whether that's a cultural thing or not I don't know, but argy bargy didn't seem to feature on anyone's agenda that night, and it was a real eye-opener.

Anyway, now we've done terror and weirdness, let's move on to a bit of pleasure, shall we, as one of the best things about working on *Fifth Gear* is that I get to visit the Ferrari head-quarters in Maranello from time to time.

Some of you will obviously have been to Maranello before, but I'd wager that the majority of you haven't. Well, if you ever get the opportunity, go. Despite it having a lot of high-tech equipment on site and there being a lot of new buildings, the whole place just screams history, and the more you get to know the history of Ferrari the more the place comes to life.

The Cavallino Restaurant, which is about 200 yards from the factory, is where all the Ferrari top brass and drivers eat. There's no menu at the Cavallino, so you literally eat what they're cooking that day, and the memorabilia they have on show is just mind-blowing. If you're a petrol-head who likes the colour red, there's no better place to eat in the world.

In the 1970s, when Ferrari built the in-house Fiorano test circuit, Enzo decided to have his office and apartment there, and when he died in 1988, the company decided to leave every-thing exactly as it was and preserve it. It's frozen in time, and what a time! The place is breathtaking. He used to write in purple felt-tip pen, and all his pens are on the desk, and his diary's open exactly where he left it.

The thing that gave me the biggest thrill was seeing the

photograph on his desk. There's just one, and it's of Gilles Villeneuve, who had died six years before Enzo, in 1982. When I was a kid, he'd always been my favourite driver, and when I saw it I almost wept. Ferrari have done exactly the same thing with Enzo's apartment at Fiorano, and with Michael Schumacher's apartment. As I said, it just oozes history.

When I first saw Michael's apartment, I struggled to believe it had been frozen in time, as at the end of his bed was a huge bust of . . . Michael Schumacher! Then, after thinking about it for a second, I came to the conclusion that it was, of course, totally Michael!

We've always had a great relationship with Ferrari at *Fifth Gear*, which is one of the reasons I've been there so many times. Again, perhaps it's because Tiff and I are professional racing drivers, as opposed to just presenters, but they allow us to do things that are not the Ferrari way. For instance, every other journalist or TV presenter who visits Ferrari, for whatever reason, will have a chaperone who stays with them constantly and tries to avert any negative feedback. Tiff and I, on the other hand, are always left to our own devices. Here are the keys, boys, there's the track, we'll see you later. Every time we've tested a car at Fiorano, they've walked away and left us to it. Knowing that a trust exists between us is a really special feeling. The top brass, too, will always come out and have a bit of lunch with us.

It has that unique mixture, though, of very traditional craftsmanship, which can be seen at the Scaglietti Factory, and bleeding-edge technology. Normally, the two would be at odds with each other, but at Ferrari they complement each other. On the first and second floors at the Scaglietti Factory there's a V8 and V12 production line where the automation on display is just astonishing. Then, just around the corner from that, you've got the foundry where they cast the engines. Does this fusion of traditional and tech happen elsewhere? Probably. But the fact that it happens at Ferrari makes it special and tells you exactly who they are.

Lastly, and this alone should have you searching for plane tickets, because they're constantly road testing new cars, all you ever hear on the streets of Maranello are Ferrari-made V8 and V12 engines, so the soundscape more than matches the view. Seriously, if you get a chance to go, go!

Before we get on to Girls Allowed, who are the subject of my next story, did you know that back in the 1990s I spent several years appearing in *Coronation Street*? It's perfectly true. I was on the wall of Kevin Webster's workshop. They don't do it so much these days, but back then advertising departments at magazines used to get in touch with up-and-coming racing drivers like me and ask us if we'd like to thank our sponsors by taking out a big advert. Being a bit young and naive, I decided to take out one of these adverts, although I did manage to get Duckhams, the oil manufacturer, to pay for it, which was a touch. Duckhams then decided to distribute copies of the advert, which featured a big photo of me on it, and somehow one of them ended up on Kevin Webster's wall! For absolutely donkey's years, every time they did some filming in Kevin Webster's garage my ugly mug would be in the background, grinning away like a Cheshire cat. What was I saying about profile? I can't think of any other racing driver who's made regular appearances on Britain's favourite soap opera.

Funnily enough, we'd done some filming up at the *Corrie* studios for *Driven*, so I actually visited the scene of the crime. I was obviously just born to be on television.

The biggest waste of money I've ever been involved in for something committed to celluloid was an advert I did for SEAT. I'm pretty sure the advert was meant for cinema audiences, and the budgets were equal to the medium. Seriously, they blew tens of thousands of pounds a second on that shoot, and the final cost was many millions. Peanuts to them, perhaps, but for the time I was in Spain for the shoot I just stood agog, thinking, *How much?*

The storyboard for the ad was simplicity itself, although they did make some alternatives. Basically, I and six other drivers run towards a SEAT Ibiza, obviously hoping to drive it, and after we try to knock each other out of the way, a gorgeous woman drives off in it and gives us the finger. Not exactly *Citizen Kane*, but there you go.

Instead of asking me to fly out there with an airline, they sent a private jet for me. As far as I know, they did the same for the other six drivers, so that was seven private jets to start with. We were out there for four days, and the hotel was one of the best I'd ever stayed in, so that too must have cost a packet.

The funniest part was when we started filming outdoors. The sun was beating down like a good'n, yet they started erecting these lights that were the size of small planets. *But you've got the frigging sun*, I thought to myself. *What the hell do you need them for?* Bearing in mind we were simply supposed to be running towards a parked car and having a bit of argy bargy along the way, they treated it like *Gone with the Bloody Wind*, and we ended up shooting the scene at least twenty times. The people, though. It was a thirty-second advert that I could have shot on my camcorder with a pal, yet there must have been at least 150 people milling around. They were seriously haemorrhaging money.

One thing I've forgotten to tell you is that one of the six drivers who joined me in Spain was – Yvan Muller! It was a good few years after our spat, so some water had passed under the bridge. Even so, we were never going to be bosom buddies, and there was only so much we could say really, as neither was going to apologize. At least we didn't kill each other!

I remember approaching him in the hotel after we'd arrived, and all I could think about was him refusing my handshake on the podium at Silverstone. I should have tried to channel some nice thoughts about Yvan, but the fact of the matter is, there weren't any.

OK, let's get on to the coolest thing I've ever done on *Fifth Gear*.

A few years ago somebody came up with the bright idea of recreating the scene from *The Italian Job* where they drive the Minis back on to the bus. OMG, yes please!

We managed to get hold of one of the buses that had doors at the back and no seats and we even had one of the drivers who'd appeared in the original film. Frank Jarvis was his name, and he played Roger, who, as well as driving one of the iconic Minis, can be seen on the back of the bus right at the end of the film when it's tilting on the edge of the cliff. Can you imagine how cool it was recreating that scene and spending a day with one of the original cast members? It was just epic.

On another occasion – this is still in the cool bracket, by the way – we were in Italy to review the new Lamborghini Gallardo Super Sport, in brightest orange, and the night before the review we thought, wouldn't it be a great idea to try and blag our way on to the test track on top of the Lingotto building? For those of you who can't remember or, heaven forbid, have never seen *The Italian Job*, the Lingotto test track features towards the end of the film, when the Minis are trying to make their getaway, and because it's so iconic we thought it would be great to get some shots of the Gallardo up there.

After managing to hide some cameras in order to film our attempt, we arrived as bold as brass at the security gates and announced that we were there to film a review of the new Lamborghini Gallardo. Bearing in mind the Gallardo is on the top of the former Fiat factory now owned by Ferrari, and Lamborghini are Ferrari's sworn enemies, this was a bit of an effrontery, but that was why we were there for heaven's sake!

Fortunately for us, the security guard was obviously a massive petrol-head, so after we gave it a few revs and invited him to take a quick look, he waved us through. A bit further on, there was yet another security guard, so yet again we stated our business, gave the Lambo a few revs and managed to proceed.

The only thing separating us now from the fated factory roof, test track and iconic movie location was a spiral road leading up to the track. Surely we weren't going to actually make it up there without being collared?

As all this had been going on, we'd managed to hide a few more cameras about the place to capture our audacity and, as with everything else, we managed it. When we finally emerged on to the track itself, I felt a tingle down the back of my spine. There's an ultra-posh restaurant up there now, and to stop people racing they've installed a few sleeping policemen. Even so, we still succeeded in getting half a lap in, and just as we'd done that, the security guards cottoned on and went absolutely orbital. Boy, did they bollock us, and all in glorious Italian! We had the shot, though, so we just smiled and said sorry.

Ciao Bella!

Right, then, it's time for Cheryl to see red.

In 2006, I got a call from the *Fifth Gear* office asking me if I'd like to do a feature with the pop group Girls Aloud. Despite not being an aficionado of their repertoire, I'd heard of them, and purely in the interests of professionalism and courtesy, I said yes. Or *wey aye, pet*, as their most prominent member might say.

This was at the height of Girls Aloud's fame, and the idea was for me to take each of them around the track at Silverstone a few times to see who the fastest driver was. It was standard stuff really, but with Girls Aloud being the biggest girl band in the country at the time, and by some margin, it was obviously a bit of a coup for the show, and I was looking forward to it.

The vast majority of our guests turn up on time for any filming jobs, but had we stopped to think about it for a second we might have come to the conclusion that getting five famous girls in their twenties to a racetrack all at the same time might just be a bit much to ask – and we would have been right! I forget how late they were, but we'd progressed from the *blimey, I wish they'd hurry up* stage to the *where the hell are they* stage.

When they finally did turn up, their entourage was enormous, but we'd been expecting that. We also had Silverstone on lockdown for the day, as had been requested, as they didn't want any punters or press hanging around. Yep, fair dos.

The first thing we had planned was for me to take them out, one at a time, in a Porsche 911. As well as saying hello to each of them, I wanted to see if we had any speed freaks in our midst and I also wanted to see how they reacted when I put my foot down. That always makes for good TV, taking people around a track at high speed. After that, we'd go out again, except this time they'd be driving, and whoever recorded the fastest lap would go out with me again, and I'd teach them how to drive a Lamborghini.

In the end the truck driving the Lamborghini broke down en route to Silverstone, which kind of threw a spanner in the works, as that was meant to be the finale. A beautiful-looking girl driving a beautiful-looking car – with me! In the end, Lamborghini said they'd try and send a replacement, as the original one had been damaged slightly, and because it was Girls Aloud we thought they'd pull out all the stops and get it sorted.

At the very beginning of proceedings the girls and I sat around and had a chat for a while, with me holding court. This was all filmed, and the topic of conversation was what kind of car they had and all that kind of stuff. Kimberley Walsh had a Peugeot 206 convertible, which was OK; Sarah Harding had a Toyota RAV4, which wasn't; Nadine Coyle had a Merc, which was fine, as did Cheryl Cole – or Tweedy, as I think she was then; and Nicola Roberts had an Audi TT.

The only one who didn't want to be there was our Cheryl, and after our little chat she went off somewhere, and nobody could find her. As I and the other girls were continuing our conversation in the foyer of the race school, we started asking where Cheryl was, and just for a laugh I suggested that she might have gone for a number two. The cameras were still rolling, and with only four girls playing ball I was trying to lighten the mood a bit. Unfortunately, Cheryl got wind of my supposition as to her whereabouts and went straight back to the tour bus and locked the door. Funnily enough, like you would if you were going for a number two!

The manager went over to speak to her, the girls went over to speak to her, and even I went over to speak to her, but she wasn't interested.

The one I clicked the most with was Sarah Harding. She was a laugh from start to finish and was the only one who got any of my cheeky one-liners. Before taking the girls out in the 911, the director had asked me to get a bit flirty with them verbally, and with the other three girls every single comment went flying over their heads. Not Sarah, though. As well as being quite laddish, she was quite obviously a latent speed freak (you'd have to be latent, driving a Toyota RAV4), as well as having a very saucy sense of humour, she was a flirt, and as opposed to squealing as I slid into a corner at 90 mph, she shouted, 'Get in!' She was my kind of nutcase, basically.

When it came to swapping seats and allowing the girls to take the wheel, Miss Harding was the only one who cut the mustard. To be fair, I probably made more of an effort instructing her, but she was always going to win. We did manage to get Cheryl to come out and do a lap, by the way, but it was under duress, and she was straight back in the tour bus afterwards.

About an hour before Sarah and I were due to record the Lamborghini bit, they called up and said that it wasn't going to be possible to get anything to us in time, and after us thinking on our feet I begged Silverstone to lend us one of their track-prepared Ferrari F355s. At first, they weren't keen, as at about a hundred grand a pop they didn't come cheap, but after a few assurances and some gentle persuasion, they relented. Thank God! The one they gave us had been on the premises a matter of days, and when Sarah clapped eyes on it she was like a kid in a sweet shop with a handful of pound coins. What could possibly go wrong?

As opposed to me taking her out first, which might have given her a false impression about how you were supposed to drive the Ferrari, we thought it best to let her take the wheel – with plenty of instruction from me, of course.

Unfortunately, instead of asking Sarah beforehand if she'd ever driven a left-hand-drive car and enquiring as to whether it might be a problem, we just strapped her in, pointed her in the direction of the track and told her to crack on. She was like a coiled spring, bless her, and instead of me concentrating on getting her from the car park to the track, I was thinking about the quick bit.

The only gap that Sarah had to negotiate between the car park and the track was between the 911 and the tour bus, and at a conservative estimate I'd say there would have been about a metre either side – had she driven through the middle! Unfortunately, Sarah became a little bit spatially confused by the whole left-hand-drive thing and ended up driving into the side of the tour bus and in doing so knocked out the wing mirror on the Ferrari and a couple of panels. Had I been concentrating fully, I might have been able to prevent the accident happening, but with Sarah being all giddy and me being all apprehensive, I just wasn't at the races. I did try and steer her to the left at the very last second, but unfortunately the damage had been done.

Bollocks!

Like a gentleman, I sat there saying, 'Oh, don't worry about it. It'll be fine', while all the time knowing that the good people at Silverstone would be sticking pins into Jason Plato dolls and asking the team I was driving for at the time if they'd kindly replace me for the Silverstone round of the BTCC. Apparently, Sarah had seen the Porsche on the left, turned away from it, but had forgotten there was a massive Chrysler on the right.

While I was trying to placate her, she then started revving the engine with the intention of reversing. 'No, no, no, no!' I said quickly. 'Please don't. Just turn off the engine. It'll be fine.'

By the time we managed to extract ourselves from the Ferrari, the car park was full of girl band members, girl band entourage people and Silverstone and *Fifth Gear* bods all scratching their heads going, 'How the hell did she do that?'

To be fair to Silverstone, they were great about it, as I think they realized that it was going to be great PR. And it was, for all of us! It isn't something I'd do again though.

Actually, who am I kidding? Of course I bloody would!

I think we should finish off this chapter with a bit of naughtiness, don't you?

By far the biggest faux pas I've ever made during my twenty-odd years on the box happened on a flight to Dubai one day to film a *Driven* item and is one of those unfortunate occasions when I let high jinks go a little bit too far.

It was before the advent of things like tablets and smart phones, so before the flight I went to the newsagents and bought a load of magazines. It was quality fare. *FHM*, *Maxim* and *Loaded*. Anyway, resting in the middle of one of these respected titles was a packet of free stickers that had been designed specifically to have fun with on a long plane journey – although probably not to Dubai. As is the way, I'm afraid the end of that last sentence didn't click with me, and after taking off I surreptitiously removed the stickers from the magazine and went to work.

The first one in the pack was a parody of the stickers you get in toilets asking if you've washed your hands. It featured a man holding his penis with the words *Have you washed your dick?* underneath. That one went straight up in the toilets, and when I got back to my seat, I let on to the production team what was happening.

What they should have done – and I blame them for the whole thing – is to say, *Now come on, JP. They're pretty strict on stuff like this in the UAE. Why not just sit down and try and have a nap, eh?* Instead, they just aided and abetted me, and after putting a load of stickers under the overhead locker doors saying *Please do not put dirty bombs in these lockers*, I sat down and told them what I intended to do next.

'When the hostesses arrive with the food,' I said, 'I want you to distract them for a second, OK?'

'OK.'

The last load of stickers were meant to go on the tin foil covering the food and said simply *May contain traces of semen*.

'OK, then, ready?' I said to my accomplice, as the hostesses arrived with the food.

As he distracted the hostesses, I went to the rear of the trolley where the meals were stacked up and managed to distribute about fifteen stickers. It was a damn good effort.

'Chicken or beef, sir?' asked one of the hostesses after I returned to my seat.

'Erm, I think I'll have chicken please,' I said, trying not to snigger.

Some passengers noticed the stickers immediately and some didn't, and the reaction they garnered was a mixture of gasps and giggles, although mainly gasps. Traces of semen tend to have that effect on people.

After the hostesses retrieved the meals from those who'd

complained, one of them ran off to the galley, where she spoke to her superior. I was still giggling myself silly at this point, as were the lads from *Driven*, but that all changed when the hostess and her superior pulled back the curtain and emerged from the galley. Despite being slim and very attractive, their faces were like thunder. Worse still, they only had eyes for me.

The last time I'd experienced trepidation like this was when I was skulking in that vaulting box at school, and I don't mind admitting that, when the inevitable tap on the shoulder finally arrived, I jumped about a foot and a half in the air.

'Can I help you,' I snivelled, trying, and failing, to feign innocence.

'Could I have a word with you in the galley please, sir?' asked the boss.

'What about?'

'Just follow me, would you?'

I did as I was told, stepped into the aisle and then walked, in between the two hostesses, towards the galley. I was the epitome of a condemned man.

As opposed to asking me what I'd done, the chief hostess got straight to the point.

'If you haven't removed every single sticker within two minutes, the captain will divert the plane and you will be arrested. If, in that time, a passenger sees one of the stickers, takes offence and complains, we will divert anyway and you will be arrested.'

Christ on a bike! Or in this instance, a plane covered in rude stickers.

'OK,' I said apologetically. 'I'll start with the dirty bombs.'

Because I'd put up so many, and over a period of hours,

I had to do an entire sweep of the plane, and the last one I removed was a *Strictly no shagging* sticker that I'd placed in one of the business-class toilets. It was a lucky escape.

The reason we were going to Dubai was to have a look at Sheikh Mohammed bin Rashid Al Maktoum's car collection. He's the King of Dubai and as well as having twenty-three children (how many?!), he's got a car collection worth tens of millions of pounds.

While we were having a conversation with a member of the Sheikh's staff, somebody from *Driven* suggested, wouldn't it be great if we could drive one of these cars flat out somewhere, not expecting for a moment that it would happen.

'This can be arranged,' said the member of staff.

'Really?'

Within a couple of hours the police had closed one of the main highways in Dubai, and I was driving a Mercedes CLR Le Mans car at 205 mph. This was work, real work!

Staying in the UAE for a second, in 2016 I and a film crew went to Abu Dhabi for the annual drag racing festival, where, as well as having a go in a dragster myself, I got to watch an American chap called Rod Fuller, who was then the third-fastest man on the planet, try and break a record that would almost render me a nervous wreck.

The dragster I had a go in first had 1,200 horsepower and could, theoretically, if it could go that far, cover a mile in just under twenty seconds. It was, and still is, the fastest thing we've ever driven on *Fifth Gear*, and about ten minutes before my run I got strapped in and tried to compose myself.

Unfortunately, the dragster that went out before me spat a load of oil on the track, and that completely messed up my equilibrium. There's a lot more to do in a dragster than just grasping the steering wheel and driving forwards. You've got to arm the transmission and then set up the transmission break before getting it into gear, etc. I'll be honest with you, I was incredibly nervous. No amount of time or concentration, however, could have prepared me for the experience itself, and I ended up completing the quarter mile in circa five seconds, reaching a top speed of 172 mph.

Impressive?

Not really.

Rod's vehicle was on a completely different plane to mine and at the time of us making the film it was the fastest-accelerating vehicle on either land, sea or air. Get these for a couple of speed stats: its horsepower was 8,000, which is more than the first four rows of an F1 grid, and it did 0–150 kph in just eight-tenths of a second. EIGHT-TENTHS OF A SECOND!

Rod was trying to become the first man ever outside the USA to do the 500 kph quarter-mile run, and it was a record he was desperate to set. One misplaced twitch of the steering wheel, however, and he'd be toast.

It's very hard to describe extreme speed, especially when it's in a straight line, and I'd have to urge you to watch the film online, as that obviously gives you at least some idea of what I witnessed.

And what did I witness?

Well, Rod ended up reaching 507 kph – that's 315 mph – in just 3.9 seconds. It was just mind-bending.

Being a racer, that wasn't enough for Rod, and as darkness fell he decided to go again. Unfortunately, his engine exploded under the force of its own power and, $65,000 later, which was the cost of a new engine – which, I have to add, was installed in just fifteen minutes – he finally gave it another pop.

With the track temperature having cooled slightly, he didn't manage to break his own record, but watching him go for a second time trackside was just monstrous, and this time I almost had a bloody heart attack. It's not often I'm lost for words, but when it came to wrapping up the film shortly after Rod's second attempt the best I could manage was, 'That man is insane!'

Going Toe to Toe with the Jolly Green Giant

Something I have to touch on in this book is my rivalry with Matt Neal, not least because we almost came to blows in the pit lane back in 2011 and have been winding each other up on and off the track for donkey's years. Actually, it's more me winding him up really, but that's fine.

I'm often referred to by some people as the pantomime villain of the BTCC, and although it's supposed to be a joke, there's actually an element of truth in it. You see, one thing I never try and do at the day job is get pally with the other drivers, and some people think that makes me a bit standoffish.

Just before the big photograph is taken of all the drivers at the start of the season, I'm usually at one end on my own and away from the group, and that's totally intentional. Don't get me wrong, I'm not rude to the other drivers unless they're rude to me, and there are plenty that I get on with. I just choose not to get pally at work and instead I choose to maintain a distance. I'm there to do a job, when all's said and done, and although I obviously respect the other drivers I regard myself as being a cut above. Call me an overconfident cocky bugger if you like, but that's the way it is, and any criticism of my behaviour – and there's been plenty over the years, believe me – is like water off a duck's back. Being a bit confident is part of who I am and so part of my success. Speaking of which . . .

Since forcing my way into the Willies team back in 1997, I've built a record that includes 97 BTCC wins (34 more than anyone else currently on the grid), 229 podiums (almost half the races I've started), 50 poles, 88 fastest laps, 2 BTCC championships, 8 BRDC awards, and I'm a two-time National Racing Driver of the Year. In terms of race wins, I'm one of the most successful British racing drivers in history, and do you know what, I don't do things by the book, but then I doubt I'd be where I am today if I followed all the rules.

The pantomime villain tag isn't exclusive to the paddock, though. Heck no. In fact, I'd go as far as to say that in terms of driving style I'm probably one of the most contentious drivers there's ever been in the BTCC. It all leads back to what I said earlier about me going for race wins rather than championships, and my attitude to it all is as direct and unapologetic as my driving style. There's no use pretending otherwise.

Which brings me on to my feud with the ginormous Mr Neal, who, if you're not aware of him, is so tall he's insured against low-flying aircraft and is a black belt in several martial arts, so I've been told.

Not the sort of chap you'd want to fall out with, then, you're probably thinking.

Well, that would be true if I were a normal human being working in a conventional job and environment, but I'm not. I do lots of very silly things for a living and lots of other very silly things in my spare time, and when it comes to my behaviour on the track I will not compromise, regardless of who's threatening to punch my lights out.

I think there are probably lots of people who work in so-called conventional jobs who have exactly the same attitude that I do, and it's probably got a lot more to do with the way you're born than what you do for a living. Having a screw loose? Being a bit unpredictable? There are certainly plenty of names for it, but in my humble opinion it has more to do with what you want and how much you want it. An all-or-nothing attitude, some might call it.

I think the aggro between Matt and me started sometime during my years at SEAT, as prior to that I hadn't really come into contact with him either on or off the track. Matt wasn't a karter, and although he's been racing in the BTCC a few years more than I have, in the early days he was a privateer, and by the time we started tussling for the same pieces of tarmac I was at SEAT and he was at Honda. That said, Matt did achieve what was considered to be the impossible as a privateer, which was to win a race outright, and because the odds against it happening were so great the purse was a cosy £250,000!

Anyway, in 2005, which is when I was at SEAT, Honda managed to find a way of entering the Integra Type R, which was a two-door sports car, into the BTCC. It wasn't a touring car, it was a grand tourer, end of story.

As a result, Honda ended up blitzing everybody that year, so much so that it became ridiculous. They were so much faster than everyone else, but their grip was also bonkers. It turned the races into foregone conclusions, and, as we all know, foregone conclusions are really bad for sport. The thing is – and this just added insult to injury for the other teams – instead of waiting to execute a manoeuvre like they could have, they just barrelled everyone out of the way and became the scourge of the championship. I remember one instance at Goodwood corner at Thruxton where Matt literally came along the inside and, instead of waiting for a gap to appear, he just barrelled me out of the way. There was no skill involved, nor was there even an element of chance. It was just Mad Max all the way, or in this case, Mad Matt. Everybody's nose was out of joint, and the atmosphere in the paddock was just crap. Everyone was angry, and everyone hated Matt and Honda.

Now, there'll be some people reading this – BTCC fans, probably – who are thinking, *Hang on a minute, you've just said that you drive aggressively, and that's OK*. Ah yes, but there's a difference. Remember what I said in the last paragraph about there not even being any chance involved in Honda's manoeuvres? That, my friends, is the difference between how I do things and how Honda and Matt did things in the Integra. With them, there was nothing left to chance, it was just, FORWARD! Like a tank, really. With me, I like to harass other drivers to the point that, when a gap does appear, they're so pissed off and agitated with me driving up their arse that they either make a mistake or make the gap even bigger. It's another form of pester power, I suppose, and sometimes it works and sometimes it doesn't. The truth is, however, that as a style of driving its main components are chance, perseverance and endeavouring to create opportunity as opposed to just out-and-out aggression.

Am I the only driver in the BTCC to adopt that style of driving? Absolutely not. In fact, you could say that all three components are prerequisites for motor racing in general, the variance being to what degree you decide to use those components and how successful you are. I have my own way of implementing them, and although it's not everyone's cup of tea, it quite obviously works.

After a while, I started remonstrating with Matt and Honda about what was going on, and, as you can imagine, it led to some pretty unsavoury encounters in the pit lane. This was great for the TV cameras and the journalists, but unless it's an isolated incident it's not going to be healthy, and to be honest it was all becoming a bit toxic.

Then, at Snetterton, Matt tried the same manoeuvre again by just barging me off on the inside, but this time I'd had enough. It happened on the final lap, after he'd managed to reduce my four and a half second lead to bugger all, and it was just a case of whether he'd play it safe and settle for second place, as he didn't really need the points, or whether he'd do what I probably would have done and go for the win. Fortunately for the punters, but not for me, he chose the latter, and so it was game on.

One thing I'm quite good at, or so I've been told, is driving my line well, and I only tend to defend it when it's absolutely necessary. Defending when it isn't necessary makes it easier for the guy behind you to get on your back, and despite my mirrors being full of Matt's orange Honda, I stuck to my line and just waited for him to try and barge through. It was only a matter of time.

Sure enough, on the exit out of a corner Matt attempted to come through on the inside, but instead of relenting, I held my line as hard as I could. This course of action was obviously at odds with what Matt had been used to and what he'd been expecting. Consequently, as he began to turn into the next corner he was only centimetres in front of me, and because I was now defending he spun sideways. The language coming out of my cockpit at the time was too rich even for this book, and I bet it was the same with Matt. The fact is, though, I'd simply administered a bit of his own medicine, and because his tactics had worked so well thus far, he didn't like it.

Despite running sideways for a couple of seconds Matt was straight back online, and before I knew it, my mirrors were full of him again.

As we came into the final corner, exactly the same thing happened again. I held my line, Matt tried the barge through, and I didn't let him. As a result, he went off, I won the race, and my new adversary finished fourth. Afterwards, Matt had the effrontery to suggest that he'd attempted two clean manoeuvres and that I'd acted less than fairly, which was just cobblers. What else could he say, though?

At Silverstone, Matt was obviously out for revenge, and this time he employed a different but even less subtle manoeuvre. Instead of taking me off on the inside, he simply barged into the back of me. It happened on turn one, and he literally just spun me around in front of a pack of about thirty cars.

I've often likened Matt's driving during that period to having an oversized bloke on the dance floor. They're usually a bit clumsy, and their dance moves tend to lack any style or finesse. It wasn't touring car racing. It was stock car racing.

Anyway, that's where the war between Matt and me began, and from then on we always seemed to be vying for the same bit of track, and when that wasn't happening, we'd be winding each other up. It was – and is, I suppose – a classic motorsport rivalry.

After a while, I think Matt and I realized that there was a little bit of mileage to be had from our feud, and we used to ham it up from time to time. It was obviously good for business – ours and the BTCC's – but while there were definitely some histrionics involved, the fact is we just didn't like each other, and as time went on it ended up polarizing the supporters even more than usual. Those who used to like Matt Neal and dislike Jason Plato now loved Matt to pieces and wanted to see me dead, and vice versa. It was pure pantomime.

I remember one day we were called in to see Alan Gow, who is the boss of the BTCC. He said, 'Look guys, can you two just calm it down a little bit? It's getting out of control.' Matt and I were both taken aback by this and ended up trying to defend our actions by saying, 'But it's good for business, Alan', which it was.

Funnily enough, during the season before the Integra incidents of 2004, Matt and I had been on the verge of becoming mates, as, after offering him a lift in my plane one day – I think we were going to a party at Brands Hatch – we got on OK. Had the argy bargy not come to pass the following year, I dare say we'd have been buddies.

What the supporters wouldn't have been aware of when the quarrel was gaining ground was all the mudslinging that was going on behind the scenes, and to be honest that became a bit tedious after a while. As well as Matt and me, the teams got involved too, not to mention family members, and there were even one or two instances where solicitors' letters had to be issued, although I couldn't possibly say by whom. It was all getting a bit serious, and at one point it seemed in danger of eclipsing the racing.

Anyway, all this culminated in us almost coming to blows at Rockingham in 2011, which was the year after I'd won my second championship. By this time, Matt and I had been at each other's throats for about five years, so it had become almost part and parcel of the BTCC championship.

Matt will obviously have his own account of this, as with our previous encounters, but this is my version of events.

During qualifying, there was a red flag, and on the out lap after that Matt and his teammate, Gordon Shedden, basically tried holding me up. They were a formidable pairing, Matt and Gordon, and worked great together as a team. On this occasion, I was the object of their attention, and instead of using the minutes and seconds we had left to post a quicker time, they were too busy trying to impede me. After finally passing them a lap or so later and then setting a lap time, I decided to return the favour and with Matt and Gordon just behind me I suddenly found it very difficult accelerating through hairpins. I can't think why. Matt in particular took exception to this and nudged me a few times and threw a few toys out of his pram before we both went back to the pits.

To add to Matt's frustrations, the driver who got pole was one Timothy Jason Plato. After parking up in the pit lane, I got out of my car, looked over at Matt, who was about three cars down from me, and gave him the finger. I also said something like *Fuck you*, but because I had my helmet on he had to make do with the finger.

Bearing in mind this was quite normal for Matt and me (not necessarily giving each other the finger, but we were forever goading each other and having a dig), for some reason he went absolutely orbital and, as opposed to giving me a mouthful and a couple back, he saw his arse and came running over.

The first thing that came into my head when I saw Matt's giant legs begin kicking into action was that you could get into an awful lot of trouble with the governing body for having a pop at somebody physically, and especially at a meeting. Also, I wasn't the aggressor in this. I was passive. It was time to crank things up a bit.

Had I not had several gallons of testosterone pumping away inside me, I might well have tried pouring cold water on the situation. But, knowing I'd wound Matt up a little bit and that it could all get a bit tasty, I started goading him. To

Matt it was all body language, as he couldn't hear me, but as well as gesturing for him to get a move on I was shouting things like, 'Come on then, you fucker, let's have you!' You know the kind of thing. It certainly worked!

By the time he got over to me, which was probably about two or three steps for Matt, my old man and Matt's team manager had arrived, as had the TV cameras. It was show-time. Lights, camera, action!

Although I was up for an argument, I was mindful of the fact that Matt was raging and had also started clenching his fist a bit and raising it. Goaded or not, this was a definite no-no in the sport, and should he decide to use his fist he'd be saying goodbye to the championship. This sent my 'goadery' to a completely different level and because I still had a helmet on he could basically hit me as hard as he liked. 'Go on then, go on then!' I shouted. 'Hit me, then!' Matt could obviously hear me now, and as I carried on goading him, Barry, his team manager, started shouting the odds. It was a proper mêlée.

The two things I remember most about the encounter are Matt raising his hand and saying something like, 'I'm going to rip your fucking face off, Jason', and then my old man waving his hands around shouting, 'Pack it in man. For God's sake, Barry, tell him to stop it. Every time I've seen the clip, that's the bit I look forward to the most. It's priceless!

You'll never believe this, but after everything had calmed down a bit, I got a message that the stewards wanted to see me and Matt. But whatever for? After giving us both a lecture about bringing the sport into disrepute, which was fair enough, I was expecting me to get a ticking-off and Matt to get a fine, but in the end they fined both of us £5,000.

'What the bloody hell for?' I asked them. 'He was the aggressor, not me!'

Thanks to the TV cameras, and the microphones, they'd heard me goading Matt, and in their eyes I was as much to blame. I'm in two minds about it really, but hand on heart it was probably a fair cop.

Anyway, it was great publicity for all concerned, and within hours of it happening it had spun around the globe a couple of times and become a huge talking point. There was a bit of afters in the form of a solicitor's letter that had to be issued after somebody mouthed off to the press – again – but that was it really. At the end of the day it was just two old adversaries going toe to toe with each other, and whenever I'm interviewed about anything related to the BTCC, other than the current season, it's one of the first things I'm asked about.

A few years ago, ITV produced a series called *Motorsport Mavericks* that profiled drivers who were a little bit – maverick. As far as I knew, the mavericks they were concentrating on were people like Barry Sheene and James Hunt, and although they'd asked Matt and me to contribute as talking heads – separately, I might add – I assumed that we were just contributors as opposed to subjects. Well, I was still half right. Unbeknownst to Matt or me, I was the subject, and Matt was the contributor, so ITV had invited Matt to talk about me on a show that was partly about – me!

I genuinely had no idea at the time but when I eventually found out I'd be lying if I said I wasn't tickled pink. Unlike Matt. According to a source he was spitting feathers when he found out, and given our history it's understandable.

I'm not sure if ITV realized that, if they had let the cat out of the bag, Matt wouldn't have contributed, but the way they went about it was genius, as neither of us had any idea. The questions themselves were either very general, so not related to anyone in particular, or about our rivalry, and after linking it all together using some other talking heads and some race footage, you were left with a very sweet fifteen minutes of primetime television – about me. We only found out when the show went to air, and one of us came out smiling. We were mugged, in a way, except he was the only victim.

During the programme, Matt valiantly tried to claim that him winning three championships as opposed to my two irked me somewhat. Hmmmm. Quite a few people have won three championships. Seven, in fact. Only one has won ninety-seven races. Shall we let that sink in a moment?

Somebody once asked me which was my most intense rivalry – Alain, Yvan or Matt – and although my opinion changes occasionally, at this very moment in time I'd have to say Yvan. With Alain it was more a case of young versus old, or older, and the fact that I learned so much from Alain and have so much respect for him kind of negates the rivalry slightly. He was still a plonker sometimes, as was I, but the rivalry was born from the fact that I'd put his nose out of joint by bagging pole on my first ever attempt, and had I been in his position my hackles would have been up and I too would have been on the offensive. We were also very different people, both on and off the track, so the rivalry was almost predictable in a way and was actually quite healthy.

It's the same with Matt in many respects. Although it's been quiet in recent years, the rivalry has become like a feature of the BTCC, and as well as everyone being aware of that rivalry, people turn up willing it to kick off. I likened it to pantomime earlier, but it's actually more like WWF. As a case in point let me ask you a question. In your opinion, how much of the above has been written with a view to me winding Matt up? All of it? Really? I couldn't possibly say.

We're actually quite cordial to each other these days, and if we have to get on, we can. For instance, both of us were good friends with the late and much-missed motor-racing broadcaster and journalist Henry Hope-Frost, and at Henry's memorial service last year we sat together and talked quite a bit. Having a common bond obviously helped matters, but it goes to show that the majority of what's gone on is stuff that's happened in the moment, and again that almost negates the seriousness of it. That said, I wouldn't trust Matt as far as I could throw him, which wouldn't be very far. It's a complicated old business.

With Yvan there were so many different circumstances concerning our rivalry, and consequently it became all-encompassing. For a start, it literally had a cast of dozens and was also driven by politics first and foremost, which has rarely been a feature with Matt and wasn't much with Alain. The political element only accentuated my rivalry with Yvan on the track, and because of the number of people involved and what was at stake – not to mention all the lawyers and hatred on both sides of the garage – it grew a much bigger head. It was an industrial rivalry, in many respects, and not one I'd wish to repeat.

But the other reason I'd have to choose Yvan over Matt is because he was by far a better driver and in that respect I'd have to put Alain up there too. Just below Alain and Yvan, but still above Matt, would be the likes of Gabriele Tarquini and Rickard Rydell, who I used to have some epic battles with.

Without wishing to be rude, Matt simply isn't up there with the very highest level of motor-racing driver I've had to beat during my career, so to all intents and purposes our rivalry is something that has been manufactured for the entertainment and benefit of the public.

A wind-up merchant. Me?

It might not surprise you to learn that I have a third string to my professional bow and that, as well as racing cars and talking into television cameras for a living, I co-own a marketing agency called Brand Pilot that I started about fourteen years ago. In order to progress in motor racing I obviously had to have a grip on the intricacies of sponsorship from a very early age to be able to make a career out of it. Rendering me commercially aware, it also turned me into a budding marketer. In fact, the reason I set up Brand Pilot in the first place was to turn my sponsorships from often short-term arrangements, where companies gave me money for wearing stickers and pressing some flesh, into long-term marketing campaigns that were measurable, professionally run and mutually beneficial. Commercial awareness left me with a desire for putting deals together, and it's become an important part of my story.

In 396 BC, my bearded namesake, Plato, came up with a proverb that, when translated into English, reads roughly as 'necessity is the mother of invention'. As proverbs go, it's pretty hot stuff and will have been adopted, either consciously or subconsciously, by just about every racing driver who's ever had to find some money in order to stay behind the wheel of a racing car. In my own case it was put to the ultimate test back in September 2008, when, shortly after the Lehman Brothers' crash, I was summoned to SEAT HQ in Milton Keynes for a 'Must Attend' meeting with the managing director, marketing director and director of communications. Having a meeting with a sponsor wasn't that unusual, but the 'Must Attend' bit was!

Having signed a new three-year deal with SEAT at the end of the previous season, I wasn't expecting any bad news, so I was taken aback to find out that they'd predicted a huge global financial crash (correctly, as it turned out) and had decided that at the end of the current 2008 season they'd be pulling the plug on all, and I mean all, UK motorsport! To say I felt like my legs had been cut clean off at the hip would be an understatement. What made matters worse was the fact that, just eight months previously, my signing with SEAT had signalled to the motorsport industry that I was off the market for another three seasons and the usual window for finding another drive had closed, which meant that I was up the proverbial creek without a paddle. Our first daughter, Alena, was just five months old at this point, which raised the stress stakes somewhat further!

While I obviously enjoy having a laugh, when the shit hits the fan I go into survival mode and Uncle Plato's proverb comes into play. When SEAT had first decided to enter the BTCC (shortly after I'd moved lock-stock to Monaco!), they'd asked me for some advice as to which team they might approach to run their programme and I'd basically introduced them to Ray Mallock Ltd, or RML. As a knock on from this, RML had been asked to design, manufacture and run the touring car programme for Chevrolet Europe in the World Touring Car Championship (WTCC), and in 2005 they'd asked me if I'd like to leave SEAT and go with them. After umming and ahhing for a while, I decided against the move and had stayed with SEAT, but because I still had a good relationship with RML I decided to approach them about the possibility of putting me in a Chevrolet for the 2009 BTCC. After many, many chats with the boss, Ray Mallock, and a great bloke who worked for Ray called Mark Busfield, we managed to cobble together a deal that would see me racing an ex-WTCC Chevrolet Lacetti as a privateer in 2009 until one of us could get some funding in place. It was literally a race-by-race deal.

With a car and team now in place, I then set about trying to get the funding. Within just a few weeks I'd managed to get some good support from companies such as Tesco Momentum Petrol and Silverline Tools (from round four the team became known as Racing Silverline), and, in addition to me finishing an extremely respectable second in the 2009 championship, I also won all three races in the final round at Brands Hatch. Not bad, eh?

Just a few months earlier I'd been on my arse and without a drive, and the fact that I managed to instigate a deal that got me into a competitive car at the last minute and finished second in the championship while bagging a full house at Brands Hatch is definitely one of my prouder moments. Had it all been handed to me on a plate, it wouldn't have tasted half as good. From the sponsor's point of view – not to mention RML and Chevrolet – it ended up paying the ultimate dividend as, after being offered a two-year factory deal with Chevrolet and RML, I ended up winning my second championship in 2010. It really was a golden period. In fact, during my three years with Chevrolet and RML I won twenty-two races and was on the podium no fewer than forty-four times! That's a lot of silverware and a lot of champagne.

This isn't just a huge brag, by the way. I think it shows that, if the shit ever hits the fan, you mustn't be afraid to get out there, knock on some doors, stick your head above the parapet and try something different. Even if you're shy, trying to overcome that could be the difference between you making it or not.

About halfway through the 2011 season Chevrolet started to leak stories to the press that this could be their final year in the BTCC and that from now on they'd be thinking only of the WTCC. With half a season still to go, this wasn't nearly as desperate as the SEAT situation had been, but it was going to require some thought if I was going to get the right deal and end up in a competitive car.

By then I'd brought in Heidi Johnson-Cash as a business partner at Brand Pilot. Heidi had come on board a couple of months earlier after impressing me – and scaring me, it has to be said – way back in 2009 while she'd been working for Pioneer UK, who were one of my personal sponsors. Heidi was head of marketing there and had invited me in to talk about a new deal.

I remember walking onto the floor where her office was based. It was full of mostly Japanese men in blue suits and white shirts who were basically just sitting there quietly and getting on with their jobs. It was unnervingly quiet. At the end of this floor was a glass wall and behind this glass wall was a tall woman of about 6 feet 1 inch marching around in a huge office, talking on a mobile phone with her left arm flailing around. Her clothes were casual and, although I couldn't hear what she was saying, I was pretty sure she wasn't ordering flowers for an elderly relative. When she spotted me, Heidi waved me into her office while she carried on her call, and when the door was opened, I was hit by a cacophony of seriously forceful and somewhat foul language. Wow! Even the mechanics at Willies had nothing on this girl. I was totally mesmerized. She was a full-on powerhouse.

After finally finishing her call, Heidi put down her phone, apologized for her language with a cheeky smile and then walked right up to me, looked me straight in the eyes and shook my hand. After uttering a quick 'Hello', she said, 'Now tell me, what's your fucking story?' That was her opening gambit! Within about an hour we'd agreed a new sponsorship deal and I was on my way, but she'd left an indelible mark on me.

Two years later – this was just after the Japanese tsunami – I decided to call Heidi to see how she was getting on, and, instead of her being profane and ebullient, which is what I'd been expecting, she sounded worried. She was concerned about the direction in which Pioneer were going, so without even thinking about it I decided there and then that I was going to offer her half of my company.

'Come up and see me,' I said to her. 'There's something I'd like to talk to you about.'

To cut a long story short, Heidi said yes, and ended up becoming a 50 per cent shareholder in Brand Pilot. From a business point of view, it's one of the best things I ever did, and in the ten years we've worked together we've had a huge amount of success. She's also taught me an awful lot and has expanded my vocabulary immeasurably.

Anyway, once Chevrolet had announced their intentions, Heidi and me sat down and started knocking around some manufacturers' names with a view to bringing one in as a replacement. At some point during these discussions I mentioned MG, who were owned by Shanghai Automotive. About a week earlier I'd had a chat with Ian Harrison from 888 (remember him?) about his plans for the coming season and he told me that he'd had some embryonic talks with MG that hadn't gone anywhere. It was hardly surprising really as they weren't involved in motorsport at the time and they were hardly making any cars. That said, something resonated with me, so I ended up putting in a cold call to them.

After a lot of perseverance I managed to get some traction with them, and two months or so later we had them on the hook. By this time, RML had put a deal in front of me for the following season with a new-found enthusiasm from Chevrolet UK, and were pressuring me to sign. But with MG being close, I had to try and hold them off. It was a proper game of cat and mouse! Because RML had no idea I was talking to MG, and because I hadn't signed for anyone else, they assumed they were my only option. They wanted their contract signing straight away, so I had to use every trick in the book to try to keep them onside just in case it went tits up with MG. It sounds like a nightmare, but I actually thrive on this kind of pressure!

After a couple of weeks, during which time RML's lawyers must have tried contacting me at least five hundred times, I finally received Heads of Terms from MG. Fantastic! The subject line of the email read 'MG HoT'. I rang up my lawyer, told him that I was going to forward him the email, and instructed him to action its contents immediately. Heidi and I were literally a hair's breadth away from bringing a brand-new manufacturer to the BTCC. We were on the verge of something huge.

Without even taking a breath I typed in the first few letters of my lawyer's email address, clicked on the one that came up and went to press send. Literally a millisecond before doing so I realized that it wasn't going to my lawyer, it was going to RML's lawyer, who shared the same first name. Unfortunately, by the time this registered, my finger had pressed the send button. When I realized what I'd done, I literally leapt out of my seat. I was in the Brand Pilot office at the time, and Heidi sat there wondering what the bloody hell was going on as I threw myself over my desk head first and started ripping out cables from the back of my PC. Yes, it was futile, and yes, it was idiotic, but I was in a state of extreme panic. 'Oh fuck!' I screamed. 'Fuck, fuck, fuck!'

'What the fuck's going on?' screamed Heidi. There was a lot of screaming.

This is one of the few situations in my life that, if I ever allow my brain to start reliving it, produce almost the same bodily reactions as when it actually happened. It's the same feeling you get when you are about to have an accident: that intense rush that takes over every fibre of your brain and body in less than a millisecond.

Basically, I had just ended my relationship with RML, and with MG not yet over the line I was officially in limbo. In fact, as far as my future racing career was concerned, I had one foot in shit street.

Within about two minutes the phones began to ring and my deal with RML had been officially withdrawn. Needless to say, they weren't happy bunnies. My stomach is turning somersaults as I'm writing this. It was one of the most hor-rifically unnerving experiences of my entire life, and if it ever happens again I'm not sure my ticker will be able to take it.

Despite the Heads of Terms eventually being signed, the negotiations with MG continued for a further two weeks, and during that time I must have had about four hours' sleep and at least a thousand cigarettes. It was worse than when I ambushed Frank!

Because they hadn't been involved in motorsport before, MG's owners, Shanghai Automotive, had to be schooled on every single aspect and, unfortunately, they tried rewriting the rule book once or twice. They wanted it written into my contract that if I was ever injured in a race they would stop paying me immediately.

'No, no, no,' I said to them. 'It doesn't work like that. You take out an insurance policy against me getting injured and if it happens you carry on paying me but claim the money back.'

'No, no, no,' said Shanghai Automotive. 'If you get injured, we no pay you.'

'Now look here . . .'

I needed the patience of Job to get that deal over the line, but we got there eventually. Triple Eight ended up running the programme for MG and we ended up having three excellent years together. Although we didn't win a championship (to be fair, we should have won in 2013 and 2014), we came bloody close and, my word, did we have some fun. MG also did really well out of it, as did our two main sponsors, Tesco Momentum and KX, who are the Tesco own-brand energy drink. During this time Heidi and I also created the KX Akademy with a view to developing young racing drivers, and we managed to secure a bursary fund in excess of a million pounds. In addition to making serious contributions to their annual racing budgets, we created and delivered monthly workshops on how to maximize things like marketing, sponsorship and social media. We also arranged media training and simulator work and taught them legal and accountancy skills. During its existence, the KX Akademy helped to propel the careers of, among others, Tom Ingram, Sam Tordoff, Josh Cook, Dan Lloyd, Ant Whorton-Eales and Stefan Hodgetts, and it's something we're both incredibly proud of.

Do you see what I mean now about life off the track being similar to life on it? OK, the physical element is different and you might not be pounding around a racetrack at 160 mph, but I guarantee that the two weeks I spent trying to coax Shanghai Automotive into motorsport while fighting their attempts to rewrite standard practice, was, honestly, the equivalent of about five seasons' worth of racing. I was dead by the end of it! I'll tell you what though, the satisfaction I felt when Heidi and I finally got them all over the line was the equivalent of any race win.

Team Plato

By far the most relevant adjective I can think of to describe my experiences as both a father and as an expectant father is *amazing*, and I'm pretty sure I'm not alone in that. Like racing a car, it's one of those things that is best appreciated with the benefit of experience and is a proper life changer.

Conversely, there is nothing more boring than listening to people waffling on about how wonderful their children are or how great it is to be a parent, so rather than do that I'm going to give you the other side of the coin, because, in addition to having words like *amazing* on my list of adjectives, I've also got daunting, tedious and terrifying. Come on, let's have a bit of honesty here! It's not all a bed of roses.

Don't get me wrong, I love my two girls to pieces, but at the end of the day the only people who want to read about ballet lessons, family holidays and school reports are the grandparents. What everyone else will want, I think, is a few insights into what it's all about and a couple of stories that are in keeping with the rest of this book. Am I right?

The first thing people usually ask me about what I call *Team Plato* – as in my family – is: was it all planned? And the truth is, no, it wasn't. By the time Sophie was twenty-five, I was touching forty, and had I asked her then if now was the right time, I dare say she would have said no. When she eventually found out that she was pregnant she gave me the news in a way that is, distinctly, my wife.

Sophie had had a hunch that she was pregnant for some time, and after finally doing a pregnancy test, she decided to break the news to me at about six o'clock in the morning.

I was having the most spectacular dream at the time, but all of a sudden a hand landed on my shoulder and started pushing me up and down. When I opened my eyes, the first thing I saw was a long blue object about six inches above me, but because I was still being encouraged to wake up, and in a pretty physical way, it has to be said, it was all a bit of a blur.

Although the sight that befell me wasn't familiar, the voice I could hear most definitely was, and as I started to come to life the two became rudely aligned.

'Jason, wake up,' said the voice. 'I'm pregnant!'

I doubt a large shot of adrenaline would have given me as big a jolt as the five words that Sophie had just uttered, and I reached up and grabbed for her wrist in an attempt to slow the object in front of me down so that it gradually came into focus.

I forget what it looked like exactly, but from memory there was a small oblong hole in the middle of the plastic object, and within the hole there was a white background with two red lines running through the middle of it.

'Is that a pregnancy test?' I said, pushing Sophie's hand away and trying to sit up.

'Yes, of course it is,' she said. 'I'm pregnant.'

'Yeah, I heard that,' I said. 'Are you sure?'

'That's the third one I've done,' said Sophie. 'Of course I'm sure.'

'Bloody hell!'

Because Sophie was only in her mid-twenties, and because I'm a caring, sharing kind of guy who rarely thinks of himself, the first thing that occurred to me was that Sophie might not be ready to have children, so once I was fully awake I set about trying to work out whether this was the case. I myself was cock-a-hoop at the news, but if Sophie was in two minds then the last thing she'd want to see was me jumping up and down in bed and acting as if it were a fait accompli.

Although naturally a bit apprehensive, Sophie seemed pleased by the news and once she knew I was, she began to relax. The more I thought about it, the more excited I became. I was now forty-one years of age, and from a timing point of view it felt absolutely on the nail.

Something that I think helped with Sophie was the fact that since getting together we'd been here, there and everywhere, and in terms of life experience she'd probably stuffed twenty years into the last five. Consequently, she was a little less jittery than she might have been, although, because she was still young, I think she had an overriding fear that from now on she'd be tied to a sink and would never drink again. Oh aye. Married to me?

Even before Alena was born, the effects of fatherhood were upon me, and from the moment I found out that Sophie was pregnant I suddenly became far more risk averse. It was almost like a switch had been flicked, and instead of tearing around the roads of Oxfordshire like a madman, or at least somebody who was comfortable driving at speed, I started driving considerately and would actually weigh up the risks of driving dangerously. OK, when I say considerately, that might be pushing it a bit, but it was a big improvement.

It was the same with television. All of a sudden, instead of leaping into a car for a test or a review and then saying, *All right, fellas, watch this*, or words to that effect, I'd talk to my colleagues first about what was to come and then work out a plan. Christ, how things had changed! I wanted to make sure I was alive to see my children enter the world and to watch them grow up.

Another consequence of the impending expansion of Team Plato was me becoming a lot more commercially aggressive. My wife she may have been, but Sophie was not and never had been my dependant, and the very thought of a person appearing who *was* financially dependent on me, or should I say on me and Sophie, made me sit up and think a bit.

Apart from wondering who I might be driving for the following season, I don't think I'd ever considered my future before, and so suddenly being required to consider the future of several people had a profound effect on me.

The only situation becoming a father didn't make a difference to, and still hasn't, is on the racetrack. Like most drivers I become a different animal in that environment, and nothing, not even the birth of a child, has ever had that much of an effect. That's not to say I haven't thought about it from time to time. In fact, it's actually troubled me slightly that when I'm driving a road car I'm now observant and respectful and have the family in mind (troubled me as in it doesn't feel natural!), whereas the moment I get on to a racetrack, where, it's safe to say, things are slightly more precarious, I don't care about anything other than finishing first. It's strange, don't you think?

I'm utterly convinced that anybody who excels at individual sport shares a very particular kind of mental quality, as, in order to possess that insane focus, that obsession and that belief in your ability, you cannot be neurotypical.

Look at free solo climbers, for instance – those crazy men and women who scale mountain faces without ropes, harnesses or any protective equipment. Are they neurotypical?

Of course they're not. They have total and utter belief in their own ability, to the point where they're willing to stake their life on it. As a mindset it's diametrically opposed to the way most people think.

One of the best examples of this I can think of in motorsport is the late, and indisputably great, Colin McRae. To compete in rallying at the highest level you have to be a special kind of nutcase, and in my opinion Colin was the benchmark.

I suppose you're expecting me to list some examples of obsessive sportsmanship now.

Not quite.

Many years ago, Sophie and I went skiing in Verbier with Colin, his wife Alison and a few other mutual friends for the New Year. I don't remember much about the skiing bit, but the après part was legendary, and Colin was at the centre of everything.

About halfway through the holiday we were in a pub one night when suddenly Colin dived over the bar, as you do. There was no warning, he just took a run-up and then dived head first.

While everyone else looked on in shock, horror or bemusement, I looked on in complete admiration, and just as I was readying myself to emulate rallying's answer to Oliver Reed, he suddenly appeared again on the bar and this time he was stark bollock naked.

WTF? I thought.

Once again, everyone looked on in horror except me and Alison. She never batted an eyelid, as she'd obviously seen it all before, and I was still marvelling at him jumping over the bar. You could tell that everybody was looking at Colin thinking, *What the hell is he going to do next?* and by the look in his eye he was capable of just about anything. Saying that, nobody could have guessed in a million years what he had up his sleeve. Or between his legs, in this case.

After getting hold of his scrotum he shouted to Alison, 'BURN MY BOLLOCKS, WOMAN!'

Eh? Not even I was expecting that!

Again, without batting an eyelid, Alison walked over to the bar, borrowed somebody's cigarette and proceeded to singe Colin's scrotum.

'AAAAAAH, YER BASTARD!' he cried, and then jumped back behind the bar.

For some insane reason, which was probably alcohol-related, I wanted in on this and, after putting down my drink, I readied myself to dive over the bar.

'What the hell do you think you're doing?' shouted Sophie, grabbing hold of me.

'I don't know, I don't know,' I said. 'I just want to do it!'

The occasion had obviously got the better of me, and I was like a child on a sugar rush with a penchant for danger-ous sports.

'No, Jason!' said Sophie. 'You're not doing it.'

In the interests of our ongoing relationship, and my scro-tum, I decided to do as I was told, and in hindsight I'm glad I did. I'm a brave old bugger but I'm certainly no masochist and if it hadn't been for Colin's strange influence over me I'd never, ever have suggested doing such a thing. I couldn't help admir-ing the man, though. I mean, who on earth decides to jump over a bar head first, without knowing what's there, before tak-ing all their clothes off, jumping back up in front of dozens of people and then asking their better half to singe their bol-locks? Colin McRae, apparently.

The following night Colin and Alison threw a party in their apartment, and Colin being Colin, he decided to hold a fireworks display. The trouble was that the fireworks were outdoor fireworks as opposed to indoor! Needless to say, chaos ensued, and in the end we left him to it.

Anyway, let's get to the maternity hospital.

Before our first daughter, Alena, was born, Sophie was told that she'd have to have a Caesarean section, and when we got to the hospital she was immediately whisked away for an epidural. I was told to wait where I was.

'We'll come and get you in fifteen minutes,' said the nurse. 'In the meantime, put these on.'

She then handed me a green cap and gown, and after putting them on and trying to avoid any mirrors, I sat down and waited nervously to be called. It was worse than waiting for a race to start.

After I was called into the operating theatre, the first thing I saw was Sophie. She was lying down, obviously, but she was also quite bright-eyed and bushy-tailed.

'I thought you'd be spark out,' I said, sitting down next to her.

'The epidural numbs the stomach area,' said Sophie. 'I'll stay awake throughout, and the doctor says I won't feel a thing.'

'Blimey!' I said. 'The things they can do these days.'

The whole thing was all completely at odds with what I'd been expecting. Not only was Sophie not unconscious, but there was a bit of music playing in the background, and everybody in the operating theatre seemed to be calm and relaxed. Where was all the noise and excitement? I was expecting screams and shouts of 'BREATHE, MRS PLATO, BREEEEATHE. THAT'S IT, I CAN SEE THE HEAD NOW!'

As I was chatting away to Sophie, the legend that is Lawrence Impey the surgeon suddenly breezed in through the double doors and, after saying hello to Sophie and me, he very calmly called his staff together and suggested they get started.

Once again, I'd been expecting nothing less than complete pandemonium by this point in the proceedings, and yet despite the doctor having fired the starting gun it was as if he'd suggested a light snooze.

Rather than worry about it, I just carried on chatting, and after a couple of minutes I decided to stand up and have a look at the business end to see how they were getting on.

You know the old saying *never assume because to assume makes an ass out of you and me*? Well, for the third time in an hour that's exactly what I did and, after getting up to view Sophie's abdomen, I was expecting to see the doctor drawing lines on it with a felt-tip pen. Don't ask me why, I just was. I must have seen it on *Casualty* or something.

Boy, was I in for a shock.

Instead of playing a game of noughts and crosses on my wife's stomach, the doctor and his nurses were about half-way through a very graphic game of Operation, and it's safe to say that I was not ready for it.

'Oh my God,' I said, stepping backwards.

'Are you OK?' asked Sophie, slightly alarmed.

'Yeah, absolutely,' I said. 'Everything's fine.'

Except it wasn't.

Coupled with the fact that I felt like I was about to die, I had to pretend to Sophie that I was fine in order not to alarm her even more, and that was not a nice experience. Had I been able to just collapse into the chair, have a drink of water and swear a few times I'd have been OK, but I wasn't. I had to stand tall, smile and pretend that everything was fine.

What made it worse, and this was apart from the fact that

I'd just seen the inside of my wife's belly, was that I couldn't get my head around the fact that she was still compos mentis and couldn't feel a thing. It just wasn't right.

Towards the end of the proceedings, the doctor said to Sophie that she might feel slightly uncomfortable in a moment, and next thing I know Alena had arrived, and we were parents! I thought to myself, *How the bloody hell does that work then?*

When our second daughter, Zia, arrived about two years later, I was prepared and stayed exactly where I was.

'Would you like to have a look?' asked the doctor.

'No, thank you very much indeed,' I insisted. 'I'm fine where I am.'

I wasn't going to get done twice.

In terms of me receiving a nasty surprise, Zia's birth almost ended up trumping Alena's, as about fifteen minutes after Zia had been born, they knocked out one of the nerve blockers from the epidural while transferring Sophie to a normal bed, and a few minutes later she just hit the bloody roof. I mean properly screaming her head off. Fortunately, the medical staff knew exactly what had happened and started pumping her full of morphine. After that, Sophie was completely out of it, so it was all a bit traumatic really. In fact, at the time, I could have done with some morphine myself. The main thing is that mother and daughter were both well, so once Sophie came around, all was fine.

One of my most vivid memories I have from the period immediately after Alena's birth is of arriving home with her for the very first time. She and Sophie had had to spend a few days in hospital after the birth, and by the time I went to collect them I was itching to get them home.

I'd made a point of asking the grandparents not to come

around for the first couple of days as I thought it would be important for us all to bond and settle in. They'd been to the hospital, so had seen Sophie and Alena, and they were fine with it.

The journey home was just lush. I had my two girls with me, and both of them were healthy. I couldn't ask for more.

My mood lasted until we reached the living room at home. After putting Alena down on the carpet, still in her car seat, we sat down on the sofa, looked at each other and said, 'Now what do we do?' We had absolutely no idea. It was terrifying!

Within about an hour we had all the parenting books out on the table; instead of allowing ourselves to become overwhelmed by it all, we forced ourselves to embrace the situation. Those first few moments, though, were seriously unsettling.

About a year later, Sophie and I were having a meal one night and, like most new or new-ish parents, we were talking shop.

'Do you know,' I said to Sophie. 'Something's just occurred to me.'

'What's that?' she said.

'Not one of our parents or friends told us the truth about what it's like having kids.'

'If people did that, then nobody would have kids, and we'd be extinct,' said my beautiful young wife, sagely. She definitely had a point.

Alena's now eleven and Zia nine, and although we've had our problems – hasn't everybody? – we're a tight little unit, and I wouldn't change a thing. Apart from seeing the inside of Sophie's abdomen! You can keep that.

People sometimes ask me if I'd like to have had a son, with the clear inference that if I'd had a son he would have followed in my footsteps. Well, the honest answer is, no, I wouldn't. I just couldn't be doing with either the pressure on him to go into motorsport like his father, which would definitely exist, or me having to support him. None of it would be natural, you see. It would all be about expectation.

With girls it's a lot different, and although some people will probably have a go at me for it, the numbers and history say that for whatever reason women in motorsport just doesn't work. You get the odd exception, of course, but generally that's the way of it, and as a father of two girls who are showing no interest whatsoever in motorsport, I'm happy with that.

Only a tiny, tiny, fraction of racing drivers make it to professional level, and you need more than just talent. In fact, in motor racing you don't always need to have that much talent, as having money can often elevate you to what is often a flagrantly false position. It's sad, but that's the nature of the beast. The inverse of that is that you can be the most talented driver in the world and go nowhere if you don't have money.

Look at golf. To get started you need some sticks, a ball and a field. Then, when you can hit the ball using the sticks you need a golf course and some clubs. It can be hugely expensive, but only if you want it to be. The point is that anyone can take it up and you can improve many of the basic skills of golf in your back garden. Then there's football. The most popular sport on the planet. All you need is a bag of wind, for heaven's sake, and a pair of boots. In that respect it's gloriously inclusive, and it's no wonder the sport's so popular. With motorsport you need an engine, a chassis, trucks, tyres, a circuit. The list is frighteningly long, frighteningly expensive and, from an inclusivity point of view, the antithesis of football.

I mentioned a lad called Kelvin Burt earlier on. He was

one of the finest drivers I ever raced against in single-seaters and he had everything: the talent and the character. He was even a good-looking bastard. What Kelvin didn't have, though, was money, and although he eventually went into touring cars he had problems there too. From a single-seater point of view he was the real deal and is always one of my examples when I talk about unrealized talent in motorsport.

In my experience, drivers who come from extremely privileged backgrounds tend to have an air of expectation about them, and the top and bottom of it is they're often not fighters. You'll also often find that they're merely playing out their father's dreams, so it's quite often a case of having all the gear, but no idea. You do get the odd exception, of course, but they're few and far between. With working- or even middle-class kids there's a difference, as if it all goes tits up, there isn't a trust fund to fall back on.

Look at Lewis Hamilton. Had it not been for Ron Dennis discovering him and then investing an incredible amount of money in him, he may not have got past first base, and the world would have been robbed of one of its greatest ever racing drivers. Sure, there'll be people out there who think that'd be a good thing, because they don't like Lewis, but for anybody who really cares a damn about motor racing, it wouldn't. He's a working-class lad, for heaven's sake, and with the help of people like Ron Dennis and his dad he has completely rewritten the rule book. The finest racing driver in the world could be stacking shelves in Tesco's for all we know and because of Lewis Hamilton he might have the motivation to try and give it a go.

A similar thing has happened in football, in that talent is now spotted at a very early age, so if young Johnny hasn't been picked up by a club the age of eight the chances are it won't happen. It's the same in motorsport. Make a splash as early as possible, that's the trick, and especially if funds are limited. Then pray for Ron Dennis!

When I realized I wasn't going to make it in single-seaters, and ultimately to Formula 1, I was obviously disappointed, but touring cars have given me a fantastic career and have allowed me to do television too, which I adore. Had I made it into Formula 1, that would never have happened (or at least not while I was active in the sport), so if anything it's been a bonus, as it's allowed me to have two careers. I'm a seriously lucky chap.

I Must See Zis Helmet Immediately!

As I write this, I'm about to travel to Brands Hatch for the first round of the 2019 British Touring Car Championship and I genuinely can't remember when I've been this excited about racing.

The last two seasons have been pretty dire, and last season, after not winning a single race for the first time, I was even thinking about jacking it in as it's been pretty desperate and the opposite of what I've been used to and what I've worked so hard to achieve.

One of the most dispiriting consequences of me winning just two races in the last three seasons is that it's played havoc with my sex life. You see, many years ago Sophie dreamed up a motivational initiative that meant we only had sex during the week after a race weekend *if* I won one of the races. She can be a hard woman when she wants to be.

At Knockhill, in 2017, which is the last time I won a race in the BTCC, Steve Rider interviewed me for ITV after the win, and when he asked me how I felt, I said, 'I feel great. The sex ban's off!'

Poor Steve. He didn't know what to say or where to look. I did, though. I was going straight home!

Thank God it's only ten weekends a year, though, otherwise I'd be joining a monastery and making my own beer.

The 2019 season will be my twenty-first in the BTCC,

and the only driver who's been around longer than I have is the aforementioned and much-loved Matt Neal.

So what's changed since 1997?

Well, my race preparation's virtually the same. It's always been this side of unorthodox, and despite my advancing years it's showing no signs of changing. Or should I say, I'm not changing it.

When it comes to the basics I'm actually quite good, and as well as eating the right foods (most of the time) I always keep myself very well hydrated. One habit I got into a while ago is fasting for one day every week, and the reason I started doing it was to make it easier to maintain my ideal driving weight of 77 kg. I've got quite a high metabolism, so with nothing else coming in my body will start using my fat reserves, such as they are. Maintaining a certain weight gets harder as you get older, and despite what you've read in this book I'm actually quite good when it comes to willpower. Sophie might tell you differently, as she wants me to give up smoking, but it only works if I want to do it! Remaining at 77 kg is obviously very important, and by fasting one day of the week I don't have to worry as much about how much I eat. It also makes me feel healthier, so it's a win-win situation.

I think I've already said that I won't drink any alcohol from the Wednesday night before a race weekend, and the only difference between now and twenty years ago is that back then I might have gone out and got a bit carried away on the Wednesday night (although not necessarily intentionally), whereas these days I'll have a few glasses of wine. I haven't turned into some kind of paragon of virtue or anything, but even I'm having to alter my behaviour slightly because of my age, and, as long as my desire to drive is still there, it'll be easy peasy. Once that goes, God only knows what will happen!

Something else I think I've intimated somewhere in this book is that I'm officially allergic to gymnasiums, and any form of physical exercise other than walking the dog, driving or the old indoor sports is a definite no-no. For some reason it's just never agreed with me, but if I felt the need to do it, I probably would.

When I get out of the car at the end of a race, I still feel fresh, whereas some of the younger drivers look like they're about to drop. I may be wrong, but I think I'm probably the only driver who doesn't indulge in some form of physical exercise (gym, cycling or both), and, although I wouldn't advocate it, it's worked for me. It must be in the genes, I suppose. The question I occasionally ask myself is: would I have been a better driver had I been fitter? and to be honest, I don't think so. It certainly wouldn't make me any faster. If I was in Formula 1, I wouldn't be able to cope, as the cars pull about 5 g, but touring cars are a different animal and require a different approach.

I do sometimes wonder what would have happened had I made it in Formula 1, and each time I come to a different conclusion. Had I been around in James Hunt's era, I think I might well have given the great man a run for his money with regards to burning the candle at both ends, but by the time I came along things had changed in F1, although only slightly. These days you have to dedicate a lot of your time to maintaining your fitness, and I'm not sure I'd have lasted very long. It's horses for courses.

One of the most important aspects of my preparation for a race weekend that I can carry out myself is the research I do. It's all about refamiliarizing myself with a track, and a few days before a meeting, I'll start digging out a few VTs of past meetings. I'm also a bit of a note-taker, so after digging out my notes from the previous year I'll then start building a picture of the weekend ahead. The weather, too, is obviously hugely important and I'm always looking for links between the weather that's being forecast for the weekend and past performances. It's a process of elimination in a way, and in layman's terms the idea is to leave yourself with a mental list of what works and where.

After that, you've got the technical stuff, which is very much a team effort and consists of something called a test plan. It mainly involves me and my engineer, and is all about swapping ideas and coming up with the best options. It's hard to overestimate the importance of the relationship between a driver and his engineer, as the engineer is the only person a driver works with on a day-to-day basis who will know the car anywhere near as well as he does. Mechanics know how to make a car work, which is obviously essential, but an engineer knows how it works and why it works and is undoubtedly the most vital element from a driver's perspective. Apart from the car!

On the morning of a race day, I'll always have a bacon and egg sandwich. The reason being that I won't eat a great deal during the day and want to put some fat in my system that my body can eat away at. If you put too many carbs in first thing and don't eat during the day, the carbs will get used up very quickly, and you'll end up having lulls in energy. That's why fat works well for my situation as, once I'm out of the door, that's it. I might have the odd banana if hunger strikes, but a meal is out of the question. I was doing a *Fifth Gear* item with a pro cycler whose name escapes me, and we stopped for breakfast, and I was aghast at his pile of grub. He then went on to explain the benefits of fat intake (providing you do burn it off).

A few weeks ago, it was suggested by one or two idiots on social media that there are too many older drivers in the

BTCC and that the likes of me, Matt Neal, my new team-mate Rob Collard and one of the BTCC new boys, Mark Blundell, should buzz off and leave it to the younger drivers. Everyone's entitled to their opinion, of course, but what a complete load of bollocks. The fact that the BTCC has such a rich mixture of youth and experience is one of its main USPs, and I for one think that should be celebrated. The youngsters want to beat us, and we sure as hell want to beat them. It's healthy, and because there's so much experience in the championship the younger drivers can only benefit. You watch, though. There's many a good tune played on an old fiddle, and, as talented as some of the new crop undoubtedly are, don't write off the old guard just yet.

As I'm about to set off to Brands Hatch, the first story I'm going to tell you takes place there and involves one of the best ever days I've ever had on a racetrack. It was October 2009, so exactly a year before I clinched my second championship, and it was the final meeting of the season. The three drivers in contention for the championship were me, Colin Turkington, who was leading, and the 2008 champion, Fabrizio Giovanardi. I was lying third at this point, and by quite some margin, so barring a miracle it was going to go to either Colin or Fabrizio.

Tom Chilton, who was driving for Ford, shocked everyone by getting pole for race one (it was Ford's first in nine years), and I started alongside him. Giovanardi got the best start, but Tom and I just managed to squeeze him out going into the first corner, and he had no choice but to back out, otherwise there'd have been mayhem.

By the time we got to the last corner of the final lap, Tom was still leading, and until about four laps before that I'd been hassling him incessantly. The reason I stopped was because I'd figured out that the only real chance I had of taking Tom would be on the last corner of the lap, which is called Clearways, but it was going to take me at least three laps to get into a position where I could give it a go. Fortunately, by the final lap, I'd managed to do just that and after getting a good run off of the penultimate corner I managed to force Tom to go on the defensive into Clearways. He defended well but ran slightly wide, which allowed me to get the undercut on the exit. From then on it was a drag race to the finish and I crossed the line just 0.015 of a second ahead of Tom, making it the closest finish in BTCC history.

Behind Tom and me were the three Vauxhalls of Fabrizio, Andrew Jordan and Matt Neal, which meant that, with Fabrizio finishing on the podium and Colin finishing down in eighth, the gap between the three of us was narrower than ever, and, with two races left, it's safe to say that one or two bums were starting to squeak.

Despite us starting race two in our finishing positions in race one, Tom managed to get the better of me, which meant that by the end of the first lap we were in exactly the same position as we had been in race one. Johnny Herbert, who ended up having a very unlucky nine races in BTCC, spun round Martyn Bell, who collided with Matt in the process.

By lap sixteen Tom was still defending from me in second and was obviously hoping to make amends after the first race. Then, while running wide at Druids, I tapped Tom, which forced him into a mistake, and after I passed him, a battle ensued involving Tom, Fabrizio, Colin, Rob Collard and Jonathan Adam. As all that went on, I managed to forge a lead, and the race finished with me in first place, Fabrizio second and Colin third. This meant that, as we went into the final race of the 2009 season, Colin led Fabrizio by four points and Fabrizio led me by four points. There were just eight points in it.

I know I sometimes decry championships in favour of race wins but I'd be lying if I said I wasn't excited about the prospect of clinching another, and especially with a hat-trick of wins, which is what I'd have to achieve, in addition to other results going my way, were it to happen.

For race three, the top eight were reversed on the grid, which meant that I was down in eighth next to Fabrizio, with Colin just in front of us and Matt Neal on pole alongside Paul O'Neill. I was going to have to go some to pull this one off.

With about six laps to go, Matt Neal was leading the race with Colin second, Fabrizio third, Tom Chilton fourth and me in fifth, so, unless something changed very quickly, the day, and the season, were in danger of turning into a bit of a damp squib. For me, anyway.

To be honest, the championship itself was looking unlikely now, and as it was partly out of my hands all I could do was go for win.

On the next lap, Fabrizio made a move on Colin by going around the outside of him into Hawthorns, and, as Colin defended, Tom Chilton managed to slip past Fabrizio. When Fabrizio attempted to make amends by retaking him at Surtees, Tom made a mistake, which allowed both Fabrizio and me through.

With Fabrizio back in third, Colin was once again sandwiched in between him and his Vauxhall teammate, Matt Neal. It was only going to be a matter of time before an attempt was made by Matt to back Colin into Fabrizio, so something had to give. Obviously well aware of this, Colin dived down the inside of Matt at Druids and in doing so he ran wide on the exit and made contact. This sent Matt wide on to the grass, moving Colin into first and Fabrizio into second, and just a few corners later I too made a move which ended up sending Matt through the gravel at Sheene.

With four laps to go, the top three drivers in the championship battle were running first, second and third on the track and in the final race of the season. It was amazing stuff.

Now sensing a win, and if a miracle happened like those two getting a puncture the championship, I decided to make my move. Actually, Fabrizio did it for me.

Shortly before the start/finish straight, Fabrizio made a move on Colin, and because he lost momentum I managed go around the outside of him and then straight around the outside of Colin at the next corner, which was Paddock Hill. It was an epic move, a proper long shot; if it goes wrong, I'm in the wall hard, but I'm havin' a moment, even if I do say so myself, and I went on to win the race and clinch the hat-trick.

The championship finished with Colin in first place on 275 points, me in second on 270 points and Fabrizio in third on 266 points. Although I was a bit disappointed not to have bagged both the hat-trick and the championship, I was happy for Colin, as he'd performed well all season and in a car that wasn't really fancied.

That's about it for magnanimity, I'm afraid. I'm all done!

My last story is an off-track version of the last, in that it involves one of the most memorable experiences I've had in my twenty-odd years as a racing driver and also features one of motor racing's biggest legends. You won't believe this one. It's true, though.

It all happened when I was invited to take part in the Race of Champions, which is a motorsport event featuring both racing and rally drivers past and present. The race itself is similar to rallycross really, and from 1992 until 2003 it was always held on the island of Gran Canaria. Since then it's been taken all over the world, and the list of drivers who've been involved over the years will make your eyes water. Let's give you a quick twenty: Colin McRae, Carlos Sainz Sr, Stig Blomqvist, Fernando Alonso, Michael Schumacher, David Coulthard, JJ Lehto, Sébastien Loeb, Tom Kristensen, Jimmie Johnson, Didier Auriol, Romain Grosjean, Sebastian Vettel, Petter Solberg, Johnny Herbert, Sébastien Bourdais, Jenson Button, Tanner Foust, Juan Pablo Montoya and, last but most definitely not least, Alain Prost. Even the likes of Valentino Rossi and Mick Doohan have taken part, so you don't have to ply your trade on four wheels to get invited. It's not a bad little list, don't you think?

The first year I got invited I couldn't make it, but I made sure I kept in contact with the organizers in case the opportunity arose again, and eventually, in 2010, it did. From a driver's point of view, unless you're a bit of a miserable bar steward, it's completely lush because as well as being put up in some fantastic hotels we all eat together, socialize together and do the PR together, so, although you're only there for a short period of time, you develop a real sense of community, and everybody's just happy to be there.

From my own point of view, I got to meet a lot of my biggest heroes and when I first saw the list of competitors for 2010 I almost had a heart attack. There were sixteen of us in all, and the names that immediately jumped out at me were Tanner Foust, Sébastien Loeb, Sebastian Vettel, Tom Kristensen, Michael Schumacher, Mick Doohan, Carl Edwards and Alain Prost. ALAIN BLOODY PROST!

The event was held at the ESPRIT arena in Düsseldorf, which holds well over 60,000 people, and the day before – there're actually two events, the Race of Champions and a team event called the Race of Nations – the drivers all had lunch together, and, without me even having to ask (although I would have – in fact, I would have begged), the organizers put me next to Mr Prost. There are plenty of people in the world I admire, but it's not often I become star struck, and I think this was probably the first time. After all, there are famous people and there are legends, and to me Alain Prost typifies the latter.

But for why, Plato, I hear you ask. Well, first of all he's got a big nose. I say that with a certain amount of humour but as a kid with a larger than average hooter I was thrilled to see that there was somebody in Formula 1 who was just as aerodynamic as I was. That was definitely an attraction. In terms of racing, I simply loved the way he went about his business. He was obviously cool, considered, and boy, could he race. My all-time favourite is undoubtedly Gilles Villeneuve, but Alain isn't far behind.

Within a few minutes of chatting about the fact that Alain had also attended the Winfield School in France, I told him that I'd based my helmet design on his, and for some reason this seemed to impress him.

'Really,' he said. 'But I must see zis helmet immediately. Where is it?'

'Well, it's upstairs in my room, Alain.'

'Well, go and get it then. Come on Jason, *allez*!'

I've never really been fond of running, but when Alain Prost told me to *allez*, I pushed back my chair and literally sprinted to my room. He was obviously quite chuffed that I'd based the design on his, and over the next couple of hours we rabbited away like old mates. Later on, at the bar, I had a few drinks with Mick Doohan, who, like Valentino Rossi, had won five consecutive 500cc World Championships. I remember calling my dad afterwards and saying, 'You'll never guess who I just met!' The event hadn't even taken place yet, but it felt like I'd become a member of the best club in the world. Never mind felt like. I had!

In the individual event I was in Group D alongside Michael Schumacher, Álvaro Parente and my new best friend, Alain Prost. I'm not sure if I became overwhelmed by everything, but I performed abysmally and ended up finishing last.

In the Race of Nations I fared much better. My Great Britain teammate was my old mate and one-time fellow BTCC competitor Andy Priaulx. This time we were in Group A together with France (Prost and Loeb), Portugal (Parente and Filipe Albuquerque) and what were referred to as the Nordic Countries (Kristensen and Heikki Kovalainen). Despite drawing against the Nordics and the Portuguese, we beat the French 2–0 and ended up progressing with them, as they'd beaten Portugal. It was the semifinal next and after beating France again 2–0 (sorry, Alain) we were up against Germany in the final. Not the Germans!

Unless it's a world war, we never seem to do that well against the old enemy, and instead of bucking that particular trend I'm afraid Andy and I fell foul of it and ended up losing 2–1. This was actually my fault, I'm afraid, because in the final race I made a mistake on the last corner which let Schumacher nudge ahead by a fraction of a second. Had I not done so we'd have beaten Germany on home soil and in front of 60,000 people. Oh well. It was a good effort.

It took a while, but five years later, in 2015, we managed to exact our revenge by beating Sebastian Vettel and Nico Hülkenberg in the final at the Olympic Stadium in London. I know it's only a bit of fun, but given the pedigree of the fields it can get a little bit competitive out there, and it was a sweet win.

What I'm about to tell you now will probably surprise many people – it did me – and although it's a good'n, it's not a story I've told very often. It involves, among others, the supremely talented Michael Schumacher, who I'd raced against in karts once or twice, and it took place directly after the 2010 Race of Nations in Düsseldorf.

Until then, I always thought Michael Schumacher would probably be a little bit stiff socially, and when I turned up to the party after the event I was half expecting not to see him there. Sebastian Vettel wasn't going and, although I hadn't heard anything to the contrary, I wasn't expecting to see Michael Schumacher tripping the light fantastic – win or no win.

The party took place in a room at our hotel. As I'm sure you can imagine, the alcohol flowed quite freely, and it didn't take long for things to get a bit loud. Anyway, while I was standing at the bar talking to Travis Pastrana, Andy Priaulx came up to me.

'I've got to take the missus up to bed, mate,' he said. 'She's had a few too many. I'll tell you what, though, while I'm gone just watch him, will you,' and then he gestured somewhere to his right.

'Who are you talking about,' I asked.

'Michael.'

'Who, Schumacher? Why?'

'He's got that look about him. Seriously, mate, just watch him.'

Partly because of the music, and partly because I'd had a few, I didn't know whether Andy meant watch him as in watch him for a laugh or watch him as in be careful, but it didn't take long to find out.

About five minutes later, while still talking to Travis, I

suddenly felt somebody grab hold of one of my back pockets, and before I could do anything, they'd yanked the back of my trousers off down one leg. 'What the hell's going on,' I said, turning around. You could have given me ten thousand guesses at what I was about to see but I still wouldn't have got it. It was just incredible. There in front of me was Michael Schumacher tying my arse pocket and half my trouser leg around his head like Rambo. My immediate reaction was to jump on him and try and get my trouser leg back, which I did, but after rolling around on the floor for a minute or so, I realized that this was futile. For a start, I hadn't brought my sewing kit with me, so wouldn't have been able to mend them, but he also kept on giggling, and I found that very disconcerting. People don't giggle when they fight. That's just ridiculous! What really made me think again about getting involved in a punch-up was that Sophie would be arriving soon from England, and if I'd been thrown out of the hotel for fighting – with Michael Schumacher – she wouldn't be happy. Instead, I got him to the ground, grabbed hold of his shirt sleeve and ripped it off, as if to say, *There you go, sunshine, have a bit of your own medicine!*

This was actually meant to bring it to an end – an eye for an eye, or in this case a sleeve for a leg and an arse pocket – but instead of then shaking hands and going our separate ways, or even him calling me a name or two first, which would have been acceptable, Schumacher smiled at me as if to say, *Shall we go and do this to some other people?*

Oh Christ. Talk about a red rag to a bull.

Before I knew it, Michael and I were marauding through this party like a couple of Vikings, except instead of raping and pillaging like the Danes used to, we were tearing off people's party gear. First of all, we'd pick a victim, and then

287

Michael would point to whatever garment we were going to remove. Then, after three, we'd attack. What a way to spend a Saturday evening!

About half an hour later, Sophie turned up, and one of the first things she saw when she entered the room was me with Michael Schumacher's shirt sleeve tied around my head and wearing what must have resembled some arseless chaps. I looked like a gay John Wayne! My shirt was also ripped to shreds, and there, with his arm around me, was a seven-time Formula 1 world champion with the look of a lunatic about him.

I've just realized, it was Breakback bloody Mountain!

'What the hell's going on, Jason?' she asked from a safe distance.

'Awwww, it's great fun, this, Soph. Seriously, get involved!'

With that Michael and I went to find some fresh meat – or fresh fabric, to be exact – with Sophie in tow so she could witness.

It turned out that this is Michael's party trick, which was what Andy had been referring to. I had absolutely no idea, though. Seriously, Michael Schumacher is an absolute lunatic when he's got a drink down him. He's great fun.

The next night, after the Race of Champions, we all got together again, and this time Michael – who it has to be said wears some very strange clothes when he's out and about – set to work on the winner of the event, Filipe Albuquerque. Like me, Filipe was new to the Race of Champions, and literally an hour or two after winning it at his first attempt he was standing in a hotel in just his pants, having been forcibly derobed by Michael Schumacher. This wasn't the best bit, though.

A bit later on, Michael was standing at the bar with me, Sophie, Andy Priaulx and his missus and one or two others, and we were knocking back schnapps and all kinds of stuff. It was epic. Then, all of a sudden, Michael spotted his wife over the other side of the room and, after turning back to us, he giggled. I thought to myself, what is this German nutcase going to do now? His wife was sitting on one of those modular sofas, and after running across the room he dived and then rugby tackled her! Both of them went flying over the back of this sofa and for a second I thought he might have killed her. Fortunately, he hadn't, but when they got up she started giving him a right mouthful. Undeterred, Michael then leaned forward and ripped off his wife's top there and then!

'Fuck me,' I shouted. 'That is unbelievable!'

Whilst Andy and I were impressed by what we'd seen, Sophie and his missus most definitely weren't, and after giving me a look that said something like *If you even think about doing the same to me, I will castrate you here and now*, Sophie said, 'That's it, I've seen enough. Come on, we're going to bed.' I didn't argue. It's best not to in those situations.

Be honest, is that how you imagined Michael Schumacher? I bet it isn't. It's funny what people do to unwind, though. Most racing drivers I know go cycling these days, which does not interest me one bit, but Michael Schumacher used to undress people.

Looking back, Schumacher wasn't the only one who had form for this kind of thing, as back in about 2003 I'd disrobed the marketing director of SEAT at a conference just because I'd got a bit too pissed and giddy. At the time there was nobody there to take me to one side and say, *Now are you really sure about this, JP?* Luckily the marketing director had a sense of humour, but in hindsight it could have gone so, so wrong.

What's happened to Michael is obviously tragic, but where

there's life there's hope. And believe me, there's a lot of life in that human being. A lot of life. The boy's just mad! When I raced against Michael in karting, if he was having a good day the rest of us might as well have gone home. He always seemed to be able to find that extra couple of tenths, and I, like the rest of the motorsport world, am praying that he makes a full recovery. Good on you, Michael.

When Andy and I won the Nations Cup in 2015 we were all staying at the Shard in London, and because the events took place in the evening we had to travel from the Shard to the Olympic Stadium – about 5 miles as the crow flies – in rush hour. Five miles might not sound like much, but in London it's the equivalent to about fifty anywhere else, and we were stuck in traffic for ages.

The drivers were being transported to the stadium on a big luxury bus, and I was at the naughty end with David Coulthard. After about an hour and a half we suddenly spotted an off licence, and after asking the driver to pull over for a minute, we got out, ran in and purchased a few crates of beer. Everyone else got on the sauce, and by the time we arrived at the stadium, which was about an hour later, we were all buzzing and ready to race. The thing is, everybody apart from the non-drinkers had been suffering from massive hangovers, so all DC and I were really doing was topping everyone up again. We were providing a service.

The following day, after winning the Nations Cup, we had to go back again for the Race of Champions, and Andy and I were both a little jaded. Amazingly, we both won our opening rounds, with me beating Romain Grosjean and Andy beating the Indy 500 winner, Ryan Hunter-Reay. After that, I think our hangovers must have kicked in (I was as sick as a dog!), as we were both done in round two, and the eventual winner was Sebastian Vettel, who, perhaps wisely, had decided to make his own way to the stadium.

Do you know, I think it's time to wrap up. I can't tell you how much I've enjoyed imparting some of my considered words of wisdom – he said, tongue firmly in cheek – and I sincerely hope you've enjoyed reading them. Getting the balance right between my careers in racing and TV and my career in high jinks has been a little bit of a struggle, but I think we've just about managed it.

On the racing front, as most of you will know, 2016 to 2018 were a bit of a nightmare for me on the track, and if I were to impart all the details we'd need another 500 pages. At least! I'm somebody who is used to winning races, so it was a shock to the system, and had it been solely down to my ability or my performances, I would have shut up shop and opened up a tearoom somewhere. Oh aye!

I did actually contemplate jacking it in at one point, for the simple reason that, if I couldn't drive competitively, what was the point? What stopped me doing so was the knowledge that I still had some beans left in the tin and because I'm a naturally competitive individual, who, over the years, has had to overcome one or two obstacles to get where he wants to be, I had no choice other than to crack on and attempt to prove my doubters wrong.

Lo and behold, I'm now back in a competitive motor for the first time in years, and, lo and behold, I'm back in the mix again. We're only three meetings in at the time of me writing, but the boys and girls at my team, Sterling Insurance with Power Maxed Racing, have played a blinder so far, and we're not a million miles away from the podium. Seriously, I can almost smell the champagne!

Something else that's chipping along nicely at the moment is *Fifth Gear*, as we've recently started filming another new series for Quest TV. TV is an area I'd like to put some effort into, as, when I am eventually dragged kicking and screaming from the cockpit of my racing car, I'll have to be kept from under Sophie's feet, and the best thing to do will be to chuck me in front of a television camera. Some of you might have seen my appearances on James Martin's Saturday morning show on ITV, which bears the mysterious and cryptic title *Saturday Morning with James Martin*. That's been a lot of fun and involves speed, a smidgen of danger and trays full of food. Confused? So was I when it was suggested to me! If you've never seen it, have a look next time it's on.

As much as I love my TV work, motor racing should have the final word, and with that in mind I'd like to use a short but very salient quote from the great Niki Lauda, who passed away recently. What he achieved after his accident at the Nürburgring in 1976 was beyond incredible and should act as an inspiration to anybody who is chasing a dream or overcoming difficulty. Perfect in its simplicity, it's an adage that has served me well over the years and still resonates with me today.

'From success you learn absolutely nothing, and from failure and setbacks conclusions can be drawn. That goes for your private life as well as your career.'

Nail on the head, Mr Lauda.

Acknowledgements

This book has been such a tonic to do. With liberal measures of gin, of course ... Firstly, I would like to thank my pal Dougie Lampkin for introducing me to the fruitcake that is James Hogg, a man whose job it has been to somehow unravel the recesses of my mind and assist me in documenting it on stuff made from trees. We began the process back in September 2018 and it has been a challenge for us both, not just in terms of finding the keys to all the different cognitive folders up there – the racing one, the high jinks one, the family one, etc. – but in terms of selecting which stories should make it into the book. If you could see how I file documents in my office, it would give you an idea of what my head's like. Bloody chaos! Anyway, thank you, James. I've loved the process and it has brought back so many wonderful memories. I would also like to say a huge thank you to Charlotte Hardman and the team at Michael Joseph, and also to my literary agent, Tim Bates. Thank you all for your patience!

Like the book itself, the rest of my thank yous will be in loose chronological order.

First of all I'd like to say thank you to Neil Hann, formerly of the powerhouse that was Mistral Racing. Neil, you did so much for me in my formative years and I remember with such fondness the endless crazy nights we spent in the workshop and working at Sportac. So many lovely memories. Thanks, mate.

Next up are three genuine legends who all gave me so much support in the early days but are sadly no longer with us. They are the great Martin Hines from Zip Kart, and Tom Walkinshaw and Hugo Tippett from TWR. God bless you all.

The next unfortunate soul, Tim Jackson, has been involved in my car-racing career right from the start and, together with John Millett, convinced me to race Renault Spiders in 1996, which opened the door to Willies. Gents, thank you both very much indeed.

Speaking of Willies. Mike Knight from Winfield Racing School was one of the two people I called when I was ambushing Frank Williams, and I value his opinion to this day. Good on you, Mike.

I simply have to give a mention to my great pals John and Mary Booth from Manor Motorsport, not only for believing in me but for making Todwick my second home. Stickle bricks! Then there's my ace mechanic at Manor, Pete Sliwinski. I got my first taste of success at Manor (and some other things!) and it's one of the most smile-inducing periods of my entire life.

I'd like to say a big, big thank you to Ralph Firman from Van Diemen for taking me under his wing and allowing me the opportunity to drive his works Duckhams cars, and to the lovely 'Rocket' Ron Carnell from Duckhams. Sorry for the wake-up call, Ralph!

Then there's Martin Sharp and Paul Hetherington from Mardi Gras, who helped launch me into the BTCC via the Renault Spiders. Where did it all go wrong?

Next on the list are Ian Harrison, Derek Warwick and everyone from 888. We all shared some massive ups and downs along the way, yet to this day we remain dear friends.

Thank you Ian and Del for your integrity in the dark moments and for giving me my first BTCC championship. And thank you to Gaz, Charlie and Martin, who I work with to this day at PMR.

Speaking of championships, if it hadn't been for Ray Mallock, Mark Busfield, Rupert Manwarring, Rod Underwood, Mark Cromack and all at RML, I might never have won a second. You're a super team of people who do motor racing at the highest level the right way. Thank you all.

To Kevin James and Mark Mckenna from my days with SEAT. You guys helped relaunch my career after ASCAR, and more importantly employed the most gorgeous woman I had ever seen. Who on earth could that be? Thank you, guys.

To Peter Cattell and David Beardmore from Tesco, for your enormous support over the years. Boy, have we had some fun!

To the lunatics that are James Goddard-Watts and Darrell Morris from Silverline. That party in Verbier after the 2010 championship win was off the scale! Thank you for your support.

To David and Lisa Flux and all at Adrian Flux Insurance. Thank you so much for your continued support. It's greatly appreciated.

Somebody I owe a great deal to is my long-time and totally ace race engineer, Carl Faux. Buddy, without your extraordinary engineering powers I wouldn't have achieved anywhere near as much as I have. Thank you, pal.

A sincere, but cautious, thank you to all the drivers I have shared a track with over the years. Well, nearly all!

OK, let's get on to the big guns.

A lady I truly adore and have learnt so much from over the years is my friend and business partner, Heidi Johnson-Cash.

Thank you for everything H. We've had fun, success and so many giggles. You truly are the sister I never had xx

To Sir Frank Williams and Sir Patrick Head. Gentlemen, by reopening your driver search in 1997 (after I'd made a bit of a nuisance of myself!), you gave me the chance to shine and changed my life for ever. I will always be indebted to you both.

To my amazing wife, Soaf, for being THE best friend and the most amazing mum on the rollercoaster that is our world, and to our gorgeous girls, Alena and Zia, for giving Mum and Dad constant smiles and giggles. Not forgetting our two dogs, of course, Joey Pickles and CoCo. When the chips are down, just knowing that you lot are there makes me feel on top of the world xx

Last but not least, I would like to pay a special tribute to my incredible mum and dad. What a journey, eh? It started in the dining room at Elmwood Crescent and is still in full flight some thirty-nine years later! Thank you both for the unbelievable sacrifices you made, and for the insane levels of support and love that you give me and the girls. Love you both to the stars and back xx

Oh shit, I'm welling up!